Practical Aspects of
BUDDHIST IDEALS

A TRANSLATION

BY

U Nyi

From

"Kokyint Abhidhamma" in Myanmar

By

ASHIN JANAKĀBHIVAMSA
Of Mahagandhayon Monastery
Amarapura

authorHOUSE®

AuthorHouse™ UK Ltd.
500 Avebury Boulevard
Central Milton Keynes, MK9 2BE
www.authorhouse.co.uk
Phone: 08001974150

First published by AuthorHouse   10/6/2010

ISBN: 978-1-4520-8027-7 (sc)

CONTENTS

INTRODUCTION	**1**
OBJECTIVE TRUTH AND THE MIND	**5**
The mind (Citta)	6
FACTORS INFLUENCING THE MIND	**13**
Unwholesome factors	13
1. Moha (Delusion, Ignorance)	14
2. Ahirika (Lack of Moral Shame)	17
3. Anottappa (Lack of Moral Dread)	18
4. Uddhacca (Jitter)	20
5. Lobha (Greed, desire)	20
6. Māyā (Deceitfulness)	25
7. Ditthi (Wrong view)	29
8. Māna (Conceit, arrogance)	30
9. Dosa (Anger)	33
10. Issā (jealousy, envy)	45
11. Kukkucca (remorse, uneasiness)	49
12. Thinamiddha (sloth and torpor)	51
13. Vicikicchā (Sceptical doubt)	52
WHOLESOME FACTORS	**54**
1. Sati (Mindfulness)	57
2. Hiri and Ottappa (Moral Shame and Moral Dread)	58
3. Alobha (Greedlessness)	60
4. Adosa (Hatelessness)	61
5. Amoha (Wisdom)	63
6. Metta (Loving kindness)	67
7. Karunā (Compassion)	69
8. Muditā (Sympathetic Joy)	70
9. Upekkhā (Equanimity)	70
10. The Three Abstentions (Virati)	74

MIXED FACTORS 77

1. Vedanā (Sensation) 78
2. Saññā (Perception) 79
3. Cetanā (Volition) 80
4. Ekaggatā (Concentration) 82
5. Jivitindariya (Life of Nāma) 82
6. Manasikāra (Giving Attention) 82
7. Vitakka (Thought Initiation) 83
8. Vicāra (Sustained Attention) 84
9. Adhimokkha (Decision Making) 84
10. Viriya (Effort-making) 84
11. Piti (Rapture) 87

CHARACTERS AND TEMPERAMENTS 91

THE TEN WHOLESOME DEEDS 97

1. Pubba, munca and apara cetanās 104
2. Sila (Keeping Precepts or Virtuous Mora l Conducts) 114
3. Bhāvanā (Meditation) 118
4. Apacāyana (Paying respects where due) 120
5. Veyyāvacca (Sundry Services) 121
6. Pattidāna (Wishing Others to Share Merits) 122
7. Pattānumodana (Taking a Share in Others' Merits) 123
8. Dhammassavana (Listening to Dhamma Talks) 124
9. Dhammadesanā (Giving Dhamma Talks) 126

GENERAL NOTES ON KAMMA 131

What is Kamma? 131
Distinct kinds of akusala cetanās 132
The power of kusala-kamma-resultant effect 135
Sampatti, Vipatti 138

4 CAUSES OF DEATH (CUTI) 150

Cuti due to exhaustion of kamma-support 151
Cuti due to both causes 151
Cuti due to destructive *(uppacchedaka)* kamma 151

PATISANDHI DEFINED   161

The four types of patisandhi   161
Some very strange way of conception   162
4 different kinds of people   164

RUPA (CORPOREALITY)   169

The 4 categories of Mahābhuta dhātu (Primary elements)   169
The fundamental and dependent rupas   172
The five forms of pasāda rupa   173

BHUMI (REALM, OR HOMELAND)   181

Niraya   181
The Birth of a Kappa   188
Deva Bhumi   191
The Good Life of a Brahma   201

[ON NIBBĀNA]   204

Appendix A - Categories of Duccaritta and Sucaritta   221
Appendix B - The Precepts   222
Appendix C - Attributes of the Buddha, Dhamma and Sangha   223
Appendix D Questions by Manle Sayadw and answers by Minkun Ale
Tawya Sayadaw, regarding the subject of male and female devas: 226
Appendix E Pārami - the Ten Perfections Practised by Bodhisattas leading
to Buddhahood   227
Appendix F -The Eleven Fires   228
APPENDIX G: GLOSSARY OF SOME PALI TERMS AND CON-
CEPTS   229
Glossary   231

PREFACE TO THIS TRANSLATION

This book is about *Paramatha dhamma*, the natural law governing the ultimate realities, consisting of the natures of the mind, its associate factors, matter and the Ultimate Wisdom. It is a study of the Abhidhama Pitaka, one of the three Baskets of the Buddhist Teaching. The book's emphasis is on putting the principles into practice.

Tipitaka or the Three Baskets of Buddhist Scripture consists of *Sutta*, *Vinaya* and *Abhidhamma*. *Sutta* is a teaching in discourses delivered by the Buddha directly to His Disciples and other audiences including lay people and celestial beings. *Vinaya* is the book of Rules of Conduct defined by the Buddha for His Order, the Sanghā. *Abhidhamma* is the broadest course of analytical study of the natural laws that govern all life forms and existences (*satta*, *okāsa* and *sankhāra lokas*), a more direct form of teaching than *Sutta desanā*, being insightful and difficult for complete comprehension for the untrained; it is in *paramattha vacana*, an unconventional language[1] The purpose of the three baskets is, as a matter of course, deliverance from all miseries, to attain the Ultimate Wisdom or Peace, called *Nibbāna*. There are intermediate stages before this Ultimate Peace, which ideally are conducive to personal, communal and world peace. These stages, though seemingly idealistic for most people, are in fact practicable for 'ordinary' lay people with some intellectual curiosity, and a subsequent firm determination to gain one or all of these stages of attainment. The immediate task, the purpose of life is, therefore, to apply all the practical aspects of *Abhidhamma*.

At the age of 42, in His 7th year[2*] of Buddhahood, Lord Buddha delivered the *Abhidhamma desanā* to an audience of a great many *devas* (gods) and *Brahmas* (nobler, higher heavenly gods) headed by *Medaw*

---

1. *Paramattha saccā, vacana or desanā,* is defined as 'Truth (or term, exposition) that is true in the highest (or ultimate) sense, as contrasted with the 'conventional truth' (*vohāra or samuti sacca*), which is the 'commonly accepted truth'. (Ashin Nyanna-tiloka, the Buddhist Dictionary 6th edition, 2003)
2.* Kyithe Laythat Sayadaw, "Jinatthapakasani" (Myanmar), Pitakattaw Pyanpwaye Press, Mandalay, 1970

Minatthar[3] in the realm of Tavatimsā[4]. The Sermon was a gesture of paying back gratitude owed to His mother, now Medaw Minatthar. It took the three full months of Lent (from full-moon day in July to that in October) on earth, from start to finish.

The exact length of the Abhidhamma Teaching is never known on earth. But the Buddha taught the full extent of the tenets, though brief, to Ashin[5] Sāriputtarā on His daily rounds for alms-food and ablutions on earth. A *nimitta* Buddha (a live replica, a virtual image, created for the purpose) remained behind addressing the celestial congregation in Tavatimsā while the Buddha was on His alms rounds on earth and teaching the abridged version of Abhidhamma to Ashin Sāriputtarā. The Ashin expanded the brief teaching to a certain length ("not too long, not too short, just enough for easier understanding"), in his re-briefings to the Sanghā. The *Abhidhamma* we learn today is what the Ashin taught with full blessing from the Buddha. It was his greatest contribution to the Buddhist Mission; his perfection in Bodhiñāna was one only next to that of the Buddha Himself – no one else could have done such a great task as this.

The *Abhidhamma* basket contains 7 volumes with the titles of *Dhammasangani, Vibangha, Dhātukathā, Puggalapaññat, Kathāvatthu, Yamaka* and *Patthāna.* Its contents are so comprehensive of all mundane and super mundane worlds and so insightful that it is difficult for ordinary people to understand. For the benefit of these people, therefore, Anuroddha Mathera[6] of South India (Kancipura) prepared what is known as *Abhidhamma Sangaha,* which was still so brief that it was, in its generality, little more than a detailed listing of the contents of the *Abhidhamma*; the essence of the dhamma seemed hidden. So, there appeared many other works in Pali, Myanmar and several other languages that divulged and opened up the *Abhidhamma Sangaha* for easier comprehension.

Some say that *Abhidhamma* is not the Buddha's Teaching but that of Shin Sāriputtara. It was not so in Theravada Buddhism. The Ashin did not teach it out of his own wisdom; he was assimilating the text, the methods and the analyses as taught by the Buddha.

---

3. This is a conventional form of address in Myanmar to Prince Siddhattha's mother as a male *deva* (a god of the heaven). *Brahmas* are higher celestial beings.
4. Abode of a class of heavenly beings (gods) in the sensuous sphere
5. A Myanmar form of address to Great Venerable Bikkhus
6. Contemporary of Shin Mahābuddhagosa and Shin Buddhadattha, 4th or 5th century AD

He was merely a faithful carrier of the message of the Master.

The characteristics of the *Abhidhamma* can be recognized from a comment by Ashin Sitthila, the renowned Abhidhajhamahāguru and Aggamahāpantita, thus: "Abhidhamma consists of the knowledge of working of the mind, of moral conduct of the enlightened, and of the insight knowledge of natural causes and effects (in the world of mind and matter). The study is beyond the scope of Psychology, Ethics and Philosophy."[7**] In fact it is beyond the reach of any study of the Arts and Sciences, the study of which are based and built up on *samuti saccā* and *paññatti paññā* (conventional, worldly wisdom), whereas the basis of *Abhidhamma* is *paramattha saccā* (the objective truth) that must necessarily make use of the conventional language and commonly accepted vocabulary lest we cause chaos in human relationships and disregard the material and conventional world we live in. *Paramattha dhamma* is the law and the language of insight meditation in seeking the Absolute Freedom and Enlightenment.

The grand, and yet seemingly effortless work, entitled "Kokyint Abhidhamma" in original Myanmar, of Mahagandaryon Sayadaw Ashin Janakabhivamsa, was meant primarily for his classes of around 650 pupils at his great Monastery in Amarapura, the Southern town of Mandalay. "Abhidhamma" is untranslatable in a single word. 'Buddhist Ideals' is my choice that inspires me to entitle this translated version as "Practical Aspects of Buddhist Ideals". The original was a popular work of religious literature in Myanmar for over half a century (it still is today), having been reprinted many times, thus giving evidence that Abhidhamma, seemingly difficult to comprehend for the untutored, can be learned and put to practice by ordinary people with some intelligence and willingness to follow up lofty moral principles. My purpose in taking up this challenging task of translating it is an attempt to contribute in some small measure to the propagation and assimilation of Abhidhamma studies among interested English-reading public, and to help further develop a serious interest and inspiration in wisdom by insight meditation (*vipassanā bhāvanāmaya paññā*).

The reader may first find it perplexing to have to read an abundance of Pali words, but they may be skipped where definitions are given on the spot. Many words that are too often recurrent and untranslatable word for word will be used on their own as the reader gets familiar with the flow

---

7.** An extract from the editorial of Myat Mingalar bulletin, October, 2007

of the text. Some Pali words are essentially basic to convey their precise conceptual meaning in Thedravedin tradition.

The translator extends his *metta* to the readers of this translation and prays that they be happy to find this work of the Sayadaw useful in their moment-to-moment encounter with the realities of life.

Let us give peace a chance to rule the world.

U Nyi,
Shwepyithar,
Yangon Division,
Myanmar.
Dated the 30th of January, 2010

FOREWORD[8]

We publish Sayadaw Ashin Janakābhivamsa's book of "Practical Abhidhamma" in homage to the Sayadaw with permission from Mahāghandhāyon Nāyaka Sayadaw Ashin Kontala, making use of computer printing and good-quality paper, for the benefit of men and women of all ages so that they may be able to study and practise the dhamma. We would like to suggest that the readers, as opportunity permits, read and study with all serious and respectful intent the three companion books, namely Ratana Gonyi[9], this book and Anāgat Sāsanā[10].

In Ratana Gonyi the three Jewels, i.e. the Buddha, Dhamma and Sanghā, and kamma and its effects have been fully described and discussed, the readers may be persuaded to become true members of the Buddhist Faith, and be in the Right View of Sammāditthi.

Whoever is a Buddhist should keep this book of Kokyint Abhidhamma in his possession so that the person may find it handy for back-reference and easy to put the principles into practice.

Anāgat Sāsanā is a book of remarks and instructions as to how to protect the Faith, and keep it pure, lasting and growing.

We wish all beings to be happy in whatever their endeavours by taking refuge in the Sāsanā,

Htein Win 28-6-94

---

8. Publishers - Ministry of Commerce, Government of the Union of Myanmar, 1995
9. The Glory of the Three Jewels (Buddha, His Teaching and the Order)
10. The future of the Buddhist Faith

SAYADAW'S INSTRUCTIONS
(*OVADA KATHĀ*)

Mahāghandhāyon Sayadaw Ashin Janakābhivamsa of Amarapura was a personality of uncommon character to whom everyone who wants the Sāsanā to sustain itself and spread wide afield, and every one who loves the country, should forever be grateful. Sayadaw loved very much being a bikkhu so as to be able to carry out tasks that would be most effective and beneficial for the cause of the Sāsanā to the best of his ability. He did not seek fame or power; he placed the cause of the Sāsanā in the forefront of all the affairs he had himself involved in.

For the sake of future Sāsanā, and for the benefit of those who would be in the service of the country, to be at ease and comfort in acquiring thoroughness and skill in the learning of the sacred Pitaka, Sayadaw prepared and compiled books on Sadda (Grammar), Vinaya (bikkhus' Rules of Conduct), Abhidhamma (Analytical Studies), and Sutta (Discourses) to the full curricular complement. Also for both laity and the Sanghā to be able to serve the public in general, and the Sāsanā in particular, in order that the public prosper and the Sāsanā prolongs and propagates and, so that the development and promotion of good moral character in general prevail, Sayadaw showed the way in his writings and class teachings such as Ratana Gonyi, Kokyint Abhidhamma, Anāgat Sāsanā, Lessons in Buddhism, the Blood of Religion, Buddhānussati, and many other works. Sayadaw always gave his pupils and lay devotees lectures and talks on the supreme attributes[11] of the Buddha, with prompting reminders on such virtues as diligence at learning, application of such learning to practice, and the prospect of miseries in the present lifetime as well as in *samsāra*[12] if precepts (and *vinaya*) are not observed and live without much thought and respect for the message of the *Sāsanā*. *Dāna*[13] is what one should do, but keeping precepts (*sila*) and observance of the rules of conduct (*Vinaya*) are the only reliable conveyance to proper abodes of life (*sugati*). Sayadaw's

---

11. Buddha Ghuna, the Properties of the Buddha as ascribed to no other person or entity.
12. The wheel of birth, old age, miseries, death, and rebirth
13. Giving, donation, charity

advice includes also starting and keeping up insight meditation (*vipassanā kammatthāna*) in keeping with one's prevalent capacity.

The extracts given below illustrate Sayadaw's thoughts.

Wholesome Thoughts First

Any one who wants to reside in this monastery shall not hold the mentalities such as those of the seniors bullying the juniors, and the juniors not respecting the seniors (*agārava*); envy of persons better than self (*issā*); envy or jealousy of those possessing keener diligence and cleverness with better chances of advancement (*macchariya*); very expressive sensuality (*tanhā rāga*); desire for status and property (*lobha*); excessive anger and pride (*dhosa* and *māna*). They will need to be in a good teacher-student relationship with due regards and love (*mettā*) for each other. They should take care of the sick (*karunā*); be glad to see others' advances in education and wellbeing (*muditā*); be keenly dutiful towards the Buddha (*veyāvacca*); generous and confident (*saddhā*); humble and gentle (*nivāta*); fearful of the four planes of *apaya*; and diligent in efforts to gain *magga-phala ñāna* and *Nibbāna*.

("One Life in the Samsāra", page 365)

On Sila and Vinaya

For a blameless, praise-worthy life, *dāna* alone is not an adequate guarantee: without observance of the five precepts[14] or the *Ājivatthamaka sila*[15] for lay folks, and the *Vinaya* for members of the Sanghā, no matter how good or high the learning may be, it is not safe now or hereafter. If members of the Sanghā do not observe the rules of the *Vinaya*[16], they are not what they are supposed to be: "the fertile land" for sowing the seeds of dāna for the laity to benefit much from. That was how I have been thinking.

("One Life in the Samsāra", pages - 356, 458, 464, 469)

---

14. The five precepts: abstinence from killing, stealing, lying, wrongful sexual indulgence and use of intoxicants

15. The eight precepts: as of the first four of the five precepts, plus vows against slander, rough language, nonsensical chatter and wrongful livelihood such as businesses in lives, drugs and arms.

16. Rules to be observed by residents of the Monastery. l

On Insight Meditation

Spending a lot of time on *paripatti* (insight meditation) is the proper way of life. Being bent on *pariyatti* (learning) alone cannot make much difference in the status of the mind. *Pariyatti* training without *sila* should not be accepted in this monastery. I have said that reminder often.

The daily routine for all the residents is to teach and learn during day time, whereas in the evening hours it is to do service in the shrine hall and enter into *vipassanā* meditation until the time of *tonekhauk*[17] signal for turning in.

("One Life in the Samsarā", pages – 458, 460, 464)

The teaching bikkhus must lead all residents of the monastery in the work of *vipassanā bhāvanā*. All shall work hard.

("One Life in the Samsāra", page – 334)

In all the ten point-instructions[18] to be observed by all the residents of the monastery, the emphasis is to have wholesome thoughts in the first place

Whenever the Ashin met his lay folks, men and women, he urged and reminded them not to forget and to strive for a better kind of life, one stage after another.

On Talk and Work

Although Sayadaw has passed the examinations for Pathamagyaw and Sakyasiha Dhammacariya, he never ascribed these titles to his name in his published works. He was also awarded the Aggamahāpandita[19] title; he never used it.

Passing examinations and gaining titles may serve the purpose of mission works in some measure. They help to make works easier than without them, Sayadaw believed. But only by dint of purity of moral conduct and by working in true spirit and in the interest of the mission, the real progress would be made. That was how Sayadaw used to instruct his pupils.

---

17. A loud sound by beating a hollow log (an implement in all monasteries)
18. To have wholesome thoughts, have respects for vinaya, be healthy, be clean, be properly dressed, be proper in composure, be proper in carriage, know proper manner of talk, be disciplined, and learn well
19. A much hallowed religious title

Celebrations for passing examinations and birthdays are not allowed in the monastery. Noisy congregations, *dāna* parties, receptions and musical entertainments are totally forbidden.

"Each and everyone should be reforming oneself in all manners of physical, verbal and mental articulation. This reformation should be carried on to the day of death," Sayadaw taught.

Sayadaw showed, as he wrote how real work can contribute to real achievements in his book on the future of the *Sāsanā*, by his personal example, the practical application of what he said, and the brilliant accomplishments in both *pariyatti* and *paripatti* performances of the Mahaghandhayon Monastery in Amarapura Township. At present, there are over 760 sanghas in the monastery, and it would not be superfluous to say that the whole monastic community is the only one, not only in Myanmar but also in the world, in being a harmonious unit, pursuing a hallowed knowledge, living and eating together on public *kusala*[20], and without any complaint or problem. This is clearly the most remarkable achievement of the Sayadaw, and an outstanding example for the *Sāsanā* and the country, to take pride in.

Myanmar nationals and researchers of other countries, wishing to study Theravāda Buddhism, came to the Mahāghandhāyon Monastery in Amerapura. Every one of them was filled with gladness of the heart and delightful confidence. The sight of cleanliness, quietness and peace, good discipline of the residents, and the prosperous state of the religious buildings impressed them all. They were awed by the tremendous achievements of the Sayadaw, witnessing his relentless and tireless efforts without let or hindrance. Apart from taking care of maintenance of the buildings, academic duties, and etc., Sayadaw wrote, one after another, many kinds of books, large and small, seemingly without a pause. His idea of so much work in his lifetime is summed up in an extract:

'Tis not for my personal gain,
I put in so much work with might and main,
But for the Buddha Sāsanā to flourish,
A follow-up on forefathers' wish
That it may fade never,
But sustain and shine for ever
("One Life in the Samsāra", page 389)

20.. Blameless, wholesome and meritorious acts

Now that the Sayadawgyi is no more, Syadaw U Mahinda, Sayadaw U Indobāsābhivamsa, Sayadaw U Aggavamsa, and Saysdaw U Kontalābhivamsa are managing the affairs of the Monastery, caring for food and general wellbeing of the resident *sanghas*. It can safely be said that the First Sayadawgyi's noble wishes for the upkeep of the *Sāsana* is in full flowering. The practical teaching and the distribution of books throughout the country was in full swing. At the very beginning, there had been some criticism and misunderstanding, but the Sayadawgyi faced them with equanimity, riding over difficulties and carrying on with a steadfast determination. On page 221 of his autobiography "One life in the Samsāra", we find how he had to manage from scanty resources the publication of his first book "Yatana Gonyi" thus:

> "When planning to print the little book of 'Yatana Gonyi', some haphazard donations of 5 /10 kyats came in making up a total of about 250 kyats. The cost was 350 kyats[21]. I did not have that much. I accepted the gift of a chest of drawers from my younger brother which we turned into cash to make up that amount."

Sayadawgyi's description gives a clear indication of how careful he was in the matter of cash accounts, and how his books were not for business but primarily for the cause of the *Sāsanā*.

"Concerning publication of the books, I was not only careful about myself. I was also mindful about whatever is related to my works. Since publication of the first book, there have been some talks making their rounds that I was going to leave monastic life. It made me think. Supposing I did leave the monastic life, and supposing I and whoever my life-partner might be are going to spend the money that might be made out of sales of the books I wrote, we would surely be sunk in the *samsarā* and miseries would follow. It occurred to me that my partner and I would not like to take that beating.

"Now also, I have often told the publishers and distributors, Maung Kyaw and nephew Maung Aung Khant, to be careful. The money accrued from sale of the books must benefit the cause of the *Sāsanā*, and not for their personal gains. If they happen to use it for a brief time due to some circumstances, they must be accounted for and repaid. It is alright for them to be paid for their services as is normally allowed nowadays. It is simply

---

21. Kyat is a unit of money worth 100 pyas, the smallest denomination.

improper to aim for gains. They were advised to try to be able to print and publish, in future, higher *tikā* works of limited demand. I wrote for the cause of the *Sāsanā*. The teaching bikkus of the monastery assisted me. So it should not be business in any case. If it is, our future generations will become devoid of human value.

"I have told them that when I am gone, I wish it to be for Ghandhāyon *Sāsanā*; that if Ghandhāyon is no more, I would wish it to be for other religious purposes."

If it is for the advancement of the *Sāsanā*, if it is for the public good, Sayadawgyi was not afraid to face poverty in the least, and would carry out his projects with full courage and zeal.

"If I am one to take pains,
And the ones after me prosper and gain,
Let me take pains and poverty;
Thus I have it in my heart truly,
Hard at work to break apart
The rumours and gossips smart,
The slants and the tales
Overflowing the ears,
Throughout the land to hear;
Only make me ponder
And brace myself up stronger.
(One Life in the Samsāra", page – 394)

Sustenance, propagation and prolongation of the *Sāsanā* were the overpowering *sammāchanda* (right wish) of the Sayadawgyi as evidently shown in his prolific writing and publications. He forbore with the brunt of such dispraises and accusations as doing business in books, saving money to leave the monastic life. His response, the way in which he took *samvega* (lessons) in *lokadhamma* (the universal law of dualities) can be seen from an extract:

"Man is only man
And what is found in man
The duality of goodness and badness,
The unfailing law of causes and effects
That is *lokadhamma* really,
Not to be glad or sorry ..... ."

(One Life in the Samsāra, page – 105)

"'Tis the way of human nature
To dispraise and censure;
Bear no enmity,
Despite difficulties,
With strong determination,
Never a backward inclination,
Red is the blood of courage,
To follow up
with one's precious lineage ….. "
(One's Life in the Samsāra, page – 289)

.

It is evident that strength from such kind of moral courage has brought about the successful implementation of his plans we find today. Sayadawgyi described the real aim of his lifetime in some place in his autobiography thus:

"*Tapyidaw*[22] would not work so hard if it were for this monastery alone. *Tapyidaw* works for the future of the country as well as the *Sāsanā*. In my mind there is no such thing as a particular monastery, a particular sect or just one *sāsanā*. It is only for the benefit of all. Tapyidaw do not work so hard for the *Sāsanā* alone, but also for the country. It is tapyidaw's overwhelming wish not only for the wellbeing of the *Sāsanā* that we inherited from Lord Buddha, but also for the wellbeing of the country that is the habitat of the people who revere, take refuge in and support, the *Sāsanā,* which (the wish or *chanda*) drives tapyidaw on. In addition, tapyidaw would very much like to take pride in the peace and prosperity of the country on the basis of the *Sāsanā*."

Sayadawgyi believed that the Teaching of the Buddha is the most correct and the noblest in the world; it brings forth benefits in both the present life and hereafter; it can become the standard bearer of the world religions in terms of reverence and confidence. This observation can be recognized in the following conceptual statement:

"If this level of maturity in human relationship – understanding, forbearance and mettā - prevails, the *Sāsanā* will shine brighter than the moon or the sun, and be looked upon as the standard bearer of the world. More than that, the believers and the practitioners will be regarded with

---

22. Address of the first person in a most humble manner: it takes the place of "I" when a bikkhu is addressing to a senior bikkhu or to a congregation of bikkhus.

respect by every one else, seeing the prevalence of the peace of mind in this life, and envisioning the assured future of the *Sāsanā*."

(One Life in the Samsāra, page – 288)

Such attitude and considerations were imparted in the talks to monastic pupils and lay devotees, with so much zeal and appeal that, it can be checked and tested for evidence today, Sayadaw's dream has been fulfilled and the success complete to such an extent that the establishment is now a beacon and standard of performance in Myanmar. On account of Sayadawgyi's fame and influence of *sila* (moral conduct), *samādhi* (concentration) and *paññā* (wisdom), men and women with strong, unshakable *saddhā* (faith and confidence) came to the monastery, a few at a time but incessantly. Thus, by allowing their *saddhā* and generosity to shower on the *Sāsanā*, the monastic compound has spread to sixteen acres; number of monastic buildings mushroomed to a total of 96 by the time Sayadawgyi passed away. Sayadawgyi himself, to his last day, dwelled in a small single-story building. At this juncture, it would be opportune to say something about Sayadawgyi's thoughts concerning buildings.

Sāsanā is not a Building

It is not the religious buildings that are capable of sustaining, propagation and purification of the *Sāsanā*. Only the *Pariyatti Sāsanā* (literature) and *Patipatti Sāsanā* (practice) based on the *Pariyatti* can sustain and prolong the true and pure *Sāsanā*.

Example- in the Second Sanghāyanā, the bikkhus representing Jetavana and Pubbāruna monasteries of Sāvatthi, and those representing Veluvana of Rajagaha, where Lord Buddha and the great arahantas had often resided, were not found to participate in the proceedings. Instead, the Great Council was led by other bikkhus who were then the real guardians of the *Sāsanā*.

Looking up at the present day situation, archaeological artifacts relating to Buddhism such as Buddha statues, implements, stūpas and other buildings are found at geographic sites stretching out from Indonesia to Afghanistan, throughout the length and breadth of all India, Pakistan and Pashwar. In those lands today, is it not rare to find a professed Buddhist?

So, it is obvious that for a *Sāsanā* to stand the test of time, making religious buildings grand and beautiful is not all that is important for they do not play the central role. The spread of correct scriptural literature that is easy to comprehend, and ample opportunities to study and practice it are the two most important factors in this regard.

Thus, the Sayadaw saw very clearly that only *Pariyatti* (learning of the Teaching) and *Paripatti* (practice of the learning) can sustain and make the *Sāsanā* flourish for a long time to come. That was the reason why the Sayadaw had written and left a great many curricular books on the *Ti-Pitaka*.

The Sayadaw did not normally write in the night by artificial light. But in the last five years, saying, "I have a lot of work left to do.", he sometimes used lights to write in the night. He was teaching classes in the afternoon on the day of his death. His pupils remember, with deep sorrow, hearing him say at the end of the class, "That is all for today. If still alive, I will carry on teaching you tomorrow."

Because he cared for the benefit of others, the Sayadaw did not seem to tire physically or mentally as he worked hard to accomplish his plans and the enormous amounts of work. He was very much inspired by the exemplary life stories of the Bodhisatta (Buddha-to-be) as he tried to fulfill all facets of a Buddha's *parami*[23] (perfection) so that he could serve all the *sattavā* (beings) for their benefits. Without reservation, he believed in and revered the Buddha to his satisfaction.

Taking inspiration from the ways the Bodhisatta tried to fulfill the *Paramis*, the Sayadaw decided to try and work hard with diligence, even willing to give his life for the cause of the *Sāsanā*.

"I do not only revere and worship the Buddha and the *sāvakas*[24] for being what they were, but I revere them even before they were the Buddha and the Sāvakas."

(One life in Samsāra, page – 357)

How this commitment was followed up without the slightest of deviation can be gauged from Sayadawgyis' words of joy in a verse, repeated five times in his autobiography, thus:

As Bodhisatta in His previous lives,
To the last, He strived
Even at cost of His life,

---

23. The ten facets of *Parami*: *dāna* (giving), *sila* (moral conduct), *nikkhama* (renunciation), *paññā* (pursuit of knowledge), *viriya* (diligence), khanti (forbearance, patience), *sacca* (truthfulness), *adhitthāna* (determination), *metta* (goodwill and love), *upekkhā* (equanimity),
24. Disciples

For Perfection[25] for all to benefit;
For the cause of the *Sāsanā*,
Let my life be a gift,
And never my mind be beaten,

I'll try,
Work for the goodness to brighten.

How to Study a Book

(Sayadaw's teaching to his pupils)

1. Upon getting a book that suits one, one should read it from the beginning to the end every day. At the beginning, it may contain a statement of the purpose of the book, and in the end or conclusion it may say something of a biography of the author, a discussion of some important issues, or a summing up.
2. As one reads on, one underlines or notes down the page numbers of the points one likes very much, those one does not find favourable, or those about which one cannot decide and would like to consult with a teacher.
3. When one has free time, one reads again, and again, the underlined phrases or points one likes very much, and asks the teacher about the phrases or points one would like to know more about, or discuss the unfavourable issues with others.

Only if one studies thus, one will have learned well and become a person of ideas and knowledge, progressive in contemplation, and balanced in thinking, so that one is convinced of having exerted a worthwhile effort.

A thought in reverse: A person who has no capacity of original thinking would find no usefulness of an authentic work of literature. How can a blind man make use of a full-view mirror of high value?

---

25. The Ten *Paramis* as pertain to Buddhahood.

A Brief Biography of Ah Shin Janakābhivamsa

1. 1. Sayadaw was born to U Zaw Ti and Daw Ohn Hlaing of Tharaing village, Wetlet Township in Shwebo District, Saggaing Division, on the 14th waning day of Tapotwe, 1261 (the 27th of February, 1900).
2. In 1266, he was initiated into *samanera* (a novice) for the first time.
3. In 1275, he was ordained *samanera* (still a novice) for the second time.
4. In 1279, at the age of 18, he passed the Pathamagyi Examination[26].
5. In 1280, in the month of Tabaung[27], he was ordained into *pabbajjita*, a full-fledged monk or a *bhikkhu* for the first time.
6. In 1281, on the Full-moon Day of Nayon[28], and again in 1282 on the Full-moon Day of Tabaung, he was ordained into monkhood for the second and the third times respectively.
7. In 1287, he won the "Pathamagyaw" title[29].
8. In 1289, the young bhikkhu passed the "Sakyasiha" examination and won the Title of "Pariyatti sāsanahita dhammacariya".
9. In 1303 (1941-42), in the waxing days of Vaso, the year of entry and occupation of Myanmar by the Japanese, the young Sayadaw established the current Mahagandhāyon[30] monastery in the town of Amarapura[31] with 5 companion sanghas, which, on the day of his passing away, was a vihara housing over 500 sanghas.
10. In 1312 (after Myanmar's national Independence), Sayadaw was awarded the "Aggamahapantita" Title (the earliest presented) by the Government.
11. In that year, Sayadaw wrote manuals of Elementary Buddhism for use in the curricular teaching at State schools.

---

26. A Government examination to qualify young bhikkhus for higher learning in Buddhist scriptures
27. March
28. June
29. The best student in the result of the Pathamagyi Examination
30. In true Pali phonetics, it should read Mahāgandhāruna Vihāra
31. The Southern town of Mandalay.

12. In 1315, Sayadaw was elected to the positions[32]:

     (a) Chatthasanghiti Ovādācariya Sanghanāyaka;

     (b) Chatthasanghiti Bāranitthāraka;

     (c) Chatthasanghiti Pālipativisodhaka;

     (d) Chatthasanghiti Osānasodheya Pattapāthaka.

13. 13. In 1337, at the whole-country Congregation of the Shwekyin Nikāya Sanghās, Sayadaw was elected Upaokkatha (Vice President) to the Nikāya Council.

14. Sayadaw started writing at the age of 30 in 1291, completing his first book in 1293. In the month of Tasaungmhone (November), 1338, he wrote "The Last Ten Months of Lord Buddha", and then his autobiography, "The Samsara of a Life time". He started writing and teaching "pañcapakarana Tikā", "Mulatikānissaya" and "Pali Nissaya" at 1:00 p.m. on Tuesday the 5th waxing day of Tasaungmhone, 1336 (11/11/74, and completed on the 12th waxing day of Wākhaung, 1339. Sayadaw took up writing and teaching Sutta Mahāvā Tikā on Thursday the 2nd waning day of Wāso, 1337 (24/7/75), completing it on the 13th waxing day of Nattaw (23/12/77), 5 days before passing away. Sayadaw wrote and taught Pātheya Tikā for a day in between.

15. Sayadaw Ashin Janakābhivamsa studied the *pariyatti* literature under Min Kyaung Sayadaw of Tharaing Village, Myaungmya Sayadaw, and the First Gandhāyon Sayadaw of Saggaing, the Second Mahāgandhāyon Chan Aye Sayadaw, Pakokku Mahā Visutāyāma Ahletaik Sayadaw U Paññā, Sayadaw Thon, U Nandavamsa, and Abayārāma Sayadaw.

16. On Tuesday, the 2nd waning day of Nattaw, 1339 (December 27, 1977), at 4:30 p.m., Sayadaw passed away in peace.

---

32. These offices specialized tasks that characterized the nature of the organizations involved in the great Buddhist Council, held in the 2500th year after Parinibbāna of the Buddha

ACKNOWLEDGMENT

This book is dedicated to the five Great Mentors: the Buddha, Dhamma, Sangha, Parents and Teachers, without whose loving kindness, kindly instructions and steadfast cultivation of a religious faith, I would not have been able to take up such a challenging task as this work.

I am immensely grateful to my good friend, U Myint Thein, for his kindly assistance in editing this translation, reading the whole manuscript and checking the text thoroughly against the original book in the Myanmar vernacular. Also thanks are due to Mr. John Neilson in Australia, who read the initial chapters and responded with some invaluable suggestions, particularly as to native usages of the English language. I am also thankful to my nephew, Aung Lawha Ling in the UK, for his invaluable assistance in computer work necessary in preparation of the final manuscript. But, of course, any errors found in the finished work are my responsibility and mine alone.

Last, but not least, my thanks are due to Saya Min Yu Wai, Poet Laureate and writer and U Aung Min Hlaing, brotherly friend of Kyaukse, who have all along been giving enthusiastic support, encouragement and other kind favours of assistance in my literary endeavours.

U Nyi
Bendar (on visit),
Brunei Derussalam.
30th of July, 2010

INTRODUCTION

pajā sabbā sussayantu, vutthahantu summangalā
dusentu, duggatin gāmin, purintu, sabbapāramin.

May all beings living in their respective abodes, sleep at ease and in peace, dreaming pleasant dreams. May they wake up and rise as the day breaks, full of grace and happiness. May the wrongful intents and wills that lead to the four lower destinations be destroyed by the weapons of noble thoughts and deeds. May all beings, assuredly, try to take up and fulfill the ten perfect moral conducts that the Bhodhisattas carry to fulfill, so as to achieve success, one stage after another.

When considering the news of people today, mankind appears to lack the noble attributes of love[33], kindness and sympathetic joy, making the world seem dry and drab. The fire causing this dryness almost completely overwhelms even the noble characters of pure mind and saintliness.

What is meant by the fire?
The fire or the heat arises out of greed, anger, conceit, envy, avarice[34], and etc., causing people to commit inconsiderate actions towards each other. That heat does not only cause the dryness in this life, it does so also in the next life and throughout the *samsāra*[35]. So, to be able to extinguish that fire as far as one can in this life, one should try to flush out the cool waters of love for all, kindness to the less fortunate and sympathetic joy for the more fortunate.

What is *samsāra*?
We have used the phrase 'throughout the *samsāra*', and so the '*samsāra*' should be given some thought. It is not the worldly loka[36] that beings live in, but the ceaseless, successive becoming of mind (consciousness), its associates and matter[37]. {*sam* = in succession, +*sara* = becoming, appearing}.

---

33. This love is meant by *metta*, the universal love for all beings, devoid of passion, or fear.
34. In Pali they are lobha, dosa, māna, issa, macchariya, etc.
35. The seemingly endless cycles of birth, old age, death and rebirth, or (in Abhidhamma) the cycle of becoming and unbecoming, appearing and disappearing of mind and matter (as observed in vipassna)
36. By *loka* is meant both animate and inanimate worlds, including all the 31 *bhumis* of existence
37. *citta, cetasika* and *rupa*

1

What are humans, devas and Brahmas?

Mind and its associates are called *nāma*. The combined effect of becoming in succession of that *nāma* (mind) and *rupa* (matter, corporeality) is called man, deva, Brahma, or, personalities - I, he, man and woman (male and female). In fact if rupa and nāma are removed, there would be no man, no deva, no Brahma and so, no *sattavā*.

How do rupa and nāma come about?

Rupa and nāma do not arise and pass away in ceaseless succession without a cause. Only on account of the impact of the external objects on our sense faculties, and the resultant effects of kammas from our previous existences, the phenomena of rupa and nāma continue to this day. Therefore, for the rupa and nāma to be, there have to be external sense objects as well as kamma or volitional deeds done in past lives.

What is important?

Out of those two causes, the external sense objects can only give us signals to cause various kinds of feelings and thoughts, and so they are not vary important. Upon impact of such external sense objects, whether they are good or bad, it is only incumbent on us to have a properly oriented, well-prepared mind, and that is very important.

Basically, it means that if our mind, the consciousness continuum, is always good, the rupa-nāma that will come into being in the next lives will always be good and noble. In spite of change of lives, it will only be good rupa and good nāma (good human, good deva and good Brahma). If the mind inside us is wicked and evil (although one may live well now due to a good-natured mind in a previous life), it will be a wicked mind in ugly looks (hell, ghosts, animals) in the next life.

Yoniso is cause for noble mind

Only if one has **yoniso**, one can have a good mind, a good heart. The habit of proper and thorough attention and wise decision is called '*yoniso manasikāra*'. Nowadays, it is 'yoniso' in vogue, instead of yoniso manasikāra. Thus, if one gives proper attention (yoniso), one does not have *akusala citta* (wicked mind), but only *kusala citta* (wholesome mind). If there is no yoniso, even in matters that could induce good thoughts, one may not be quite happy. Therefore, for a great many bhikkhus and laity, the most important thing is to be in the habit of 'yoniso'.

Causes in a chain

Whether a person has yoniso or not depends on whether that person reads good literature, or takes lessons from the wise and the learned. If one studies good books and takes training from the wise (being in association with the wise), one's knowledge and wisdom grow. If this one, receiving growing knowledge, makes a determination such as "I must have a good mind in my heart," that one is likely to have yoniso in every situation encountered. The one who does not read good books and does not take lessons from the wise is likely to have little knowledge, and does not know how to orient his mind properly. Therefore, I would like to see a great many people

1. to take to heart a proper yoniso in any situation they may get in, and get ahead in association with others with mature minds, holding fast to the *brahmacora dhamma*[38] in every situation of life one encounters;
2. to stand the impacts of rises and falls of fortunes in life, with firmness in resolution and in good grace, well composed with a clear mind, and without change of usual attitude and thoughts;
3. to make efforts and put hard work to whatever fulfillment of perfections in dāna, sila, etc. that one is committed to in this life so that lives in the next existence and beyond may be bright and high-standing, until the attainment of Nibbāna.

With these three basic aims in mind, "Kokyint Abhidhamma"[39] has been compiled for a great many people so as to make themselves practitioners of high moral conduct.

Looking into the mirror
To see daily
The image of self to repair;
Like the mirror, read this book,
See how fair one would look,
Daily contemplate how one fares,
And take care . . . .

---

38 (P) The four articles of *metta, karunā, muditā* and *upekkhā*.
39 "Ko kyint Abhidhamma" is title of the original book.

namotassa bhgavato arahato sammā sam buddhassa
CHAPTER ONE

OBJECTIVE TRUTH AND THE MIND

The four categories of paramattha dhamma

Paramattha is Pali. It means "noble principle", not in the senses
of preciousness, goodness, royalty and the like, but in the sense that it
holds the firm truth, never changing in its intrinsic nature - (*parama*
= noble, *attha* = principle of nature; *paramattha*[40] = noble principle of
nature.) Paramattha principle consists of four categories, namely ***citta***
(mind, consciousness), ***cetasika*** (mind-associates or factors influencing
the working of the mind), ***rupa*** (matter, corporeality), and ***Nibbāna***
(enlightenment, final deliverance from *dukkha*, the endless cycle of birth,
growing old with pains, death and rebirth).

The principle of non-changeability
The kinds of cetasika include *lobha* and *dosa*. Lobha is craving or greed,
and dosa violence, anger, aversion. Lobha, as appears in the noble and the
wise lot, is the same in nature of greed as that appears in the evil and the
foolish people, and even that in a dog; there is no difference in the nature
of greed. Similarly, the non-changeability in the nature of dosa and all
other cetasikas and other categories of paramattha dhamma should be
understood.

Thus, because paramattha dhammas do not change, being not
dependant on the social, intellectual or bhumi status of the beings and,
because they show their firm nature so, the readers should learn diligently
the instructions that will be given in the sections to follow so as to

---

40. Current 'common' usage is *paramattha saccā,* meaning 'unchanging nature of the objective truth' or simply 'the ultimate truth' that is unchangeable. Commonly also,
dhamma takes the place of *sacca.*

understand and gauge the true nature of characters and temperaments in the hearts of oneself and others.

(Maxim)   - 1. Truly unchanging,
                         unwavering and forthright in nature
                         is the paramattha in its noble stature;

                         2. Citta, cetasika, rupa and Nibbāna,
                         these four are paramattha dhammas.

THE MIND (CITTA)

Consciousness of sense objects (ārammana) is citta.

We are conscious of many objects detected by our senses all the time. The state of consciousness of those sense objects is called 'the mind'. Although we call this 'knowing', actually it is not knowing by way of insightful knowledge called ñāna, but merely taking on and putting the objects into the field of consciousness.

6 kinds of objects and 6 of consciousness

1. All sights including colours are   *rupārammana*;
2. All sounds are   *saddārammana*;
3. All smells are   *gandhārammana*;
4. All tastes to the tongue are   *rasārammana*;
5. All bodily contacts are   *phutthabbārammana*;
6. All others to be aware of   *dhammārammana*.

When adopting the rupārammana, it is consciousness of seeing. When adopting the saddārammana, it is conscious of hearing. When adopting the gandhāramana, it is consciousness of smelling. When adopting the rasārammana, it is consciousness of taste. When adopting the phuthabbārammana, it is consciousness of something coming in contact with some part of the body. The ārammanas other than those five are dhammārammana, and it is consciousness of whatever comes into the mind. The taking of ārammanas into consciousness thus is the knowing function of the mind or citta.

The properties of citta

Dhammapada Pali text says that citta can go to a far-away place; it roams about alone, on its own; it has no material body, no size or mass; it dwells mostly in the **hadaya** cave (the heart). For evidence pertaining to these properties, read on.

Going to a distant place

The mind cannot go to a distant place as though it has feet to walk on. But it can take an āramana of an object at a very distant place as if it goes there and reaches that far. For example, when a person in Mandalay has an āruna of an object in Yangon, the mind does not really get to Yangon, but it only takes on the virtual vision of the object. So, it goes far by virtue of its ability to take on an ārammana of a distant object, and we say, 'the mind goes far'.

Roaming alone on its own

The mind is extremely quick in the way it produces many thoughts in sequence. This gives rise to the thinking that there can be 2 or 3 thoughts or more and takes on 2 or 3 ārammanas or more at one and the same time. Actually, the mind cannot do that; it can only take one ārammana and know its presence in one thought at a time, and then only takes on more ārammanas, one after another in sequence.

A person, while sitting on a perfumed silken bed, with a sweet in his mouth, and looking on a dancing and singing artist, has all the five arammanas of sight, sound, smell, taste and touch, all around and near him. He does not know all the five arammanas at an instant. He takes on in his mind his favourite arammana first, and after experiencing that only, he would switch onto the other arammanas one after another.

Because many thoughts cannot occur in parallel but only one at a time, we say, 'The mind roams alone on its own.'

Furthermore, 'roaming' here does not imply actually moving from one location to another. It is only catching a distant ārammana in the mind. In taking an ārammana in the mind, a category[41] of the mind alone cannot take it to a complete knowledge. To catch the knowledge of the ārammana to a certain extent would require many other kinds of mind to play in succession. Although many kinds of mind come into play in the

---

41. There are 89 categories of mind.

cognitive process, the process takes place so quickly that it seems to the people the sights, the sounds, the smell, and so on take place at one and the same instant.

No material body, size or mass

The mind has no spatial body, size or mass so that we cannot say it is white or black, fat or thin. It has the only attribute of catching and knowing the ārammana.

Dwelling in a cave

The mind that knows the sense of seeing occurs in the eye. The mind that knows the sense of hearing occurs in the ear. The mind that knows the sense of smelling occurs in the nose. The mind that knows the sense of tasting occurs on the tongue. The mind that knows the sense of knowing the touch occurs at the spots of touch on the body. Although some of the minds occur in the eye, etc., a great many minds take place in the housing of the **hadaya**[42] heart. Thus because most cases of knowing take place in the cave-like heart, we say 'the mind dwells in a cave'

In short, the mind has no physical shape, but only the property of adopting and knowing ārammanas. In receiving arammanas, the mind does not at all leave the hadaya cave, but can take ārammanas at distant places. In so doing, it cannot take up 2 or 3 ārammanas at one and the same time, but only one after another in a serial order.

(Maxim) -
1. Take, hold on a sense object, note how the mind knows and acts;
2. Going far, alone roaming, with no shape or mass in the showing, the mind is a cave dweller, these properties all there are.

How good and evil minds can mix

The minds work so fast that in about 5 minutes good and the evil minds (kusala and akusala cittas[43]) can occur together, in a mixture. Early in the morning, while paying homage to the Buddha in the shrine room, and having many wholesome thoughts, a call from downstairs for business comes up, and a lobha-mind appears. If, while the Buddha was in the arammana of the devotee, somebody comes to talk an abusive language, dosa appears in his or her mind.

---

42. (P) same as heart, sometimes referred to as hadaya vatthu
43. (P) Wholesome and unwholesome minds

Even while doing lobha-oriented business, one may want to do *dāna*[44] (one might be planning to do so), and thus *saddhā*[45], a *kussala citta* or wholesome mind appears. While being angry due to some dissatisfaction, one may remember some teaching from one's mentors and thus *sati*[46], a *kusala citta* or wholesome mind, appears. While in a pleasant conversation (*tanhāpema*[47] lobha) between husband and wife, a quarrel develops (dosa), but one partner reverts to tenderness and both become kind to each other (lobha). Thus the mind changes so fast that one should, with mindfulness, know the difference between the good and the evil minds, and prepare oneself to be in a good framework of mind at all times.

Different minds and different looks

Just as people differ in looks and appearances, so also their minds are different. Just as there are dull and sharp looks, there also are dull and sharp minds. There are also other differences: the beauty and sharpness of looks differ in degrees, ranging from low to the matchless class. On the base kinds, they can be as ugly as the ghosts and the *petas*[48]. Likewise, good kinds of mind can range from the low to the best, noblest and incomparable class of mind; evil minds can range from a little evil to the most wicked of monstrous proportion and the dullest, useless kind.

How to reform

Born in a remote country and brought to a city, a young man or woman can copy the manners in dress, eating, living and every thing else of the city folks. If healthy habits of body and mind are also taken care of, his or her looks will have changed in a matter of one or two years, even to the point of a personality-change, unrecognizable and mistaken by people who knew him before. Thus, if, with some skill and will to change, the difficult and slow task of changing of looks can be performed, then there is no reason why the mind that changes very fast and is easily shaped cannot be reformed, so long as the will to change is really there. If one notices what minds are occurring in oneself day in and day out, and eliminate the unbecoming kinds, one will become fair-minded soon and in 2 or 3 years time, one will be prepared to respect and even venerate oneself.

---

44. (P) To give donations
45. (P) Confidence, faith, generosity.
46. (P) To remember, be mindful of wholesome teaching
47. (P) Loving fondness
48. (P) *Petas* are the ugliest of all beings.

The reasons why the mind should be reformed

There are many reasons why one should reform one's own mind. One knows best how evil and how wicked one's mind is, and in what respects it is so. The person, who has that kind of mind, even if he is in the top echelons of society, belongs morally in the low class. Because he is morally poor, although he may have honours and riches in this present life, he will be debased in the next life. In view of that prospect, one must reform one's mind to be really honourable and noble.

One who has an evil spirit cannot respect oneself. Friends, brothers and sisters, husband and wife, bhikkhu and devotee and associates can have no respect for the person of evil mind. In order to avoid such low opinion from people around one, one should reform one's mind to be pure, forthright, and noble.

Besides, the person of an evil mind, in whatever outwardly good performances he may be doing, whether it is in charitable deeds, keeping precepts, or meditating, cannot be taken as clean and honest. His *kamma*[49] will not result in clean benefits. In order to avoid such unclean results from unclean habits, one should try to keep one's mind clean and noble.

Besides, the person who is wicked and evil will be wicked and evil not only in this life, but also because his whole being exudes wickedness and evil, he will be infected with a chain of wickedness and evil in his many later lives, so that it would be hard to call him a mature person of **perfections**[50] at any stage. So, in order to become a person of accumulating perfections, one should also try to keep wickedness and evil out from one's mind. Thus, there are many reasons for the reformation of one's mind.

How King Milinda reformed his mind

King Milinda[51], after asking Ashin Nāgasena[52] some questions regarding certain problems[53], planned to ask more important insightful questions about the Buddha Sāsanā. He entered into a seven-day retreat to gain control of his mind before asking the questions. It was an exemplary action of a man of purity and saintliness.

---

49. (P) Volitional acts with resultant effects in this or later lives
50. *Parami* in Pali (there are ten perfections the Bodhisatta cumulatively fulfilled in his entire samsaric life)
51. King Milinda was the Greek king Minandros who ruled North-Western India in the 1st century BC.
52. Ashin Nāgasena was the bhikkhu who answered all the questions on Buddhism asked by Milinda
53. His problems of faith in Buddhism

His method of attaining self-control: he rose from bed early in the morning, did his ablutions, including a bath, and, discarding the kingly garments and paraphernalia, put on bark-dyed yellow clothes with a scalp hat to keep his hair in and to look like a shaven head. Thus assuming some form of a look-alike bhikkhu (he was not a bhikkhu), he made a determination to keep, and kept 8 vows for one whole week:

1. not to carry out any kingly duties;
2. to refrain from any sensuous desire;
3. not to be angry;
4. not to be led by ignorance;
5. not to be high-handed but be humble towards his subjects, servants and employees;
6. to watch and keep physical and verbal civility;
7. not to let unwholesome thoughts arise as reactions to sight, sound, touch and mental aramanas, and so to keep out reactionary moves;
8. to extend loving kindness and goodwill towards all beings.

He kept all these eight vows strictly for seven days. In the morning of the eighth day he ate his breakfast and, with a lowered eyesight like that of a well-composed bhikkhu, a peaceable and clear look in his face, and well-prepared as to what to say, approached Ashin Nāgasena, and began to ask meaningful questions.

How to follow the example

Taking the way King Milinda kept his vows to train his mind for 7 days as an example, the good and the virtuous men and women of high moral stature should observe, very often, vows in like manners in their own homes, marking out a time frame like a full 24-hour day, a day, a morning or so, so that unwholesome thoughts would not have a chance to occur in their hearts. Repeating this process for a great many times would entail in the growing scarcity of those unwholesome thoughts and in ascendancy to the status of a saintly personality, naturally endowed with generosity, confidence and an unwavering faith. For many days in a stretch, the unwholesome thoughts that used to come in before will not appear.

"The mind carries the world.
The mind enchants the world.
All beings follow the will of the mind." (Dhamma)

11

"Before doing anything,

one gets oneself preparing,

so everything may be proper,

and fall into a good order;

Likewise,

in traveling through the samsarā

one must reform and be prepared,

day in day out train the mind

so as to gain a better kind,

so that one day one may reach

the safest town of Nibbān peace."

CHAPTER TWO

FACTORS INFLUENCING THE MIND

How cetasika affects the mind

We have seen "the good mind and the evil mind" in Chapter One. But since the mind's work is only to know the ārammana, the mind by itself cannot be good or evil. Because it meets up with different kinds of cetasika, depending on whether they are good or evil, the mind becomes good or evil. It means, "For the mind to be good or evil, concomitant cetasikas come in to play and influence the mind." Observe this analogy: water is colourless or neutral in colour. By addition of dyes like red, yellow, blue, black, the clear water becomes red, yellow, blue or black. So, to understand the good and evil kinds of mind, the factors influencing its nature must be studied.

(Maxim) -   'Tis the mind's nature
              To know the object pure,
              'Tis neither good nor evil, sure;
              But the cetasikas colour the mind neutral,
              To be white or black, and good or evil;
              But people say
              It is the mind good, and the mind evil,
              But cetasikas are the factors that drill
              The mind to do what it does.

UNWHOLESOME FACTORS

14 *akusala cetasikas*

1. *moha*	8. *dosa*
2. *ahirika*	9. *Issā*
3. *anottappa*	10. *macchariya*
4. *uddhacca*	11. *kukkucca*
5. *lobha*	12. *Thina*

6. *ditthi*   13. *middha*
7. *māna*   14. *vicikicchā*

(Summary) - **moha** is ignorance; **ahirika**, shamelessness; **anottappa**, fearlessness; **uddhacca**, restlessness; **lobha**, craving; **māna**, conceit; **ditthi**, wrong view; **dosa**, anger, hatred; **issā**, envy, jealousy; **macchariya**, stinginess, avarice; **kukkucca**, remorsefulness, worry; **thina**, sloth; **middha**, torpidity; **vicikicchā**, sceptical doubt. All these 14 kinds of cetasika are conducive to all sorts of **akusala kamma**, the unwholesome manners.

1. MOHA (DELUSION, IGNORANCE)

kinds of moha

Not knowing the truth is *moha*. There are two kinds of moha, namely *anusaya moha*, and *pariyutthāna moha*. *Anusaya* means quiet and dormant, whereas *pariyutthāna* means active. The moha that always lies dormant in oneself is *anusaya moha*. The moha that appears together with the mind is *pariyutthāna moha*.

Anusaya Moha

The poison tree has certain inherent property that makes it bear poison fruit. Likewise, there is a kind of *dhātu*[54] property in all beings, which hides from the intellect certain knowable truths. That dhātu property is called anusaya moha. Because anusaya moha hides the three characteristics of *anicca*, *dukkha* and *anatta*, the ordinary man or *puthujjana* does not properly and deeply appreciate these characteristics. People thus do not clearly understand the *paticcasamuppāda*.

Puthujjanas cannot comprehend this anusaya moha. Those modern people, who may have read and come in contact with such vocabulary as *anicca*, *dukkha*, *anatta*, can only guess some ideas about them, not the real insightful meaning of the terms. Even the sotāpana, sagadāgāmi and anāgāmi persons have only less and less of anusaya moha dhātu as their magga ñāna ascends. Only at the stage of arahanta, this anusaya moha is completely annihilated. So, take note, "for as long as one is not an arahanta, even at the moments of wholesome deeds, this moha is present and dormant in every one."

---

54. Intrinsic, inherent nature (like that of a chemical element)

Pariyutthāna Moha

When moha is roused, concomitant with the mind, a devilish mind would have arisen. People cannot see future miseries resultant from current evil actions because this pariyutthāna moha is hiding them. They cannot see the immediate effects of their demonic behaviour that is being acted out now. Even the wise and the noble would commit akusalakamma on account of the influence of this moha. So, moha is the very devilish cause of all unwholesome actions. All foolish actions of devious consequences in the world have their origin in this moha.

How a wise man suffered from Moha

Once upon a time, our Bhodisatta, then by the name of Haritaca, renounced and left the wealth of eight hundred millions, became a forest-dwelling ascetic, and achieved supernormal powers by dint of hard work at meditation. To escape from heavy rains during the wet season, he moved away from the Himalayas to the king's garden in Barānasi. The king of Barānasi then was future Shin Ānandā, the co-aspirant and parami-partner[55] of our Lord. The king felt so revering toward the hermit at first sight that he requested the hermit to stay there under his care. The king supported the hermit with the four essential materials[56], personally proffering food every morning.

Once, there arose a rebellion in the country, and the king, before leaving to personally suppress it, asked the queen, repeatedly, not to forget the venerable hermit. The queen punctually proffered food to the hermit. In one morning, as the hermit had not come yet, she took a perfumed bath and put on soft silken clothes and waited, reclining on the royal couch.

Meanwhile, the hermit, by virtue of his psychic powers, came by the sky-way. When he entered the palace by the ventilator door, his robe of plant fibres made a noise that alerted the queen to rise suddenly, causing her loose garment to slip from the waist down. The hermit, seeing what he saw, had the anusaya moha that had lain dormant in his pure mind awaken and now arisen into pariyutthāna moha; as the concomitant lobha came into play, the hermit, taking the queen by her hand, behaved like a demon.

---

55. All disciples of the Buddha were aspirants of deliverance in His final life-time, and happened to meet and serve each other in the countless number of their previous lives. *Parami* is a striving for perfections.
56. Food, residence, robes and medicine.

Comment on the story

In this story, the foolishness and unruliness should be noted with a grave seriousness. If this kind of moha had not entered his mind, the hermit would not have committed such an unjustified, wrongful action, should even the king himself have generously allowed it. But now the darkness of moha had descended and prevented the intellect to see the present wrongfulness or its later consequences in the samsāra: the life-long practice of jhāna-abhiññāna was no way to destroy the darkness; this darkness had in fact caused the disappearance of the powers of jhāna-abhiññāna.

But the hermit was a man of character, endowed with some *parami dhātu*[57]; he was greatly remorseful on the king's return. He worked hard to gain the psychic powers again. Drawing lesson from the incident that it happened the way it did because he lived too close to the people, he returned to the Himalayas, far away from the human habitat.

Not every kind of ignorance is moha

As moha is ignorance in its generalized definition, the facts of not knowing a place one has never been to and a name one has not learned before are also thought of as the real moha and so, unwholesome. In fact, such ignorance is simply a matter of the lack of prior learning, not moha and not unwholesome. It is only a matter of cognitive process called *saññā*. It is so not only with ordinary men and women, it is also true with the arahantas.

Ashin Sāriputtarā was second only to the Lord in the matter of wisdom. But the Ashin had once given a young monk a wrong instruction in meditation. As the monk was young, the Ashin gave him *asubha kammathāna*[58], thinking it would be best suited to the youth; the youths are normally prone to *kāma-rāga*. But it so happened that the method did not work - he was diligent in his meditation for 4 months without seeing any signs and images[59].

When he was taken to the Lord, the Lord, knowing suitability of different objects of meditation to different temperaments, created and gave a lotus flower to the young monk who had a fondness for it. Very soon, when the Lord made him see withering of the flower, the monk became full of apprehension so much so that as the Lord taught him the three

---

57. The strengths of character accrued from previous and present efforts at Perfection
58. Meditation with attention on the ārammana of corpses, unpleasant objects
59. These signs and images normally arise during concentration training, useful in the assessment of the level of concentration achieved.

characteristics of *anicca, dukkha* and, *anatta*, his ñāna ascended to the arahantaship. Note the Lord's incomparable ñāna.

Thus, if even Ashin Sāriputtarā could not know what was beyond him, it was not moha in not knowing what one has not learned and what only an affair of the prior knowledge is. It is only a matter of one's calibre in intellectual prowess. For example, the fact of not being able to see a very distant object in broad daylight while the sun shines is not because there is something hiding it, but due to the incapacity of one's eyesight.

The gentle and the rough *moha*

In the story cited, the real moha was very thick and rough so that there was a complete lack of understanding of the difference between the unwholesome and wholesome acts. There is another kind of moha that hides the knowledge of mind and matter as revealed in the characteristics of anicca, dukkha and anatta; it does not know the four Noble Truths to any extent, has no concept of *paticcasamuppāda* (compared with the rough moha, it is not so thick and heavy). All the same, the mind that arises, concomitant with moha, is called "mohacaritta" or "foolish mind". Any one who is strongly affected by this moha is called some one "foolish, black, dark, thick, idiotic, stupid, dull, wild, inferior," and so on.

> The whole world is in complete darkness. Only a few beings could see through it, extraordinary as they are. Only a few of all the birds caught in a net could get free, so also only a few of all the dead people could get to the abode of the devas.
>
> (Dhammapada Pali)

2. AHIRIKA (LACK OF MORAL SHAME)

Lack of shame is *ahirika*. All unwholesome deeds are like human excretion. Ahirika is like the village pig. The excretion is something loathsome and hateful. Even an accidental smearing on one's body with it is something to be shameful about in the public. The village pig, however, does not think it is loathsome, but something he would eat with relish. He is not shameful of getting it on his body - he would roll in the latrine pit. He would, in fact, take pride in his ability to eat a lot of it.

Likewise, the unwholesome deeds such as killing are loathsome and hateful in the view of the noble characters. Even an inadvertent wrongful action is worthy of shame in the midst of the noble-minded. But people with ahirika are not shameful to do the unwholesome deeds - they are not ashamed of having done such wrongs. In fact, in the midst of those ahirika-lovers, the greater the number of wrongs they can do, "the grander the pride" they can take in.

Since moha is accompanied by ahirika, even the wise and the learned may do unwholesome deeds without feeling a whit of shame. To see whether that is right or not, those who are often referred to as wise should look back on and think about their own life experiences.

Remark on the Haritaca story

In the behaviour of the hermit as has been shown in the section on moha, the nature of this ahirika is also evident. The hermit, having gained supernormal powers, was a person of first-class noble character. What he had done, however, was a most shameful thing, a sex scandal, in the presence of all the ladies in waiting on a floor of the royal palace. Because of the over-powering darkness of moha accompanied by the shamelessness of ahirika, the hermit committed the misdeed with supercharged energy.

All wrongful actions[60] are shameful

All unwholesome actions, not only this sensuous kind of the hermit, are shameful. Shouting, roughing up and using abusive language on account of anger and aversion; arrogance and haughtiness, behaving like a mad man and looking down on every body on account of conceit and pride; censuring, blaming, grudging, criticizing on account of envy or jealousy; these are all shameful acts. The mind concomitant with ahirika is called "ahirika citta", and the person of that mind, the "shameless person".

3. ANOTTAPPA (LACK OF MORAL DREAD)

Lack of moral dread is *anottappa*. Unwholesome deeds are like burning flames. Anottappa is like moths. Flames are extremely fearsome. But the moths do not think so, and rush into the fire without a whit of fear. Likewise, unwholesome deeds are the cause of many kinds of dangers and harm. But these dangers and harms are hidden from view by moha,

---

60. Akusala kamma

making it fearless. The dangers and harms that come with unwholesome deeds[61] are:

1. *Attānuvāda* (self-accusation, loss of self-respect) - "People respect me for my social position and by thinking I am a good man, but I know my self. Contrary to what they think, I am not good actually. I do misdeeds stealthily. I am a bad man," one may accuse oneself, and thus has no faith in and respect for oneself;
2. *Parānuvāda* (accusation by other people) - "This is a wicked man. He is carrying on with all sorts of misconducts," other people may say, censure and look down on him;
3. *Danta* (punishment) - Killing others may end up in being killed. For taking things not given, one may be beaten, or even killed. The thief may be caught, convicted and sentenced to a term of imprisonment by a court of law;
4. *Duggati* (destination to lowly forms of life) - the persons of unwholesome conduct remember their gilts and feel remorseful at the time of death; they are destined, in their next lives, to the four *apāyas* (the abodes of hell, animals, ghosts and half-ghost-half-gods).

Remarks on the Haritaca story

Here too the story of our Bodhisatta, the hermit Haritaca, should again be considered. The hermit's hideous gilts were enormous. There was a great loss of self-respect. The scandalous news of "the king's guru committed adultery on the queen" spread throughout the city, and the immediate effect was the accusation and censure

If the king were not Shin Ānandā-to-be, for his insult on the queen, the hermit's life would not be thought as much as a blade of grass. Because the king was noble, his life was spared. It was anottappa that made him dare do such sexual misconduct, punishable with death. The mind concomitant with anottappa is called "anottappa citta" or "fearless mind".

Just as the village pig is not loathe to human excrement, so also the shameless person is not ashamed of committing unwholesome actions. Just as the moth is not afraid of fire, so also the anottappa person is not afraid of doing evil deeds.

(Tikā-kyaw)

---

61. Akusala ducaritta

4. UDDHACCA (JITTER)

Restlessness and uneasiness of the mind is *uddhacca*. When a stone is dropped on a heap of ash, the ash is thrown about and scattered. Likewise, the mind is scattered about, taking ārammana of all sorts one after another, so that it cannot be gathered and concentrated on a single ārammana. The mind, concomitant with uddhacca, is a drifting one. When its influence is powerful, the body becomes restless and the person a jitterbug.

The unstable mind of Nanda Thera
When Prince Nanda[62] was about to be married to Princess Janapada Kalayāni, the Buddha took away and robed him into the Order. Bhikkhu Nanda's mind could not be calmed and settled down on the duties of a bhikkhu; it was more often than not drifting to Janapada Kalayāni. In this story, the unsteadiness of the mind is the work of uddhacca.

Uddhacca the weakling
The inherent nature of uddhacca is its inability to keep the mind concentrated on any particular object. It grasps this ārammana and that, too fast too often, and thus the attention span is short and scattered, with the result that its effect, unlike that of lobha and dosa, is not so strong as to pull a person down to the apāya bhummis.

5. LOBHA (GREED, DESIRE)

Wanting to get something is the nature of *lobha*. But here, by "wanting' is meant only the wishes and desires related to the attributes of the *kāmaguna*[63]. The wishes for such noble ideals as realization of Nibbāna, the experience of dhamma, the learning of literature, the gathering of material properties for giving them away to the poor, and etc. are not lobha; they are simply wishes for something to be done later.

Other names of lobha
Lobha has various other names, namely *pema, tanhā, rāga,* and *samudaya*. Pema is used for the kind of love between parents and their offspring, brothers and sisters, husband and wife, the kind of loving among members of a family and relatives or close friends. It means "fondness". This kind of love is also called *"samyojana"*, literally meaning "rope" - people

62. Prince Nanda was younger brother of the Buddha
63. Active properties of kamma conducive to unwholesome volitional actions (*akusala kamma*)

are bound up in loops or network of ropes and do not want to part with each other.

Sights, sounds, smell, taste and touch are the five sense objects people desire, so they are called "the five kāmagunas" [kāma = desirable + guna = tie, tether]. If the desires for these ārammanas of kāmagunas, unlike the regular hunger and thirst, are so strong as to urge one to pursue to get them by hook or by crook, they are called "tanhā"; in cases of man and woman one of whom clings to the other, rather feverishly, it is said to be "tanhā-yu"[64]. The word tanhā carries the meaning of "passion, starving". Of those five ārammanas of kāmaguna, the over-zealous desire for the touch ārammana commonly known as *"methuna*[65]" is termed *"rāga"*. Rāga also means "entanglement with obsession" (Rāga = lobha that sticks to people the way dyes stick to fabrics.) [These expressions are not of literary usage, but rather of our common language.]

In the classification of the Four Noble Truths, this lobha is termed *"samudaya*[66]", meaning "dukkha-to-be or the cause of *dukkha"*. Because we are not free of these elements of lobha, namely pema, tanhā and rāga, we go round the *samsāra*[67], hugging the inalienable dukkha, the suffering. The various forms and extents of suffering we come across in this life have their origin in samudaya, the tanhā-lobha. So, "if lobha is large, dukkha is large; if lobha is small, dukkha is small; if there is no lobha, there would be no dukkha." The mind concomitant with this lobha is called lobhacitta, tanhācitta and samyojanacitta; the person, correspondingly, "the person with large lobha, large tanhā, large rāga and strong samyojana".

Tanhā-lobha does not retreat

This element of lobha called tanhāpema-samudaya-samyojana, if let loose on its own without the controlling factor of dhamma, would never recede or disappear. Like the new horn of a young bull-calf that grows and grows, so also the in-born lobha grows with the age of the person: the older the person, the bigger the lobha. For the elderly people who know no way of deterring their lobha, there is a saying "As hair-knot on the head grows larger[68], it hangs down lower; as one grows old, foolishness grows many folds."

64. Tanhā-yu (M) = a sex-maniac
65. (P) The act and the joy of sexual union
66. (P) Truth of the origin of dukkha
67. (P) The recurring cycle of rebirths, on the 31 planes of existence
68. (M) A century ago or so, Myanmar man had his knot of hair above the forehead. As hair grew, the knot grew and hung down one of the temples.

Drinking brine water

Since birth, one has loved one's parents and relatives, and later on one loves one's playmates and then friends; it is the way of an inborn nature, signaling the advent of enjoyment in sense objects (kāmaguna-ārammanas); it is like a thirsty man who finds brine water, drinks it and ends up wanting to drink more and more of it. As people starve for and pursue the sensuous world of joy and happiness, they cannot see any fault with it, and go round in the whirlpool in the sea of love.

"Love, love, love and love again, not satisfying the love in the main,

Drinking dirty brine water once and again would not quench the thirst so plain;

'Ties pema-tanhā that wraps round one, no fault is seen in loving the other one;

Bethink to be happy to share in love, 'the way of nature, and the way of love."

(A poem of ancient wisdom)

Lobha, if alone, drops one to lowly worlds

Unsupported by any wholesome deeds, lobha alone, however small it may be, can destine one to the worlds of apāya. For instance, a stone by itself, however small it may be, will sink in water. Therefore, clinging at the time of death to one's husband or wife, or to one's children or the property one owns, one is destined to be a *peta*[69] after death. During the lifetime of our Lord, a bhikkhu was much attached to his new robe when dying, and became a louse in the robe upon death. He was freed from that existence only after 7 days, it was said.

The support of wholesome deeds

The love between two people, tanhā-pema, cannot pull the couple down to the apāyas, if assisted by some wholesome deeds. For instance, although a stone by itself may sink in water, with the assistance of a boat, it cannot sink. So, we find in the Jataka stories in which couples in love, tanhā-pema, supported each other by fulfilling the deeds of perfections.

Food for thought

When husbands and wives are of the same kind of mind, they do not want to part with each other; but rather they want to assist in each other's parami (perfections) and enter Nibbāna together. When our Bodhisatta

---

69. (P) Ghosts, hungry beings

was Sumedā, a woman of good descent, by the name of Sumittā, prayed that she wished to be always together with Sumedā. Ashin Mahākassapa and Maibaddā together fulfilled their paramis for many world cycles[70]. In such cases, it should be given some thoughts as to whether it was in the nature of plain chandda (wish) or tanhā-pema lobha.

Determination

The personalities cited were, in fact, puritan characters. The wish to associate with such characters at all stages is a wholesome sort, and one should wish for such association on purpose. Those ashins were of proper moral conduct (sila), trying to fulfill perfections[71]. In the literature, it says, "One, in keeping with sila, can always achieve one's wishes - if chanda is there, it will be accomplished." Therefore, although there certainly was tanhā-pema that bound them, their kusala-chanda was so great that they became close cooperators in their quest for perfection (parami) together.

> "Oh bhikkhus, one who keeps sila (since one's wish is perfectly
> pure) would achieve whatever one wishes."[72]   (Pali Text)

Nakulapitā and Nakulamātā

The wealthy man, popularly known as "Nakulapitā" during the life time of our Lord, and his wife "Nakulamātā" were always together in their past lives. Now in this life too, they were together when they first saw the Buddha and became sotapanas. Because that couple had been in previous existences our Bodhisatta's parents, uncle and aunty living closely together, they loved the Lord as their son and used to say to him anything they wished to say. So, one day, the man said to the Lord,

"I took Nakulamātā since youth. Since the time I married her, I have not behaved or thought wrongfully towards another woman. I want to be looking at her all the time in this life, and so also throughout the samsāra."

Upon hearing this, Nakulamātā, feeling not to fall behind, joined in,

"Since youth, I followed Nakulapitā to his house. Since then, I have not thought of any other man. I want to be seeing him all the time in this life, and so also throughout the samsāra."

---

70. A world cycle is one in which a world is born, lives and dies to be reborn again - that takes thousands of millions of earth years. (See later)
71. Paramis or moral perfections, aiming to fulfil for the purpose of the Ultimate Wisdom or Deliverance.
72. *Ijjhati bhikkhave silavato cetopanidhi visuddhatthā.*   (Pali Text)

In response to the couple's statements, the Lord said,

"Like-minded and supportive of each other in this present life, man and wife must have the same attitudes in respects of saddhā, sila, cāga and paññā[73], if they want to be bound together in the next lives."

Just as the man is generous, so also the wife must be. Just as the man is pure in the upkeep of moral conducts, so also the wife must be. If one wants to give, the other must not bar the giving - the man must be glad of the wife's donations and alms giving. One must also match the other in the pursuit of knowledge and wisdom. With reference to this sermon, Pancāvudha Pyo[74] sings,

"In the realm of man, man and wife, thinking alike, praying alike, never wavering in the acts of charity, in keeping precepts and matching confidence in the faith, will have lots of influence and fame, praised by gods and angels, destined to be together, bound in the bliss of love that stretches far for long in the samsāra."

Remarks on the story

In this story, a consideration should be given to the reciprocal love that had existed between the man and wife who were already sotapanas. Because they were truly and nobly in love with each other, their minds had never gone astray for other persons. Because their minds were so pure, they adored each other so much, never wanting to part with, and always wanting to look at, each other all along the samsāra. Although it was the lobha that made them want to be seeing each other all the time and bound them together, the wholesome deeds they did together would send them to the noble, desirable realms of existence.

---

73. (P) Saddhā = faith, conviction; sila = morality, virtue; cāga = generosity, liberality; paññā = wisdom
74. (M) A variety of ancient Myanmar poem

6. MĀYĀ (DECEITFULNESS)

In some cases, tanhā-lobha is called *"māyā"*. So, māyā would be explained here. Māyā is like a juggler-magician. A juggler would pick up a stone, and make it appear to be a gold nugget. Likewise, māyā also tricks a person into misunderstanding and covering up the trickster's fault. It means, "One pretends to be innocent, in spite of one's wrongful conduct."

Feminine māyā

Once upon a time, there lived a university professor who had a certain pupil whose wife was in the habit of going astray with one other man. On the days she was about to see that other man, she was particularly good and tender to the husband. On other days, she used to treat him like a nut, a slave, and insult him. The husband was so confused and unable to understand the behaviour of the woman that he told his teacher a complete account of the affairs. The professor explained the nature of the feminine behaviour.

Remark on the story

The woman in the story assumed a superfluous tenderness towards the husband on the day she did her mischief, because she wanted to cover that up. That pretension of tenderness is māyā. This māyā in some other cases is called *"tankhanuppatti ñāna"* (quick-wittedness). [Tankhana = at the instant +uppatti = occurring. It is not the true wisdom really. The true ñāna (wisdom) applies only to the wholesome affairs.]

The quick wit

A certain housewife was in the habit of playing with a young male servant. One day, the householder saw the woman kissing the youth. The woman knew the man saw that. So, she went to her husband and said,

"My man, this boy is dishonest. Today he stole and ate the cake I had kept for you. When asked, he lied saying he did not take it. Now, when I smelt his mouth, it smelt cake. We should not keep a dishonest servant in our house."

Remark on the story

In this story, her kissing of the servant was a great wrong. And yet, to cover that up, she suddenly got a clever idea of deceit. It is māyā. This māyā belongs not only to women, but also to men.

Hermit's māyā

Once upon a time, there was a hermit worshipped by a villager. As a measure of safety from thieves, the villager one day dug a hole and buried a hundred nikkhas[75] of pure gold in the ground near the hermit's dwelling, asking the hermit to look after it. The hermit in response said, "Dayakar[76], you should not ask a monk or a hermit to look after such a thing."

But then the hermit thought, "A hundred nikkhas of pure gold is sufficient for a comfortable living." He moved the gold to a place near the road by which he would be traveling. After the morning meal, he said to the man, "I have been dependent on dayakar for some time now. Staying longer would cause attachment. Therefore, I am moving away to some other place." The villager tried to dissuade the hermit from going away repeatedly, but to no avail. He saw the hermit off to the village gate.

After he had traveled some distance, the hermit returned and said, "Dayakar, some roofing thatch of your house was caught in my braided hair. Monks and hermits should not take what is not given to them, not even a blade of grass." The simple villager became more reverent of the hermit, thinking the hermit was "so full of sila!"

But at the time, there was a clever visitor in the villager's house, who said, "Friend, was there any thing you entrusted and kept with him? If so, go and look." So he went and looked, and found no gold at the burial spot. Together with the visitor, he ran after the hermit and caught him with the gold.

Remark

In this story, the return of a blade of roofing thatch by the hermit to cover up his theft of gold was nothing but māyā. The occurrence of this deceitful māyā, or "cheating and lying", is thus so widespread even among some monks and hermits that so few could be trusted; the chance to have associated with upright, honest people would depend on fate or the wholesome kamma in the previous lives.

Various kinds of māyā

In covering up one's own fault, there are various methods other than those shown in the stories above. In pretending to be free of guilt, the culprit may appear to be violent and angry, threaten to cause fear, flatter to persuade sympathy, and so on in trying to cover up his or her guilt.

---

75. (P) A measure of weight
76. (M) A form of address by monks and hermits to male laity, especially donors.

These various kinds of māyā can be found in residential monasteries and homes. Having excreted in the night at places other than the (outhouse) toilet[77], the guilty one pretends it was not him. Having made wind in the middle of a crowd, the guilty one might make some other sounds to cause confusion, or even tries to make a belief that it was some one else.

Just because there are so many kinds of māyā, there is an age-old saying, "a thousand feints, a hundred thousand ruses, and uncountable guiles, added with sand grains on nine mats, and more with the leaves from nine cutch trees." (all these feints, ruses, and guiles are kinds of māyā.)

Sātheya (Pretension)

Sātheya is to be noted in association with māyā. To persuade other people to have a high impression of one with the kind or kinds of property or abilities that one has not got is a variety of lobha that is called "sātheya". Māyā pretends to be guilt-free by covering up one's own guilt. Sātheya pretends to possess the kind or kinds of property and quality that one has not got. Both characterize falsehood, deceit and wickedness.

Monks and sātheya

Pretence of sila without observing proper moral conduct, honour without really being honourable, and knowledge without much scholastic learning are sātheya really. Smart people distinguish such pretenders, but they may think, "What has that got to do with me. Let him lie as he likes." Or, it may be that because the pretender is a master and benefactor, the smart people at close proximity and familiarity are afraid to reveal such pretensions. And thus, the pretenders go on gaining footholds in society.

The laity and sātheya

There are a great many people who make great shows of morality, honour, capability, education, property, and so on without really possessing much of those virtues and qualities.

The evils of māyā and sātheya

These māyā and sātheya are worse than normal natural desires and wants. In the case of monks, because they have none of sila, samādhi and paññā they would have to brag so as to appear on the same level as the venerable monks who actually possess those virtues. For such boastfulness, great damage is already done to their lives in the samsāra. The lay men and women who support those monks get no intellectual and cultural

---

77. Toilets were located outside of traditional dwelling houses and monasteries.

advantages; not only that, but also the donations to those monks amount to little or no merits.

For worshipping those hypocrites, there have been instances of young women being ruined. On account of the corrupt livelihood of those so-called gentlemen, citizens of their villages and towns become corrupt.

Having followed the so-called leaders with pretension of leadership capabilities, but in fact, lacking those noble qualities, their followers not only suffered losses in lives, but also the loss of sovereignty and nationhood. These days, there have been instances in which, believing and marrying with people with pretension of wealth and riches ended up not in the joy of life (*mangalā*[78]) but in sorrow and ruination (*a-mangalā*).

If marriages involve, either on one or both sides, covering up of faults (*māyā*) and pretension of prestige and wealth (*sātheya*), they will be found out after the marriage. Then, will the misled person (and family) be able to adore such deceitful person (and family)? If, in spite of all that, a marriage holds, will there be happiness? In addition to being in love with each other in the nature of *tanhā* and *pema*, marriage partners should have the purity of *metta* and caring for each other.

For Buddhists, marriage mangalā is an affair that does not end in this life. If the partners have like minds and are happy with each other, the actions together of attending to shrines, visiting monasteries, giving in charity and doing other meritorious deeds can carry them to great benefits to enjoy together in their future lives in the samsāra. (It does not mean an absolute certainty, but rather a likelihood.) If marriages were founded on māyā and sātheya, because there would be no genuine meritorious deeds, there could only be some meagre benefits, throughout the samsāra. Therefore, right from the time a marriage is planned, it should be a mangalā that is nothing to do with māyā and sātheya.

Thus, as māyā and sātheya can lead astray a single person, many people, a nation or the world (like the *titthiyas*[79] who assume the status of the Phras[80], without being so), they are the two very base and wicked kind of cetasika. That may be so, but nowadays those two rogues are so common that those who have decided themselves to be good and saintly should reconcile themselves not to be included in such lot, and take great

---

78. A virtuous and noble deed that leads to great benefits and happiness in this life and beyond
79. Ascetics and others holding wrong views concerning the phenomena of natural causes and effects
80. (M) A term for holiness, professing attributes of Bhagavā, another term for the Buddha.

care not to have those dishonest and wicked cetasikas in their hearts; they should also urge their families and associates to do likewise so that their minds may be always clean, pure, sharp, fast, upright and noble.

7. DITTHI (WRONG VIEW)

Wrongful knowledge or view is *ditthi*. Today it is commonly called "wrong view". It means viewing not only "what is there as is not there, what is not there as is there, what is right as wrong and what is wrong as right," but also "his view is right, and the others' wrong"[81].

The views that the world and all the living beings are created[82] by an omnipresent creator, and that there is *atta*[83], the soul in the bodies of these creatures, are speculations of imagined "truth" about something that does not really exist. It is ditthi, holding, "what is not there as is." Ignorance of the continuum in the living beings of their volitional actions, good or evil, carrying their corresponding effects to a future date, and of reality of *Nibbāna* as mind and matter come to naught, and of the existence of life hereafter for as long as Nibbāna is not yet attained; such ignorance is the sort of ditthi that holds the view of "what is there as not."

Killing lives and sacrificing them at an altar is a great wholesome deed. Bathing on very cold days in winter; sitting in the middle of four bon-fires on very hot days; living the way of an ox or a dog; all these practices are morally good, and meant for cleaning one of defilements. To bathe in the Ganga River on auspicious days is a good custom of washing down all of one's guilts and faults. These beliefs are ditthi, viewing "what is not right as right."

There are views that giving in charity, observing moral precepts and meditation as a way of life for desirable destinations and for Nibbāna do not make a proper way of life. Those views are ditthi, holding "what is right as not." Such ditthi views are widespread. The mind concomitant with ditthi is known as "ditthicitta", and the person holding that view "micchadltuhi". [Note that similar logic and terminology will be applied to the cetasikas to be shown later.]

81. The right view is one supported by observable evidence and objective evaluation (or contemplation), not by way of intellectual speculation or some-body-says-so...

82. Creation in the Buddhist teaching is only a speculative idea, contrary to the three naturally occurring characteristic phenomena of *anicca, dukkha* and *anatta* = impermanence, suffering and non-self as found in the observation of the interactions between mind and matter (nāma and rupa) - a result of insight meditation. ..

83. (P) the self, the soul

8. MĀNA (CONCEIT, ARROGANCE)

Māna is conceit, pride, arrogance and haughtiness. The person in the habit of pride tends to be arrogant towards other people like the banner on a pole. There is haughtiness. If better than other people in official status and prestige, wealth and property, education, looks, health and so on, that one would look down on those people, thinking highly of one: "Am I like them? Are they a match to me?"

On equal status the haughty person takes pride in oneself thinking, "What is the difference between him and me? I get as much as he gets." If lower in official position and possessions, not being able to match up, the person might think and say, "What do I care about his being better? I eat what I have. I get what I earn. Who is there for me to beg of?"

Common prides and methods of their removal

Pride in birth (*jāti māna*)

Pride in being one of good descent is 'jāti māna'. Nowadays, there are people of some good descent, but not to be as good as to breed conceit and be pompous and think other people are lowly, only to be trodden under their feet. In the olden days, didn't the common men and women love the people of royal blood, if the latter did not show their pride, being not haughty but smooth and pleasant in their dealings with the commoners? The saying, "Familiarity breeds contempt," may be true as some people may be rude and take advantage. But the fault lies with the improper manner, and its perpetrators are the ones to lose. Think ahead and look backward for reasonableness, and remember not to be proud of high descent.

Pride in wealth (*Dhana māna*)

The pride of people with some wealth is "dhana māna." Nowadays, there are people in possession of some wealth. But they are not so rich as to be of inexhaustible riches, and not to think of the lesser people as not worthy of association by way of walking, eating and talking. Like the proverbial man who thinks the small creek of Mu to be a river, a man may think he is rich. But would it not be better if he could be kind and generous towards the poor? Would it not help in safe-guarding his property? The smiles on the faces and pleasant words from the mouth of the wealthy could be a kind of relishing tonic for the poor.

Therefore, in order not to let the present wealth that is supported by some charitable acts in previous lives, send one down to lowly births, and the evil pride be the backdrop of lives hereafter, try to remember to cultivate a serious mind worthy of a man of riches, and be somebody other people look up for some aid and assistance. There is a great deal of dangers to the riches of the present life. Even if free from danger, it can be useful only in this life, unless one applies that to charity.

"The luxuries and pleasures of a king, sitting regally on a throne under a tiered parasol, surrounded by a retinue of officials in a great golden palace, last but for a lifetime, like the way a bubble pops on the surface of an ocean[84]."   (Anantasuriya)[85]

Pride in learning (Paññā māna)

Pride of the learned is called "paññā māna." Literature imparts knowledge to make humans discern the wrongs as wrong and the rights as right; it gives education - it trains to cultivate culture and peaceable human relationships. It is extremely shameful to find some one with pride of monstrous proportion founded on education. It is not particularly extraordinary that someone learns and gains some great knowledge from someone else. Many fortunate people can learn well from proper teachers.

So, it is incumbent on the learned people not to be haughty and boastful, but instead, sympathetic and kind towards those who could not find the opportunity to learn, and other less fortunate, not so clever, people. There was once, it is said, a very distinguished bhikkhu who had, in his past life, taught with great patience, and in the present life, he became a famed personality, well-learned in both mundane and super-mundane affairs. Therefore, use your acquired learning for benefits in the samsāra.

The two lanes of education

Since the vocational and professional educations are meant for the worldly purpose of livelihood by design, there is no need of scrutinizing them for our purpose. For bhikkhus in the service of the Sāsanā, however, there are two lanes.

84. One span of a life time is only too brief in the long stretch of the samsāra.
85. This court official of Bagan Period composed the classic poem at the nick of time before he was executed by royal decree. The improbable comparison alludes to immeasurable expanse of samsāra and an extremely brief lifetime.

The lower lane

Great learning would bring fame. There would be many people flocking around him to proffer donations: food, robes, monasteries, and medicines, plentiful and good in quality. The situation is very inviting, but lobha would be associated with dosa and māna. Thus, hugging lobha, dosa and māna, the young monk may begin to learn the literature. When he has much learning and built up his fame, taking the lead from his original purpose, he works hard to gather plenty of alms and donations (*lābha*) - being wealthy and proud, he can be haughty and looking down on others, thus making his knowledge unwholesome, leading him to take the lane to the lowly worlds. It is said in the books that it would be better to have slept than learned something in such a frame of mind.

The upper lane

If learned, one would come to know the Lord's teaching, and be able to teach others in turn. Looking in the mirror of Pitaka literature, one would be able to scrutinize one's own frame of mind so that one could repair it to be pure, righteous and noble. When learned with that purpose, one would not care about the abundance of alms, donations and donors, but work hard in pursuit of the original aim. The learning of such a personality is wholesome, leading him to take to the upper lane.

Some monks who aim for passing examinations and gaining fame at the beginning changed their minds when they have learned the literature and become good at heart. They are like the proverbial pot of water that sloshes about when not full, but becomes still when full. Their learning is wholesome, leading them to take to the upper lane. May the young learners take to the good lane when they have accomplished the learning.

Pride in good looks (*Vunna māna*)

Taking pride in one's good looks is "vunna māna". Good looks in this present life is due to minimal dosa, donation of flowers, sweeping and cleaning of pagoda and monastery precincts and so on in the past life. Such beauty is some thing to be proud of.

But one guesses and looks back at one's past life, and sees one was a good kind, a donor of water and flowers in a purely charitable mood, and so one should not be too proud of one's beauty and show haughtiness towards others. Try to breed continuum of a clean mind in a beautiful body, and be a saintly person, gentle and well composed.

A Summary Reminder

The saintly persons who had entered Nibbāna could have taken great pride in their descent and so on as already shown and climbed to the sky to hoist a banner of pride without the assistance of a ladder. They were brought up as princes and princesses on the hands of kings and queens; there was every reason to be proud. In the matter of learning and wisdom, such persons as Mahosadhā went far beyond worldly norms.

On the side of the ladies, such bhikkhunis as Uppalavana, Khemā, and Yasodharā were saintly ladies born of good families, endowed with properties and wealth, learning and wisdom, and beauty that were wonderment beyond imagination.

Whilst such top-class saintly men and women did not take pride in their births, etc., it is, if thought deeply, very shameful to find those who are like "the hares, common in every bush", and "the fish, a little bigger than the other", and yet behaved like "the wobbly castor plant that rules the wood of no substance," with what little they have of birth, wealth, learning and looks.

Arrogance, haughtiness and show of pride are the behaviours of the man of pride many people abhor. They are not only valueless, but also a cause for lowly descent in the next life. They are nothing but unwholesome. Therefore, although the status of birth, wealth, learning and looks that one has now is as high as it could be, aiming to better them in the next life, one must break the fang of pride and behave like "the snake with a broken fang, the bull of an ox with broken horns, and the rug with which feet are wiped."

9. DOSA (ANGER)

Harsh and rough nature of the mind is *dosa*. Although it is said to be harsh and rough (anger and aversion), dosa has one other image, its low side, namely sorrow - unlike the clean mind, it is not at ease, a little rough and ruffled. Troubled, depressed, and frightened states of the mind are all in the same nature and classed as dosa.

In short, sorrow, unhappiness, fear, disappointment, sulkiness, anger, grudge, vengefulness, threatening with abuses and shouts, fight, conspiracy to kill, these are all in the nature of dosa. Since fright and violence are both classed as dosa, a man in the habit of great anger is susceptible to fright if fallen in a frightful situation. Take notice and make character assessment of those people. [Violence is waxing dosa; fright, depressive.]

The story of a woman

Something about the nature of various forms of dosa is exemplified by the story of a young woman in India - the story also reminds us of marriages that did not involve love, but were forced upon them by their parents. The two youngsters in the story did not know each other. By an arrangement of parents of both sides, they were wedded. The bride was a girl of good descent, staid and dutiful. But the groom did not care or think well of whatever she did. There was no kindness or tenderness on his part.

Because the husband did not care about her dutifulness, the girl began to get disappointed. She was puzzled and unhappy, often moping in listlessness. Not satisfied from the very beginning, and now seeing her in such an unpleasant state, the husband hated her, some times resorting to violence. The wife was hurt and unhappy. But as she could do nothing about it, she carried on with her duties as usual.

But then, she was flesh and blood, and full of consciousness, not made of stone, and so, every now and then she thought of committing suicide. Her life was hell in the present world, a continuum of anger, disappointment, confusion, unhappiness and fright. She bore it all till she had given birth to two children, when at last she made a decision and sent a letter to the husband who was visiting one other town on business. The letter read:

"Master, although we were wedded by the arrangement of our parents, I had loved you and tried to win your love. But my efforts bore no fruit, and instead they were thought of as deceptions. I was so hurt and unhappy that I often thought of suicide, but without success on account of the two children. Now I have come to the decision that to carry on living would only stretch my unhappiness. After writing this letter, I have poisoned the children's cakes, and also ended my life."

After receiving the letter, the husband came to realize all the virtues of his wife, and immediately returned home, where he found the three properly emplaced corpses of his family, He had his gun handy with him and ended his life. [How various forms of dosa came about has been shown in this story.] Considering this story, as people only meet in the present world for one reason or another, it would be well and good to have mature, generous minds and try to be proper and reasonable in the affairs of personal relations.

Makkha (Ungratefulness)

In connection with dosa, there are other common cetasikas such as *makkha, palāsa, soka, parideva, dukkha, domanassa, upāyāsa* - their natures should also be noted. One of them, *makkha,* is the kind of dosa that does not know the debt of gratitude one owes to others. Since youth, we have owed debts of gratitude to our parents, to our teachers, to our friends and so on, as they have brought about benefits to our advantage. Some people may not think so; not appreciating any beneficence done for them, they may say, "What has he done for me?" and cancel any gratitude that they owe.

Some others, besides not knowing how to be grateful, do damage to their benefactors the way the proverbial dog eats the cowhide it has been sleeping on. Such people are called "*mittadubbhi* = friend-busters - wicked people," very much to be censured. "Someone's kindness" is something to be paid back for. Even if that gratitude, on account of inability, cannot be paid back, it must be appreciated and always thankful. When opportunity and circumstances permit, it should be paid back with all heart and soul.

Lesson: say, a person takes to the shade of a tree for rest and breaks some branches of it. This person and, like him, the friend-busters are two of the same kind, base and wicked.

The son who served a debt of gratitude

There was once a young man in a town, earning his living by carrying and moving loads on his shoulders, while looking after his widowed mother. His mother, however, was not a good sort, having a secret affair with a man and hiding it from the son. Friends who knew about the affair (being kind to the young man, an honest worker and a good son) told him all. But the son said, "Kindly allow mother to do as she wishes and be happy. It is alright if she is happy. Whatever she may be doing, my part is to take care of her." [Just as good sons and daughters are rare, so also there are not many good parents.]

Remark

The mother's baseness was her responsibility. To take care of her was the son's duty. Such caring of the mother must not be taken as caring for the mother as a person, but as a benefactor that she was once. Thus a good character, envisioning the benefits due in the present life and hereafter, should try to pay back the debts of gratitude they owe to others. [There was once a young white elephant that looked after his blind mother. He was caught and taken away by a hunter king who later released him as he went on a hunger strike and, when asked about the reason of his hunger strike, told the king of his mother.]

Palāsa (False pride)

Vying with another person (trying to keep up with or be better than every body) is a kind of dosa called *palāsa*. Not wishing to be anything less than others by way of sila, samādhi, paññā, wealth, beauty, good descent and cleverness, the man or woman of palāsa thinks, "What difference is there between him and me," (notwithstanding whether the other person is actually better, or better by common knowledge). It is an attempt by word of mouth to be on equal terms in personal abilities and qualities. But comparing oneself with another person, thinking one actually has those qualities, is not palāsa.

Soka (Sorrow)

Sorrow is called *"soka." Domanassa vedanā cetasika*, described later, is also "soka" as it is the experience of unhappiness. Every time this soka is experienced, there is dosa with it, requiring one to note dosa as well. Sorrow comes many times during a lifetime: sorrow due to loss of loved ones; loss of wealth and riches; loss of wealth and livelihood of friends who wish one well.

A kind of domanassa

There is a kind of *domanassa* that is mistaken for soka. The fear that loved ones may be sick, that they have not returned home when due, that any thing may happen to babies and young children, these are imagined fears with an accompaniment of a thinking, "If I am not here, they will be in trouble," an ordinary kind of domanassa, not soka.

What good does fear do?

The fears cited above are not easy to bear. They make havocs in the heart and cause a deeply troubled mind. It would have been somewhat bearable if some good comes of them. Actually, there is no good done but a burning heart. Instead of hugging such baseless fears, one should plan ahead and arrange things with much care to avoid them. For instance, for the young ones, instead of fearing for their sickness, one should arrange a proper transport and food in prevention of accidents and sickness.

If something happens, in spite of these precautions, then one is only responsible to send for a doctor.

If danger in traveling to a certain place is really a possibility, then the responsible step would be to stop the young one from going. If it is a must, then action should be taken to arrange a safe passage. If the responsible person is still thinking "if I am not here, what will happen to them?", then one should make sure to find some one to take care of the child. If, in spite of such responsible planning and execution, there is no compliance of the rules on the part of the youth, and harm strikes and kills him, then do not worry. If one continues worrying about such a non-complying person, better note him as one belonging to the class of foolish, useless people. Nowadays, we find so many youngsters who do not pay heed to words of teachers and parents. Because they are so, many of them get into deep troubles. Is it worth, on the part of teachers and parents, worrying for them?

Parideva (Extreme sorrow)

Weeping in despair is *"parideva."* It is actually "weeping with sounds of sobbing or wailing". But the source of the sound is dosa domanassa from inside, and so parideva should be noted as dosa. If one loses or is in the prospect of losing one's official status and privileges, or close relatives, one becomes very sad and dejected. This sadness and dejectedness are domanassa called soka mentioned above. When that sadness cannot be kept down inside, a weeping sound called parideva comes out. What we call "fire of parideva", however, does not mean the weeping sound, but the severely burning dosa domanassa inside the bowel cavity.

Does weeping do any good?

This weeping, like the imagined fear, does not do any good to any one. It is not to blame the one who is stricken with grieve since it is a natural reaction as a loved one or some one dependable suddenly disappears from under one's eyesight. Shin Ānandā wept upon the Buddha's passing-away. But weeping with loud wailings seems like māyā to attract attention for sympathy and pity (it may not be quite so, though). The loud wailings in weeping can hit the hearts of others and make them equally sad. Even some happy people lose their happiness and suddenly become sad when they hear some one weep.

Then why do some people want to yell out in weeping, moving one or two people near by, and, perhaps, more in the next house, some more in two or three more houses, and (may be) the whole village? In so weeping, it amounts to admitting that one has no way, no training, of controlling one's mind, Therefore, once the unavoidable fire of parideva burns, it is essential to finish it with the quiet tears that come down. The nobler and more saintly people who know how to keep their minds under control would take *samvega*[86] from the experience of dukkha so encountered.

How the bodhisatta soothed emotions

Future Gotama Buddha and future Princess Yasodayā were once a millionaire couple who gave away in charity all their possessions to become forest-dwelling ascetics together. The beauty of the young she-hermit was extraordinary in that a seeming smile on her graceful face was an attraction for many people to adore and respect her.

The tender millionaire-turned hermit had to be content with natural fruit and roots and what people gave her, entirely unlike the kind of food she was formerly used to. So, as time went by, she suffered hemorrhage of the stomach and was getting weak day by day. The Bodhisatta helped her lean and rest her weight on his side and took her to a public rest house near the gate of the town, where he placed her down gently and went into town for alms.

While he was thus making his round for alms food, she was unable to stand the strain of the pain any longer and died before he returned. People coming out of town saw the situation, wept in earnest, though not related by blood, and prepared the corpse in proper form for burial.

The Bodhisatta returned at that time, and saw the unexpected funeral affair, the sorrowful sight and a personal blow to him. But he was well composed when he stepped onto the rest house and sat at the head of dead body of his wife. He ate the meal for two, alone, and then gave a talk to the crowd, the way cool water sprinkled over the fire, quieting the parideva of the people.

Malikā, wife of the General

The mental attitude of Malikā, wife of General Bandula was an inspiring one. Bandula and Malikā had thirty and two sons, born as twins. Sons of the extraordinary parents, they accompanied their father together with their attendants on his attendance at the king's court, making a big crowd by themselves.

---

86. (P) a prompt for contemplation, some logical lesson learned from an observation which prompts further thinking or insight meditation

Some court officials, not liking the situation, told the king, "One day, General Bandula, together with his sons, will try to take over the country." The king, thoughtless as he always was, believed it readily. He made a deceitful plan, made the father and sons gather in a building, and killed them by setting fire to the building.

In the morning after the night of the murder of the father and sons, Malikā had planned to give alms food to bhikkhus headed by Ashin Sāriputtarā. When the time of donation was close, she received a letter telling her, "The father and all the sons had died last night," it would not be a surprise if she wailed and cried, but she kept her tears back, put the letter away, and carried on with her charitable work as planned

Remark

Referring to the two stories, one might leave the Bhodisatta's lack of parideva be, as he was already a mature perfectionist. But the ability of Malikā to keep back the fire of parideva was commendable as it was something of inspiration for many. In this human world, one may not live to a hundred years, but may easily find a hundred problems, and so it would help, if one can have the parideva under control to one's utmost ability. Also, in such cases of parideva, one can gauge one's level of perfection on the touchstone of dukkha one meets up with and make an assessment like, "How well do I fare in the matter of fulfilling perfection?"

Dukkhadomanassa (physical and mental pain)

Bodily pain is called "dukkha", and mental suffering "domanassa". Restricted movement in traveling, at work and home, attack of diseases and beating, injuries from accidents, and so on are the cause of bodily pains and physical tiredness; and so, they are all dukkha. If the body suffers pain, one may complain, "Oh, it is painful, dukkha, dukkha." Although the body is painful, the mind may not be unhappy. In fulfilling the moral perfections (the ten paramis), Bodhiattas like Mahosadhā and Vissantarā took bodily pains without a complaint, but because they aimed for the wellbeing of all beings, there was no question of unhappiness: there was no domanassa.

Sadness, unhappiness, puzzlement, dejectedness, and so on, mean dukkha of the mind, called "domanassa." This domanassa vedanā is a disease of the mind. Therefore in saying, "hearing about him makes my mind ache, please don't come and tell me about him," unhappiness was referred to as "mind-ache". Unhappiness and mind-ache occurring in this way may not necessarily be associated with bodily pain. In the middle of good life in association with friends, servants and companions, people may still be disappointed because they "do not get what they want, and not want what they get". That is domanassa. The dimension of this domanassa is bigger than the suffering on the body.

"Unable to bear the strains of domanassa in living atop 'a pile of gold', some young couples left it and took the beating of poverty in a rickety old hut."[87]

Depending on various situations, there are ways one can adopt a happy life. But there are no easy solutions to suit the individual situations for some people with limited intelligence. In short, one must be able to envision and prepare a detailed scheme on every aspect of life for a lasting wellbeing. One must be diligent in trying to fall in line with the scheme. If, in spite of intelligence and diligence, misfortune comes (the target is missed), do not be disappointed. Change course and try again. Diligence is the way of a Buddha-to-be. Besides, it is important not to be shaken down by *loka-dhamma*[88]. Loka-dhamma is after all the kind of natural law that man must meet up with in the course of a lifetime. (Loka = the world + dhamma = nature, the course of nature]

Loka-   dhamma consists of
1. *lābha* -   having an abundance of food, money, assets
2. *alābha* -   not having and abundance of food, money, assets
3. *yasa* -   having companions
4. *ayasa* -   not having companions
5, *nindā* -   getting blames and censures
6. *pasansā* - getting praises
7. *sukha.* -   good health in body and happiness in mind
8. *dukkha* -   suffering in body and mind

Thus there are eight articles of loka-dhamma, four desirable ones and four undesirable. When one gets the desirable items, one is glad, interested and high in spirit. But when one meets with the undesirable items, one is sad and depressed, looking painful. Both types of emotion are natural responses to the impact of loka-dhamma. The one keen to be happy is also very easy to be sad. The one of great happiness can be easily turned into one of great sorrow. Sadness is domanassa.

---

87. Young couples lived with rich parents in law in a not-too-distant past.
88.   Worldly conditions, vicissitudes of life

Therefore, if one wants to be happy, be very careful not to be greatly affected in one's mind on account of the eight articles of loka-dhamma (desirable or undesirable). Details follow.

Lābha – alābha

One must work hard in all fairness to earn a living worthy of one's efforts. But do not be too showy so as to make others hate the sight of you. Some seek profits that could not be made, but instead, might even lose the initial capital, like "losing the water from the bottle." Do not lose heart and be sorrow-stricken. But there are numerous losers that way; even some had lost thrones, changed status from that of masters to slaves wholesale, and there are others who did not answer 'yes, sir..' when called Maung Maung, but said 'phra' when called Aung Kyaw[89]. Therefore keep at all times a firm resolve as not to be moved by the loka-dhamma, regardless.

Yasa – ayasa

Benefactor gentlemen and womenfolk look well only if surrounded by some companions[90]. The companions take care of security inside and outside of the courtyard, and also assist in every other need. To have that many companions, one must distribute one's wealth or income among those people. In Myanmar language, it is 'chwe-yan' for companions: 'chwe' stands for give, and 'yan' for surround; so, 'only if one gives, others would come around one'. One should not treat them like domestic servants, but rather regard their wellbeing and progress in life as dependent on one. One should also regard one's own paid servants as companions and look after them for their progress and betterment in life. In spite of that attitude, if one does not have companions, do not worry. If one has many companions, do not be too proud.

Fame and popularity are important not only in this life but also in every other life. When thinking of doing some noble kind of work, it should be noted that prestige and fame are necessary to achieve success. "*Gunavante passanti janā* = only men with prestige are thought as men," says a Pali text. Therefore proper fame and prestige must be established by knowledge and diligence first. If they are gained, do no brag, and if not, though due, never mind.

---

89. Calling Maung Maung is polite, calling Aung Kyaw or a name without an honourific of Maung or endearing Maung Maung is rude. 'Phra' is a word equivalent to submission..

90. This is a customary view since ancient times in Myanmar, not necessarily adaptable to a modern democratic society, except perhaps by way of friendship which is different by definition.

Nindā-pasamsā

Nowadays, many people are so hateful and jealous, and habitual in making it their business to dispraise others, so much so that it is on rare occasions only anyone may get praise, but certainly and frequently, a censure. So, firstly, take care there is nothing to be blamed for. But then, note that even the ox the king of gods created was criticized for its dung being soft. It is the age of "blame if you hate, praise if you love, and confide if you adore." So, if there is no scarcity of hateful people, there certainly are many who find fault with any body.

But are those people, who easily find fault with other people, flawlessly intelligent and beautiful like Amarā, Kinnari, Maddi, and Sambula[91]? Or, are they real perfectionists like Mahosadhā and Vissantarā[92]? Or, are they as pure and venerable as Ashin Mahākassapa, Ashin Sāriputtarā and Ashin Ānandā[93]? Are they perfect? The little son from a village who came talking about stammering of a lady neighbour, "Fa … Fa… Father, th.. the.. the wo .. wo .. woman f .. f .. from th .. th.. that hou .. hou .. house s .. s .. sta .. stam .. stam .. stammer," found himself stammering. Actually the fault-finder has already been censured for his faults, and so he "must find company".

Or else, it could be that they are doing their utmost to hide their faults like the proverbial "saintly cat." Why is that so? It was because "thieves are wont to accuse others of theft." Other cases are gossiping out of "jealousy of better people," although they may not like to be faulted themselves. Why is that so? For instance, it became the gossip of the town when a young gentleman of some prestige began regularly visiting the place of a young woman; it was actually because the young man was not visiting the gossipers' homes. Thus dispraises and defamations are the unavoidable course of loka-dhamma, but the talks may have no foundation. Even if true, it is more likely that the fear is self-made and exaggerated to a degree over and above the shame and fear one really deserves.

It is like someone who feared ghosts. The sight of the stump of a palm tree in the darkness of a night made him think, and cling to the idea, of a ghost. He became transfixed to the sight and got in a trance so much so that he thought the ghost was chasing him and so ran fearfully, dropping faeces as he ran. Similarly, in some instances, imagination breeds fear and makes one intolerably frightened. Therefore, in Samyutta Pali, "Like the <u>young deer that</u> ran every time it hears some slight sound in the wood,

91. Great beauties in Buddhist literature
92. Buddhisattas of great virtues
93. Disciples of Gotama Buddha

the person, afraid to be a subject of blame and censure, has a mind that is unstable, infirm and negligent," said the Lord. Just as the young deer that runs every time it hears a slight sound does not get enough to eat, so also the man of imagined fear brings about nothing of benefits. As the original aim of blame and censure is to cause shame, if the perpetrator knows the victim is really affected by his slanders, then it would be like "the more pronounced the coma, the more the witchdoctor likes."

Another way of thinking is that it is encouraging to be a subject of gossip. Why is that so? People would not want to talk about the lice on the dog or the grass that grows in between bricks, the mediocre. They would only talk of people with some fame. Therefore, just as the tallest amongst many trees is the one most attacked by the wind, so also the higher the status of a person, the more the attack of the storm of gossip there is. So, instead of caring and being sad about the slanders, one should be glad about them as they are actually the signs of one's higher social or professional standing.

Therefore, whilst not taking much notice of slanders and not being affected like 'a man who rises and looks about every time the house dog barks,' one should try to study well how to nurture a stable and firm mind with mindfulness and concentration. Whenever one is the subject of gossip, one should contemplate, "How well can I stand it?" and try to get used to it. But be careful not to have done any blame-worthy actions.

Just as slanders and gossips should not shake up a man, so also when praised, one should not smile too broadly. In such a situation, one should react with a thought, "It is the natural outcome of my good work," and with a wish to share one's fortune with others, honestly thinking "May others be also praised and honoured." [Sukha and dukkha have already been explained.]

Summing up, in the 8 categories of loka-dhamma, there are 4 desirable kinds called "*itthārammana* (desirable sense objects)", and 4 undesirable kinds, "*anitthārammana* (undesirable sense objects). In all our past lives, we have committed good and evil kammas (kusala and akusala), and now in this life we are bound to find those itthārammanas and anitthārammanas. Finding them thus, we must stand those loka-dhamma storms by all available means, and defend ourselves by dint of hard work and wisdom, and aim to reach the safe port of call named Nibbāna.

For instance, a sea-captain cannot expect to pass the time in crossing an ocean in peace and quiet: he will come across regular breeze and slight waves, often strong winds and waves, and some times mighty storms and high seas that could endanger the ship. Skilled captains with hard work and reasonable wisdom would steer the ship, fighting the storm and high seas to reach his destined port of call.

> *Katattā nānākamānam,*
> *Itthānitthepi āgate.*
> *Yoniso tittham sandhāya,*
> *Tareya nāviko yathā.*

Meaning: Because various kammas, wholesome and unwholesome, were, without a doubt, committed in the samsarā, desirable and undesirable sensations accordingly appear now in this life. But like the sea-faring captain, using appropriate methods and procedures, diligence and wisdom, one must paddle swiftly and overcome all heavy seas and storms of loka-dhamma, right from this port of flaming dukkha here on this side, aiming straight to the safe port of call named deliverance over yonder.

Thus those, who show little reaction to the eight articles of loka-dhamma, plan their life with vision, and work diligently to achieve success, would do well in freeing themselves from physical and mental suffering, and in the performance of perfection in kamma, worthy of human beings.

"Loka-dhamma is nature's course, various in kind and source;
Emòtion not to rise, cultivate the mind to be wise.

Upāyāsa (severe dosa)

The severe dosa that is aroused when one or other kinsfolk, prestige or wealth, is ruined or lost, is called "*upāyāsa.*" In the cases of ordinary dosa (anger or aversion), one wants to kill. But in the case of upāyāsa dosa, it is severe grief. The heat from that stricken mind impacts the heart that pumps out more blood, spreading heat throughout the body, possibly causing a pass-out. The victim may probably suffer fits.

On the death of a loved one, the parideva, causing weeping, can be so extreme that weeping stops and the victim falls into fits. The cause of such fits is upāyāsa. Therefore upāyāsa is more severe than soka-parideva. The searing heat of soka is like that of the oil frying in a pan, while the weeping sound coming out of parideva is like the oil overflowing from the pan. But the extreme heat in upāyāsa is like the oil drying up in it.

Those susceptible to upāyāsa

The faint-hearted and the highly dependent people are susceptible to upyāsa. It is true with the woman-kind, generally. Women's mind, in most cases, is not as strong and reasonable as men's. Most of them are physically weak and ignorant[94], and not eager for knowledge essential in the cultivation of their minds[95]. They are wont to depend on other people. Therefore, when soka strikes, pariveda follows. Those fires of soka and parideva easily set the weak rupa afire, and thus, in a short time upāyāsa takes hold, and the victim may pass out. [Even men, when physically weak, cannot bear the strain on the mind. Therefore, when someone passes away and grief comes in, try to eat nutritious food so as to stand the strain on the mind.] So, men and women, when met with some grievous trouble, must, in the fastest possible speed, extinguish the soka-parideva fire that strikes first Then only, they will be saved from the attack of upāyāsa.

[The way of easing soka-parideva has now been shown. This ends the discussion of the associated articles of dosa]

10. ISSĀ (JEALOUSY, ENVY)

Grudge and jealousy are the nature of "*issā*". When someone tells how one other person is beautiful, wealthy, learned, good of moral character, and so on, the second person's reactions may show not only the apparent jealousy (not wanting to hear), but also say, "Every other bird is as beautiful as the owl", or "Oh, this kind of hare is in every other bush," with distorted looks and eyes askance. All these are issā. [In the villagers' language, it may be "This kind of toddy palm-nut can be picked up from under any other toddy palm-tree."]

"Jealousy for being better: animosity for working in competition; grudge for doing the same work;" these traditional encounters refer to the sort of issā that one might have for another person engaged in the same kind of livelihood. A fish-monger could hardly be jealous of a jeweler. But jewelers might be jealous of each other. Also amongst each group of fish mongers, monks, scriptural teachers, and abbots of monasteries, jealous talks and gossips fly about. A person of good work, intelligence and diligence is not affected by such talks; only the gossipers would be looked down on by thoughtful people - they are bound to suffer in samsāra, being

---

94. Applicable to the time of writing this book
95. Sayadawgyi wrote this in compassion, not in discrimination He had said and written words of great praise for women of high intellect.

destined to lower forms of life. So, issā is an evil dhamma that should be entirely eliminated.

The pigs and the emerald cave

Once upon a time, there lived a lion in an emerald cave in the Himalayas. Many pigs lived near by. The pigs, seeing the lion in the cave, are afraid at all times. They blamed the emerald cave for their fear. One day they consulted among themselves, rolled in a pool of mud, and rubbed their muddy trunks against the walls of the cave. aiming to make them fade.. The cave did not fade, but instead, got polished and shone brighter. Similarly, talking bad of another person out of jealousy only places one in an awkward position. it would only enhance the other person's status.

Praising self and condemning others

Praising self (revealing one's attributes, etc.) every so often is called *"atthukkamsana."* [Attha = self, ukkamsana = put forward, raise] Condemnation of others by word of mouth or in writing is called *"paravambhana."* [para = on others, vambhana = condemning] In atthukkamsana, it could mean taking pleasure in self-praise, amounting to māna. In paravambhana, it could mean issā and jealousy amounting to dosa.

Self-praise

In speeches and write-ups, self-praise can take different forms such as how knowledgeable one is, how wealthy, and how good by lineage; what university degrees one is holding; how one has beaten an opponent in a competition; how one has been in high places although one may be lowly now; (in the case of monks) how one is preeminent[96], and how rich his devotees are; how officially important one is; how one has passed an examination, how good one is in dhamma-talks, and how well one can teach; how one can make gold and silver[97]; and so on (never minding the truth or otherwise). Those self-praises may impress some thoughtless people, but others would think little of the braggart, saying, "That man is kind of queer, isn't he?" Therefore talks and writings in the way of atthukkamsana should be avoided.

---

96. Phone-kam (M), poñña-kamma (P), power status as a result of meritorious deeds in past lives
97. Presumably this refers to alchemy that some monks may engage themselves in.

When occasion calls for self-description . . .

Occasionally, self-descriptions may be necessary for reason of giving others an assurance of one's competence in earning a livelihood or in talking dhamma, and as a caution against low opinion from others. But then, reveal honestly and only as much as may be necessary. Such self-description or -praising is not māna, but skill in rendering a certain type of work effective by way of talks.

Condemnation

Words of condemnation may be found in some writings and talks of careless writers and speakers. Condemnation of a person so that the person may fall to the low opinion of other people is evil and wicked. But when the really wicked person is in the high opinion of many people or one's friends and relatives, one should condemn that person so that the public or the people (associated with one) may not be misled. But in talking of a person's wickedness, if no proof can be produced, there is a possibility of misunderstanding even by one's close associates. So, take great care not to have criticized unworthy cases.

A story was told of an abbot of a monastery, who was very much revered by devotees as if he were an arahanta. One day, at an alms donation gathering, his devotees did not find him among the monks in attendance. So, one of the devotees, thinking, "He may not be well," went to the monastery to find out. But he found the monk in the monastery kitchen, frying eggs by himself. With goose flesh all over, he returned to the gathering and told his wife what he saw. The woman was suddenly taken to fright, thinking, "My husband has gone mad," and called out loudly, "Oh folks, come, come, I don't know what has happened to my man." The man was much ashamed and pretended he was alright now, and told every body that there was nothing the matter. At bed time, he told the woman for the second time. This time too, she was about to shout again, and he had to plead with her not to do so. From then on, the man never again dared to tell anybody about the abbot frying eggs in the kitchen.

Thus, in criticizing others, one may sometimes be thought as mad. Therefore, tell the story if you must, but only at times appropriate.

But then it would only be wise to tell close associates, including members of one's family, of the wickedness (no matter whether they may or may not believe it), so that they may be on guard.

Macchariya (avarice, stinginess)

Stinginess is the nature of *macchariya*. Nowadays, those who are not charitable, and those who are reluctant to give any thing to any body are called people with macchariya. But actually, macchariya is not the lack of a will to give or be charitable - it is a wishing that others do not get anything. Not wanting to give is only the clinging to one's possession - it is lobha. Macchariya is the wish that others do not get any thing, by way of material gains or in attributes, regardless of whether or not the materials or attributes belong to one. Literature mentions five kinds of macchariya:

Avāsamacchariya - Not wanting to give or share one's private place of residence, monastery, bed, and so on and, not wanting to share sanghika paccaya[98] such as monastery, bed and other places with other monks, are all macchariya. But if applied to visits by monks of loose character, it is not āvāsamacchariya. Such macchariya characters, when they die, may, probably, become ghosts (*petas*) at that monastery, or else fall into the hot iron-cage (*niraya*).

11. *Kulamacchariya* - It is the macchariya on own relatives and devotees, or not wanting own relatives and devotees to have any relationship with other monks. But if applied to monks of bad character who would corrupt the faith and confidence in the Three Jewels[99] (*saddha*), it is not kula-macchariya. The monk of this type, when he sees other monks meeting with his devotees, would be unhappy, his bowels becoming extremely hot and may cause vomiting of blood, bowel movement, severing of the intestines, or else extreme poverty in the next life.

12. *Lābhamacchariya* - It is macchariya in other people's material gains, wishing others not to gain any material advantage. But the wish that monks who squander alms do not get any alms, but wishing good monks get alms enough is not lābhamacchariya. Monks of this character can fall into the kind of niraya where they eat and live in the wells of excretion in their next life. [A story to illustrate this point will be told in the section on *kamma*.]

13. *Vannamacchariya* - It is macchariya in other people's physical stature and looks, and intellectual reputation. It is a wish that nobody else be better than one in looks and in social

---

98. Materials and amenities meant for the monks, the donated materials and amenities
99. The Three Jewels are the Buddha, Dhamma and Sangha

recognition. This character is likely to look very ugly and be notorious in the lives hereafter.

14. *Dhammamacchariya* - It is macchariya in dhamma scholarship (also art and craft) that one has mastered. The person of this character does not wish to share with other people the knowledge, literature, art and craft, and techniques of talks one has acquired, and so would not properly answer questions when asked, or show what one has collected in writing, or would not tell all in his lectures and instructions, fearing others may know as much as he does. But applied to those who would misuse the learning and those who would do some damage to the Sāsanā, the wish of withholding knowledge is no macchariya. The character of macchariya is likely to be intellectually handicapped in the next lives, or else, he may fall into the hot-ash niraya.

Food for thought

Thinking of the five kinds of macchariya, they are most likely to occur among some monks and nuns who live on alms and in the monasteries donated by their devotees. Indeed, such incidents are now evidently rampant among some of those people. Among the laity too, the fear of other people to be better than themselves in housing, in wealth and in commerce, in kinship and friendship, in looks, in social stature and fame, in learning and knowledge, and so on, is quite common. These features are the characteristics of macchariya. The characters, the subject of those macchariya, do not actually suffer. To the person entertaining macchariya, though, the mischief is quite apparent and so he should uproot the habit completely out. If people do not stop entertaining this macchariya now, then they must better be prepared to make a trip to the land of the petas.

11. KUKKUCCA (REMORSE, UNEASINESS)

Regret, repentance or remorsefulness is *kukkucca*. It is a troubled conscience, remorseful in worrying over "Oh, what a great wrong I have done!" as well as regretful over "Oh, what a great good I haven't done!"

How it comes about

Four sons of rich parents, commonly known as "Du - Sa - Na - So." had enough wealth to do wholesome deeds in their lifetime, but instead, they went all out for *micchācāra kāma*[100] (sexual misconduct). Upon death, they fell into the hot liquid-iron niraya, known as "lohakumbhi niraya." They rose to the surface of the molten mass once in every sixty thousand years, each able to utter a single sound of a word to mean something before sinking back into the liquid mass, Now, the first one could only say "Du-" that is interpreted as, "We had a lot of wealth in our lifetime to do wholesome deeds that are dependable refuge, but instead, we had only indulged in a wrongful way of living." This man was regretting for having not done wholesome deeds.

The third man[101] could only utter "Na.." that is interpreted as, "Our suffering in this hell would never end. We had done unwholesome deeds in our human lives." This man was regretting for having done unwholesome deeds.

But regretting and remorse may not wait for the next life like the case of those four Du-Sa-Na-So men. It can happen now in this present lifetime. The remorsefulness in the mind can be so intense as to make the body sweat.

How not to regret

Once an unwholesome deed has been done, it cannot be erased by regretting. It only adds new uneasiness of conscience. Therefore, without worrying over the regret, it only remains for one to act so as to overcome the resultant effects of those akusala kammas by not committing such unwholesome deeds again. For one who makes a heart-felt determination, "I will not commit those unwholesome deeds again," and actually keeps the promise, the akusala kammas (if not too heavy) will not take effect. This was the Buddha's utterance as quoted in Mahāvagga Samyuta.

Using time to advantage

Youth is that part of a lifetime in which opportunities are all open in pursuing and achieving education, wealth and meritorious ideals in accordance with one's intellect and wish,. If "one puts plowshare to ground past the rains," one may reap little or nothing. But for one who takes notice of "having not done any meritorious deeds", there should be no regret. It is a lot better to remember late than never to remember.

---

100. (P) Also called *kāmesumicchā cāra*
101. Apparently, the author omitted the second and the fourth men for the sake of brevity.

There was once an old man by the name of Tambadāthika who, in his prime of life, had earned his living in a king's employ, as an executioner. He was retired when too old to carry on with the job. He met with Ashin Sāriputtarā when he was near his death. He was unable to pay attention to what the Ashin said as there was a great difference between what he was hearing and the type of work he had done for a living.

The Ashin understood then, and asked the man. "Dayakar[102], did you kill because you wanted to, or because the king asked you to?" The man's answer was, "No, Ashin, I did not want to kill. I did so, as the king asked me to." The Ashin asked in a feint, "If that were so, are you at guilt? and carried on talking dhamma. The man was relieved, thinking, "I don't seem to be guilty," and concentrated his attention on the talk, thereby achieving the level of a "*culasotapana*" (lesser-sotapana), and rose to the abode of gods as he died. [In this story, although the killing was done on the king's order, both actions, the ordering and the killing, were wrongful. But only to relieve the man of guilty-consciousness, the Ashin asked the question as a way of gaining attention.]

Remark

The old man had done too many killings, and so it is certainly *pānātipāta*[103]. But the question was asked on purpose, though cleverly designed, to free him of kukkucca. Indeed, the kukkucca was removed and the man was able to concentrate on the dhamma. Due to this wholesome mental action, he became a god of the heaven upon his death. So, no body must worry over the unwholesome deed already done, and regret for having not done wholesome deeds not yet done. One must try not to do any new unwholesome act, but try to engage in wholesome deeds at any age, any time, as soon as one gets to know.

12. THINAMIDDHA (SLOTH AND TORPOR)

Sloth and sluggishness in both body and mind is "*thina*". Torpor or drowsiness is "*middha*." These two cetasikas usually occur together. Under their influence, diligence is lacking while laziness is apparent. There is no eagerness at work, but only hesitancy and reluctance. They are evident when about to fall asleep and, for some people, while listening to dhamma talks.

---

102 (M) A form of address to a lay devotee
103 (P) the taking of life, a wrongful kamma

Not all cases of sleepiness are thinamiddha. Some sleepiness is due to physical tiredness after much hard work. This type of sleepiness exists even with aranhantas. Trees are withered with drooping branches and shriveled foliage in the heat of the sun as if they are sleepy. Therefore every case of sleepiness is not thinamiddha. Only in other cases where the mind and its associates are not fresh and alert but sluggish and torpid, it is thinamiddha. Nowadays, the one who is lazy and dull is talked about as "man of extreme thinamiddha".

13. VICIKICCHĀ (SCEPTICAL DOUBT)

Skepticism about the Buddha, Dhamma and Sanghā is "*vicikicchā*". It is not a total disbelief but a half-hearted belief. The doubts are:

1. Is it true of the Buddha being omniscient, knowing all and sundry?
2. Is it true that the abodes of gods can be accessed and Nibbāna attained by following the path shown by the dhamma?
3. (Looking at well-behaved bhikkhus) are they properly practising sanghās?
4. Do our observation and upkeep of precepts and vows, moral uprightness and the sanghās' code of conduct, bring about any real benefit?
5. Have we or have we not been in the previous lives? (Is this present life created by the eternal God?)
6. Is it correct that there is life after this one? (Will we be finished after we die in this life?)
7. Can it be true that wholesome and unwholesome actions remain in the continuum of khandha as good and evil kamma? (Doubt about kamma)
8. Is it true that kammic actions carry resultant effects? (Disbelief in effects of kammic actions)
9. Is it true of the dependent relationship of *avijja* causing *sankhāra*, and so on? (Disbelief in Dependent Origination of mind and matter) Note that not believing in the Buddha and etc. is thus vicikicchā. It is also called "suspicion".

False vicikicchā

There can be doubts about whether certain affairs are correct and proper: for example, the meaning of a passage in a letter, the method of doing a job, and the road to take in traveling. Even arahantas sometimes were not sure of applications of certain rules of Vinaya, thinking "Is this manner proper?" This kind of doubting or uncertainty is not vicikicchā. In some cases, it is contemplation, and in others, it is only *vitakka* (initial thought), or simply getting an idea or a sense. Only the doubting of the Buddha, Dhamma and Sanghā that should certainly be believed, is true vicikicchā. When vicikicchā is thus aroused, one should ask the learned teachers. Only then, one can be free of vicikicchā, fully confident with one's belief in the Buddha, Dhamma and Sanghā.

Conclusion

Every one of us can detect in our consciousness continuum the akusala cetasikas shown above. The whole world is troubled by them as seen in all the various forms of suffering every day.

For this work of great effort in trying to describe, and make people understand, the cetasikas that influence the minds to be evil, may I, in the continuum of my thoughts and behaviours, progress with less and less of evil nature and wrongfulness. May my associates, old and young, be of good mind; may readers of this book be the same.

> I have written with efforts to contribute
> To change the attitude
> From evil to the noble attributes;
> May I be endowed with the grace
> Of a noble mind
> To do away with the wicked kind;
> May my associates, young and old,
> Be likewise endowed,
> And destined
> Straight through the Nibbāna threshold.

This ends the Chapter on Mind Associates that influence the mind to be evil and wicked.

CHAPTER THREE

WHOLESOME FACTORS

Cetasikas that influence the mind to be noble and wholesome

(1) *Saddhā* (defined below)
(2) *Sati*
(3) *Hiri*
(4) *Ottappa*
(5) *Alobha*
(6) *Adosa*
(7) *Amoha*

(8) *Mettā*
(9) *Karunā*
(10) *Muditā*
(11) *Upekkhā*
(12) *Sammāvācā*
(13) *Sammā-kammanta*
(14) *Sammāājiva*

[Summary] - **Saddhā** is faith and confidence; **Sati** mindfulness; **Hiri** moral shame; **Ottappa** moral dread; **Alobha** greedlessness; **Adosa** hatelessness; **Amoha** nondelusion, wisdom; **Mettā** love and kindness for one and all; **Karuna** compassion; **Muditā** sympathetic joy; **Upekkhā** equanimity; **Sammāvācā** right speech; **Sammā-kammanta** right action; **Sammāājiva** right livelihood; These are the cetasikas that influence the mind to be virtuous, noble and wholesome.

1. SADDHĀ (FAITH, GENEROSITY)

The nature of trust, faith and confidence is saddhā. It is "**yonkyi**" in Myanmar. In saying "yonkyi", each of the two syllables, "yon" and "kyi", has its own distinct meaning.

How "yon" means

In ditthi, there is no causal kamma and so it carries neither good nor evil effects; there has been no previous life, and will be none hereafter; there is no such thing as God-like perfected man who knows all the phenomenal laws of nature[104] or Dhamma, and so there is no such doctrine as Dhamma and consequently, no Sangha. This, indeed, is a wrong view,

104. This is a reference to the omniscience of the Buddha

completely devoid of belief in the processes of kamma. In vicikicchā, the belief (yon) is 50-50 either way. But in saddhā, it is a complete trust and faith (yon) in "the actuality of causal kammas and their effects". This principle is interpreted in the scriptural literature as "saddhāmokkha = decision based on belief (yon). Note that only this kind of belief (yon) in the evidently right view is the real, wholesome saddhā.

How "kyi" means

While giving alms and donations, while keeping precepts and meditating, and while doing any other wholesome deed, a clear (and pure) ('kyi") saddhā is there in the mind. When a piece of ruby is placed in muddy water, the clouding particles settle down and the water becomes clear (kyi). Similarly, when the ruby-like saddhā appears in the mind, the dirty vicikicchā and other defilements disappear, and the mind is completely clear. Such is the property of saddhā in its ability to make the mind clear.

It is difficult in some animals and children to have saddhā as they do not understand causal kammas and their effects, but their minds may become clear when imitating the elders in bowing down in reveremce to the Buddha and the Sanghā, in giving gifts and assistance to others. Those with wrong views also have this true kyi-saddhā, a true kusala kamma, in giving donations for hospitals, homes for the aged, leprosiums, orphanages, schools and so on.

Note: For better understanding of the behaviours regarding this true saddhā, continue reading "Saddhā-caritta" in the Chapter on Carita[105].

False saddhā

As shown so far, it should be sufficiently clear that saddhā in its final analysis is a blameless, pure faith, a faith in the right view. Some people, their livelihood being dependent on pilgrimage to a pagoda[106], tell tales of miraculous lights issuing from the pagoda; belief in such tales is no true saddhā. Believing people who tell of imitation relics of the Buddha or arahantas as true is no true saddhā. Also believing in what people of wrong views tell of their view is no true saddhā. It is naivety, simplicity, and so unwholesome moha.

---

105. (P) Habitual thoughts, talks and actions, trait, inclination, moral character
106. They work in the precinct of a pagoda or in the vicinity - the pseudo-trustees or the small entrepreneurs.

Some women and men say, "We venerate him so much", about a hermit or a monk, because the subject has the attractive qualities of talk, voice, looks, service, doctoring, and so on. That cannot be a true saddhā. It is only intimacy and liking, not free of tanhā-pema. Such veneration is mentioned in scriptural literature as *"muddhap-pasanna[107]"*. [Muddha = naive, pasanna = veneration]

Warning

There is so much falsehood around and about nowadays. There are strange teachings in other religions. So also among the so-called Buddhists, there are some people who mislead the public by distributing strange teachings, strange meditation practices, and strange medicines. Donating and offering alms to these people ate not of true saddhā. They are the gifts of tanhā-love, the giving of naive people.

Because men of wisdom think these shams are "not worth caring", they are now sitting in shrine rooms. Rightly or wrongly, some ladies are leading in the affairs of the dhamma. Therefore, regarding all aspects of human life, careful consideration as to what to believe and what not to believe should be exercised, and a progress made in the context of correct religious cultivation (beginning with the ladies).

How saddhā and pema are mixed

Nowadays, there are some virtuous people who cannot distinguish between saddhā and pema. The person of venerable composure and manners, talks and teachings are venerated for the person's personality. That is saddhā. For his teaching, the devotees love him like a relative. In this context, veneration is saddhā; loving is pema. The devoted Vekkali venerated and loved the Buddha. Chanda Mathera, known by many as the Buddha's childhood slave, loved the Lord as his master.

The principle of saddhā is true kusala, truly wholesome; love is *samyojana[108]*, true akusala, truly unwholesome. That samyojana, or personal attachment, can be channeled into knowledge and kusala dhamma. According to a Pathāna Pali text[109], unwholesomeness of minor consequence can be a good foundation for substantial wholesomeness. But

---

107. *yo babavatiyā saddhāyā samannāgato avusadañāno so muddhappasanno hoti na avicca pasanno, tathāhi avatthusamin pasidati, seyathāpi titthiyā.*
(Ekanipāta Inguttaratikā)

108. (P) Threads, ropes, fetters or bonds

109. Quote: *"akusalodhammo kusalassadhammassa upanissaya paccayo."* (Pathāna Pāli)

only if the master talks and teaches earnestly, and the pupil follows up just as earnestly, benefits can be harvested.

2. SATI (MINDFULNESS)

Remembering and keeping in mind is the nature of *sati*. Sati takes many forms. Suppose there was a wholesome deed done in the past. Now that affair comes back to the mind. While listening to a dhamma talk or taking instructions, one listens with attentiveness so that one may understand and remember what is being said. While at meditation, one keeps in mind the sense object (ārammana) with full alertness and effort so that the object may not be lost from one's attention.

One thinks, in advance, of a kusala kamma one will do tomorrow or some other time later. One takes care not to breach the precepts one is observing. One watches oneself so as not to flare up or indulge in lobha, dosa, māna, and etc. One remembers the teacher's instructions and homilies. Such remembering and keeping in mind are true sati. It is also called "*appamāda* (= not forgetting)". Therefore, when monks give precepts to their devotees, they always urge them to have sati, saying, "*appamādena sampādetha* = Mind, do not forget, and have sati in having done wholesome affairs." The Lord had also spoken, "Bikkhus, sati is indispensable in all affairs."[110] [Basically, it meant that saddhā, viriya, etc., may be in excess, but sati can never be in excess, and so, in every manner of life, one should have sati.] Also on the verge of His passing away, the Lord said, "appamādena sampādetha."

False sati
Thinking of relatives, missing each other while husband and wife are apart, remembering the appointment with a friend, coming to mind of someone who has done some favours, and the like are related to tanhā-pema. Besides that, thinking of taking a revenge on the oppressor, remembering the time for killing, remembering dangers on the road, and so on, are related to dosa and domanassa. Those remembrances and coming to mind are not true sati. They are categorized as good memory in the nature of saññā and the ability to take up an idea on the mind in the nature of *vitakka* (thought conception) to be shown later.

---

110. Quote: "*satinca khavāhan bhikkhave sabbathktam vadāmi.*"

3. HIRI AND OTTAPPA (MORAL SHAME AND MORAL DREAD)

To feel the sense of shame to do unwholesome deeds is *hiri*, and to be afraid to do unwholesome deeds is *ottappa*. Just as hiri is the character of those who keep their honours intact, so also ottappa is a distinct characteristic of those who respect parents, teachers, senior relatives, etc., and other virtuous people.

Thinking, "I am a man of good family. If a man of my breed is doing something unwholesome (for instance, fish mongering), then it would be something to be ashamed of," one feels ashamed to do anything unwholesome, and would avoid doing it as an act of protecting the honour of one's clan. An educated man would think, "A learned man like me would shame myself if I do this base, unwholesome act (taking other people's belongings unfairly)." An elderly man also thinks, "It would be shameful if an old man like me do this unwholesome thing (say, lying)." Thus, hiri is distinctly evident as a source of self-respect.

If I am one doing unwholesome deeds, my mother, father, relatives and teachers will all be the subject of gossip and censure in the spittle-pool of others, suffering like the proverbial "all the fish in a boat, getting rotten for one single fish gone bad." Thus, ottappa is the evident fear of one who has such concerns towards one's kith and kin. This is the second source of self-respect. There is neither hiri nor ottappa in the man who has no self-respect, nor any concern for one's teachers, family and relatives; that man would show contempt for virtues and carry on with his customized unwholesome habits.

And so, because these two cetasikas, hiri and ottappa, protect human race by drawing lines between sons and mothers, and brothers and sisters, they are called "*loka-pāla* = world-protectors". And, because they can manage purity and blamelessness, they are also called "*Sukkadhamma* = puritanical principles." If the human world were devoid of these two principles, it would not be much different from the animal kingdom, but a chaotic world of unspeakable manners. Even today, as we intermingle with people who lack the virtues of hiri-ottappa, we see a great many with scanty dress and indecent manners, making unsavory scenes. If this continues, we will, very soon, see tails sprouting out.

False hiri-ottappa

Although the feelings of shame and fear are said to be hiri-ottappa, not every bit of the senses of shame and fear is true hiri-ottappa. Only the sense of shame and fear in doing unwholesome deeds is true hiri-ottappa. Feeling ashamed in going for Sabbath and Dhamma talks; that of having to appear to talk or read to an audience; that of having to take up a lowly job, but not feeling ashamed to die of starvation and be a good-for-nothing jobless loafer; the shyness between a boy and a girl; these are not cases of true hiri. They are only, pretensions, deceits and haughtiness. According to Abhidhamma, they are only tanhā by nature.

The 4 cases of freedom from shame

In the books that instruct guidance for worldly benefits, there are 4 situations in which there should be no sense of shyness or shame -

(1) when paying out interests in commercial transactions;
(2) when approaching teachers and learning from them;
(3) when eating;
(4) When husband and wife are making love.

[In these situations, there is no question of wholesomeness or unwholesomeness. It only means not to feel shy or ashamed in the pursuit of worldly happiness.]

The feeling of fear for the judge in a court of law; the fear of villagers riding trains and steamers for going to toilet; the fear of a man for another man, for dogs or for ghosts; the fear about visiting a place one has never been to before; the fear of young man and women in meeting each other; the fear of the elders and the fear to talk in front of them; these fears are no true ottappa. They show the weakness of character on the bases of unwholesomeness, defined as *domanassa*.

The mid point

From the foregoing, it should be understood that in the cases of non-akusala kamma, there should be no shame, and no fear. But it does not mean that one must be a devil daring to do anything, shameless and fearless. The devil of a fool has no respect for others, deep in dosa and māna, and the dare-devil is steep in dosa and moha. Therefore, one must avoid the shame and fear that should not be there on one hand, and the dare-devilish non-fear and non-shame of foolhardiness and disrespect for parents, teachers and elders on the other. One must choose to apply oneself to be clever, knowledgeable, and amenable to wholesomeness so that one stands at the mid-point of gracious, virtuous non-shame and non-fear.

[In this world, people fear what they should not. They do not fear unwholesomeness that they should.   - Dhamma][111]

4. ALOBHA (GREEDLESSNESS)

Not desiring or wanting to get something is the nature of *alobha*. The nature of alobha is the antithesis of lobha. The two cetasikas are archenemies like fire and water. Whatever lobha wants, alobha does not. The difference between the persons of lobha and alobha can be noticed by sight.

The monk of lobha
If the person with lobha is a monk, he would want material things. He would talk to his devotees, persuading them to donate. When he gets them, he is reluctant to give them away in charity, and holding on to them, he would think, "Well, well . . . I am so great," and be self-opinionated. Actually, he was base and lowly, because he had to beg the wealthy devotees for their charity, and this he does not notice, poor monk.

The men of lobha
Men of lobha are of the same kind. They seek material gains by hook or by crook, without any consideration of fairness. When they get what they seek, they are not contented - it is like "the more the ghost gets, the more it wants." Of the wealth one has gathered in a lifetime, one thinks, "These are mine, they are mine," and clings to them till death after which these riches become nothing but something to send one to the realm of the ghosts. Lobha is such a wicked factor of consciousness influencing the mind in bringing one to such a lowly state of affairs.

The monk of alobha
Alobha is not like that. If the person is a monk, he does not love the wealth or materials. It is not pleasurable to get material donations so readily. He seems to think that it is shameful to be greedy, and that the getting of alms, given by devotees for the purpose of their kusala merits, is a great thing, even as a gentleman, if not as a monk. It seems to be characteristic of the "gentleman" to think he would rather give to others

---

111. Quote: *"abetabbamhi bhāyanti, bhāyitabbe na bhāyare."*

than take charity from others. Therefore, a monk of principles would not take pleasure in the receiving of material donations.

The man of alobha

In the case of the laity, one has to seek material wellbeing as a matter of course, but would not seek gains unscrupulously. He is not in the habit of indulging in sensual pleasures. In doing business, one is habitually kind and considerate towards the poor, habitually charitable, never hesitant in his charitable deeds, and completely detached as to the outcome of his generosity. The like of such a personality could leave mansions and palaces, completely unattached, and take to the monastery of a thatched hut, absolutely contented and happy.

Thus, as there is a vast difference in principles between lobha and alobha, they are like running back to back. Those people who think themselves to be saintly perfectionists[112] should make self-assessments in line with the foregoing discussions to see which one of the two kinds they really are. They should ask themselves, "What kind am I, man of lobha or man of alobha?" If still a man of lobha, then make amends now, in this lifetime. If on the side of the man of alobha, then one is already on sound foundations, but take care and make efforts to be truly on the track of alobha in all aspects so as to progress further onward.

5. ADOSA (HATELESSNESS)

Not being rough and violent is *adosa*. Adosa is in opposition to, and an archenemy of, dosa; it is like the way a snake would turn away from its archenemy, the gecko[113]. Just as man of dosa is rough and violent, the man of adosa is gentle and pleasant. Since his mind is at ease and peace, he can forbear all the insults as might be inflicted on him, and can cool down the heat of the dosa. It is not only the cool in his mind. His face is also, unlike the tense features on the face of the angry man, clearly lit like the silvery moon in the sky, clear and pleasant to look at. His usage of words is also so pleasant and effective that others cannot help but like him. The inherent adosa brings forth enormous power over people. *Metta*, the world's most favourite virtue, is actually this adosa.

[Metta will be shown soon.]

---

112. Those aiming for fulfilling the Ten Perfections of Bhodisattas
113. The black lizard, *tout-tai* in Myanmar

The alobha and adosa of Bhodhisatta

Once upon a time King Brahmattha of Bārānasi took on a young queen when his Chief Queen passed away. He placed his grown son, Prince Mahāpaduma, as Crown Prince. One day, as there was an uprising in the country, the king personally led a compaign to crush the rebellion, leaving the Crown Prince to take charge of the palace. After the rebellion was crushed, the king returned. The city gate was duly decorated to welcome him. When the king was approaching at the gate, the prince, in preparation for reporting to the king, went to the queen for any instruction as to "what ought to be done." The queen, already enchanted with the looks of the prince, took him by the hand and indicated to the throne. The prince refused, and refused the urging three times. The queen then said, "Very well, for this refusal of my wish, you will learn when the king returns." When the prince left, saying, "Do as you wish," the queen tore herself with her own claws and pretended as if she was bullied and physically abused by the prince.

As soon as the king was in town, he asked after the queen as he did not see her. The queen's ladies in waiting replied that the queen was indisposed. So he went to her bed chamber. The queen showed all the scratches and told a tale of how the prince had molested her, how he had clawed her all over because she did not let him, all that was in her woman's māyā (learned without a teacher), sobbing.

The king, angry in the manner of "Touch my wife, and get my sword," was unable to contain himself, and so ordered the prince to be dropped off a mountain top into the abyss. Then, afraid that people who loved the prince might take the prince away by force, the king went with the executioners and saw the prince dropped from the cliff-top. But for the power of the prince's metta, the guardian spirit of the mountain saved him from being killed.

Remarks

In this story, at the time the queen and the prince met, the queen's desire, *tanhā-lobha citta*, was strong. The prince's non-desire, *alobha citta*, was evident. After that the queen had self-protecting *māyā citta*, and again, in presenting her case to the king, the scheming of māyā citta (*musāvāda*, lying). The king, from the beginning of hearing the false story to the end of throwing down the prince, had extreme *dosa*. The prince had *alobha citta* in not desiring the young queen, *adosa citta* in not hating the king and the queen, forbearing *khanti* citta, and *metta citta* in loving kindness or *adosa citta*. The prince in the story was the Bhodisatta, the queen Cincamānavikā to-be, and the king Shin Devadattha to-be[114].]

Epilogue

After the episode, the prince was taken away by the king of dr agons[115] and let him stay in their abode for one year. Then he returned to the human world to live a hermit's life. A hunter found him in the forest and reported to the king. Now knowing the truth, the king called the son back who refused to return. He could not get over the fact of the queen having made him act wrongfully, so he thought the queen must pay back for what she did[116]. The queen was thrown down from the peak; she did not die immediately but suffered injuries and pains, rolling and twisting over and over, alive in niraya.

6. AMOHA (WISDOM)

Amoha is wisdom or *paññā*. Whatever moha hides and covers up, paññā or amoha does its utmost to uncover and reveal the truth. Thus, moha and amoha are arch-enemies like the proverbial "brown hawk[117] and the crow".

The true paññā

In ñāna paññā (wisdom), there are two types, namely the true and the false paññā. Among them, the knowledge of causal kamma and its effects, understanding of the true import of books and literature, vipassanā ñāna, the Buddha's *sabbaññuta ñāna*, and all the rest of innocent, civilized learning and wisdom are true paññā.

The false paññā

Those who are dubbed as "smart people" are clever in making others fall for them by the techniques of manners and verbiage, in hiding and stealing, in deceit and stratagems. That kind is not true paññā. It is falsehood and circumvention called "*vancanā* (false paññā)". By the principle of paramattha saccā, it is tanhā-led akusala. Besides, there are also such kinds of cleverness as how to attack, how to kill, how to make

---

114. Cincamāna and Devadattha were two principal villains in the lifetime of the Buddha
115. They are a class of dragons having the supernatural powers of gods. (devas)
116. In Myanmar it is "one suffers the way one makes another suffer = karlawibak naukpotet".
117 Khinboke in Myanmar.

and use good weapons. They are also not true paññā, to be shown later as *vitakka,* clever unwholesome thinking.

But dull and intellectually handicapped people have no such false paññā. Only those who have inherent and latent true paññā, and those with wide general knowledge can be that clever. The true paññā is the basis of this false paññā as assisted by *pakatupanissaya,* a pathāna causal factor. Therefore, just as those with inherently sharp intellect are capable of reaching to the highest point in the domain of wholesome endeavours, they are also capable of the utmost in the domain of unwholesome deeds.

Jātipaññā and pavattipaññā (Inborn intelligence and acquired knowledge)

There are two types of true paññā, namely jātipaññā and pavattipaññā. The person who was conceived in the mother's womb with alobha, adosa and amoha is called *"tihetuka puggala,"* meaning "the person with 3 hetukas at conception" The amoha also called paññā of that person is jātipaññā (inborn intelligence). That type of person is easy in learning since childhood. He can think and contemplate this way and that.

Without the inborn paññā, the wisdom accumulated from learning since childhood from good parents, learning at school, learning by more studies with the assistance of the wise teachers, and acquiring wide general knowledge in adulthood are all pavattipaññā. So, a person without jātipaññā can cultivate pavattipaññā. The person who has not only jātipaññā, but also pavattipaññā can reach the top class in human society.

How to prepare jātipaññā

The gift of ñāna since conception is not only beneficial in the worldly life, but also it is an advantage in meditation. A person with jātipaññā can achieve success in meditation. So, to be gifted with inborn intelligence in all the existences to come, people should prepare themselves for it in the present life. Here are some methods: one must, in the first place, want to be a sharp-witted, well-learned person; to justify that, one must pay earnest attention and read with all heart and soul the literature written to provide knowledge and wisdom; one must keep in touch with the learned people and ask for, and make note of, their advice. That much of effort would lead one to growing pavattiñāna, and pave the way for a well-developed intellectual. Then it would have cultivated a predisposition to wisdom, an imprint in the structure of one's causal kamma, to be carried in the continuum of the samsāra. But then, one should not be contented.

To be fresh and open to learning, one must be clean, neat and tidy in all manners of life starting with one's body, dress and bed. Every time one gives in charity, one must wish in mind and say , "I wish to be sharp in wit and wisdom." When offering alms to the sanghas, one should have a wish for them, "May you learn, teach and write." If circumstances allow, one should establish a teaching monastery, have a qualified teacher, worship and support him with all the facilities and amenities required for the teaching.

One must also support schools for lay people, assist people in their education, and want to share with others what one has learned. If one has such keen interest in education thus, one can be a great man of learning and wisdom all along in the samsāra. That is how to prepare and acquire jātipaññā in the continuum of one's life in the samsāra.

The difference between saddhā and paññā

The nature of saddhā is such that it is satisfied so long as charity can be performed with the important idea of one's wellbeing all along the samsāra. There is not much consideration of patriotism and religion. But the nature of paññā is such that it places emphasis on the kinship (patriotic spirit) and religion, and charity is offered only if it is beneficial along that line of thinking. A trust in good causal kamma and its good effectual consequence (kamma and its effects) would eliminate the thought of beneficence to be realized in the next life.

Thus, the difference between saddhā and paññā is fundamental and vast. The nationhood of Myanmar may be looked at from differing points of view. But one-sided and biased view, instead of a balanced one, is no way for either saddhā or paññā. It is only proper to take a look at both sides of a coin. "Too much saddhā is tanhā (passion), whereas too much paññā is māyā (wickedness)", reads a customary saying in literature.

[Note: To write fully on how people look at things with one or the other of saddhā- and paññā-eyes, it would take a full-length book. So it is over-looked here.]

Urging

No matter whether the knowledge and wisdom of the people are genuine or false, it is only important that they have the seedling of that quality. For people to live, the heart is the most important part of life. Similarly, wisdom is the heart of the matter in development and progress of life at present and beyond. Only people of wisdom can know and see through the benefits of perfections in dāna, sila, etc., and only by way of the wisdom that those perfections can be pursued and fulfilled.

In life, doesn't domestic peace depend on knowledge and wisdom of man and wife? In managing the affairs of the children, business development and progress, only couples with knowledge and wisdom would understand the advantage of work and diligence, and make life pleasant. They would, "dare appear with wisdom in the midst of a public show, and be admired." Other people, not particularly intelligent but rather idiotic in verbiage and mannerism, can hardly be classed high, although they may be rich, enjoying themselves well enough.

It is this power of paññā (knowledge and wisdom) that overwhelms and rules the world. Capitalists took their share of the riches by assisting those men of knowledge. From insignificant arguments to the global wars between nations, the side of the wise usually wins victory. In the Catudhamma jātaka, in the battle field of his homeland of River Ganga, the Bhodisatta king of monkeys beat his enemy the crocodile by way of a clever deceit. [In this story, deceit is a false paññā. But in the business of improving situations in life, it is a very useful tool.]

In the Mahosadhā jātaka, the power of paññā of the Bhodhisatta handsomely defeated the huge forces of Kevut Brahmin and King Cularmani, like the way crows were driven away by merely frightening them. Myanmars had little or no interest in the pursuit of worldly knowledge when men of technology and knowledge annexed the country[118] for its riches in petroleum, gemstones and forests, the way snot-eating children were cheated. It was the power of knowledge with which they took over the country.

Even today[119] foreigners, sharp witted in commerce and business, are exploiting our local men and women; even those foreigners, thought to be of lower class, are doing retail business with their enterprise and talents. But our local people are still asleep like the proverbial "Po Thu Taw[120] who sleeps all day long under a banyan tree on the mound."

Oh ... people, there is no need of advice from a fortune-teller to know that any country with few learned people are outclassed and outsmarted by others. School teachers, who love the people, please give good guidance. School children, work hard and learn well. Men of riches and members of Sangha, please support and encourage education to develop on all fronts.

118. This refers to aannexation of Burma by Britain in 1885
119. This refers to post WW II years
120. Man in whites, living in a monastery, running errands, and eat
Man in whites, living in a monastery, running errands for the head monk

Only if the whole country works hard thus, the people can rise above the status quo, and advance as sharp-minded owners of jāti-paññā into the continuum of the samsāra.

7. METTA (LOVING KINDNESS)

There is no separate cetasika as "*mettā*". *Adosa* cetasika that wishes the wellbeing of all beings is called "*mettā*". Therefore, mettā is kindly love that wishes the wellbeing (the wish to assist and facilitate in the welfare) of all beings.

The false metta

The love extant amongst members of a family and between man and wife also wishes the wellbeing of each other, and to protect and aid each other. People say they "have mettā" for the people they love. But, such love is not the true type of mettā; it is, as we have seen in the Section for lobha, "*gehassita pema* = home-dependent love".

Once upon a time, a devotee asked his mentor monk, "Ashin Phra, with whom do I begin to extend mettā to?" The Sayadaw said, "Begin with the one you love most." So, the man sat outside the bedroom and began his mettā kammatthāna, with the mind attendant on his wife. His love for her grew and grew. He rose and went to his wife, but the door was bolted from inside, and he could not get in. So the poor man spent the night outside the room, with his head butting against the walling. That is "home-bound love".

A certain cow's metta

It should not be said, however, that the love in the way of such tanhā-pema "cannot always be true mettā and kusala citta". Quite often, it can be true mettā and true kusala citta. Once, a mother cow, whilst feeding her small calf, was speared by a hunter; but for the cow's power of mettā, it was said, the spear became like a palm-leaf, soft and supple, unable to pierce the cow, and dropped to the ground. Thus, amongst the kinsfolk, parents and offspring, and between men and wives, true mettā is quite possible.

The mettā of Sāmāvati

King Utena of Kosambi had 3 queens, namely Sāmāvati, Māganti and Vāsuladatthadevi. Sāmāvati was a devotee of the Three Jewels[121]. Māganti, before she was queen, had a grudge to settle with the Buddha

---

121. Buddha, Dhamma and Sanghā

since her youth as a young Brahmin girl. So, she was always trying to find fault with Sāmāvati. Sāmāvati was one who particularly practiced mettā kammatthāna. King Utena visited the bedchambers of the 3 queens in turn. He was a harpist by nature.

One day, when the turn for the king to go to Sāmāvati's chamber was drawing near, Marganti, with the assistance of her uncle, got a highly venomous snake, put in the hollow of the harp, and its venom drained off. Then she closed the hole with some threaded flowers. Next, she went to the king and made her plea that the king should not visit Sāmāvati as she had bad omens in her dream. The king would not be persuaded, and went to Sāmāvati's chamber; Marganti went along, pretending she was concerned.

When they arrived in the chamber, the king had his royal meal and rested on the couch. Marganti, pretending to be busy, pulled the threaded flowers from the hole of the harp. The very angry snake came out, hissing, and got close to the king's head. Pretending to be a great deal frightened, and pointing to the king, Marganti blamed Sāmāvati and her companions, saying this so happened because the king did not listen to her.

King Utena did not understand Marganti's schemes, but he was so frightened and angry that he picked up his bow and arrows, ordered Sāmāvati and her maids to fall in a straight line. Meanwhile, Sāmāvati told her companions,

"My girls, do not bear a bit of anger towards the king or Marganti. At this kind of moment, we have nowhere else but mettā to take refuge to. Only, try to carry on extending your usual mettā to the king and Marganti.

The women, already tamed to the core, not regarding the danger of life as urgent, had their minds on mettā meditation. The king, his anger still not abated, already had aimed and, with all his strength, pulled on the bow and released the arrow. But the arrow, for the power of mettā, stopped short of the target, returned to the king and dropped at his feet. Then, the king took hold of himself, dropped down at the feet of Sāmāvati and apologized.

Remark on the story

Marganti had a jealous heart, issā, on Sāmāvati for being better; māyā in scheming; and dosa in wanting to get the other queen killed. King Utena was overwhelmed with anger, dosa on seeing the snake; and much frightened, dosa and domanassa, when the arrow returned to him. The maids and Queen Sāmāvati were able to keep and maintain mettā citta on the enemy.

What should be copied

Noble people, having aimed high in life, keeping in mind the tradition of Sāmāvati, should try to improve your own minds to be better and better, not reacting to the actions of those who have unjustifiable envies, *issā-macchariya*, on you. If opportunity permits, do whatever you can to help and serve wholeheartedly those jealous people, making proper use of the invaluable weapon of mettā. Only if such utilization of mettā is made, you can be thought of as perfectionists[122]. [Mettā is like water, and dosa fire. The more the water, the less the fire is. Therefore, to reduce the dormant dosa, people should try to cultivate mettā, and make it grow.]

8. KARUNĀ (COMPASSION)

The kind of kindness that arises when one sees poor "disabled beings" is called *"karuna"*. It bears the sense of pity. When thus the true koruna appears, one wants to rescue, or help to ease the suffering of, the disabled being. If one is unable to do so, one feels very sorry. It feels as if there is a source of heat in the chest. Although it is not true karunā, it is the kind of domanassa that can arise in the consciousness continuum of noble people, with its source in karunā. This akusala is not the evil sort, but the usual kind of habit peculiar to the noble lot.

The false karunā

Sometimes when we hear or see people associated with us suffer poverty or miseries, we wish to save them from such suffering, as if we were affected in true karunā. Then it may not be true karuna but soka. True karunā is kindness and pity; it does not cause worry. False karunā is accompanied by worry and anxiety.

Attitude of saintly people

The people we call righteous nowadays are kind to the people of disability when they see them in such a state of affairs, and they are capable of mettā only for the dear relatives and associates. But the top-class perfection-seekers, such as Bhodisattas and the mature righteous people, were filled with karunā towards all beings, foreseeing their possible fall into recurring miseries and the lowly worlds of apaya just like the way

---

122. Those in pursuit of paramis (perfections).

parents feel pervasive karunā when their children are in miseries. These noble people have great love for all beings put in a nutshell by virtue of the power of mettā, again the way parents apply their love, equally deeply and unfailingly, to both the good and bad types of children.

Such lofty, noble elements of mettā and karunā had taken root in the consciousness continuum of the Bhodisatta when he was still seeking to fulfill the faculties of perfection, so much so that when He became the Buddha, He was able to look at the Mara Deva[123] with mettā, and have compassion for Devadattha who sought to kill Him. So, every one seeking to be righteous and noble should copy the attitude of the Bodhisatta, not letting the attitude of "Only if the other is good, I will be good" persuade one, but rather try to be mindful of the true mettā and true karunā, no matter whether "the other one is good or not".

9. MUDITĀ (SYMPATHETIC JOY)

Gladness in seeing, and hearing of, the prosperity and general wellbeing of other people is *muditā*. When those with covetousness and envy see other people enjoying prosperity and prestige, or being of good kinship, looks, health, and education and so on, they become possessed of unlawful acquisition and jealousy. But the noble people would be glad with true muditā and say, "Oh what a great fortune! They are so good. Sadu, sadu! They are thus endowed on account of wholesome deeds they did in their previous lives."

The false muditā

Sometimes one is happy seeing one's related people in prosperity and success in life. That state of affair is something closely similar to muditā, but in fact it is gratification, piti-somanassa, not free from tanhā-lobha. More than that, one may even be so extremely pleased that tears may come down. Take note of such emotions as "false muditā". But then, it does not mean to say that every one of such occurrences is false muditā. Quite often, they are genuine muditā.

10. UPEKKHĀ (EQUANIMITY)

Regarding all beings with indifference is *upekkhā*. This indifference is unlike the loving kindness of mettā, the compassion of karunā, the

123. The evil god that came from Vassavati Deva Bhumi and tried to unmake the Buddha in all ways he could

sympathetic joy of muditā, or the hatred of dosa, but rather, without a hint of reaction, it is leaving whatever may come into attention as they really are, because it is something no one can do anything about, being "the work of kamma, wholesome or unwholesome", and so, it is best leaving all eventualities to the inevitable effects of kamma (*kammasakā*). [*Kamma* = only the kamma that one has committed is *sakā* = one's property or root cause.]

Nowadays, people talk of facing away from their own offspring or pupils of incurable characters. That kind of indifference is to ignore the pupil (or sons and daughters), leaving them to the work of their own kamma. Such slovenly neglect is not the kind of upekkhā as shown here. The indifference in upekkhā has some thought about them. But it takes to neither side of hate nor love, but rather keeps in the middle. This upekkhā is possible with ordinary people. The upekkhā required in jhāna absorption is only possible with people who have accessed to one of the three domains of mettā, karunā and muditā.

The Four Domains of Brahmavihāra

The cetasikas already shown as mettā, karunā, muditā and upekkhā are the four domains of "*brahmavihāra*" [brahma = noble and pure; vihāra = living]. Living with any one of these domains extended to all beings at all times is a noble, *brahmacariya*[124] way of living. This way of living is not dry and drab like the way of abhijjhā[125] and issā[126], but rather warm and pleasant. (It is often said that, brahmacariya is translated as *brahmaco* in Myanmar, -co meaning warm and pleasant.)

Extending mettā

If one has in one's continuum of consciousness mettā at all times, the mettā-oriented mind grows and grows. This growth of mettā in one's consciousness is called "mettā bhāvanā", growing or multiplication of mettā for others.

With one's attention directed at someone, wishing nothing but the wellbeing of that someone, the attendant mettā is actually connected to that person. Then it is like sending the mettā directly to that person, and so the term "sending of mettā" is used for the growth, in one's consciousness, of mettā for the person.

124. (P) The way of living of a pure one, Brahma.
125. (P) Covetousness
126. (P) Jealousy

The Common Method of Sending Mettā

Pali - "*sabbe sattā averā hontu,*
abyāpajjā hontu,
anigā hontu,
sukhiattānam pariharantu".
Meaaning - 1. May all beings be free from dangers and harms;
2. Be free from worry, and be happy;
3. Be free   from suffering, and be healthy;
4. Keep well and live long.

The right way of sending mettā

A wish for the wellbeing aimed at one or many, only if genuine, actually amounts to sending mettā to the target. Full of other thoughts, chanting "averā hontu" and so on, the way one has learned by rote, does not really mean sending mettā. Therefore, sending mettā by saying in Myanmar (one's own language, in a way one really understands), rather than saying in Pali, is basically most effective. So, inserting the name of the person one intends to send mettā to, one should wholeheartedly say, "May my mother be free from all harms, be happy, physically fit, fresh and pleasant; and may she live long." For the father change to "May my father be ....", and for the teacher, "May my teacher ....". For all beings, say, "May all the beings ....". This is a direct translation from Pali. If that is thought too long, then say, "May my mother be free of harm, well and happy." Sending of mettā to father, teacher and others will be treated similarly, and in full attention.

Method of sending karunā

The nature of karunā is the wish to save and free the poor from miseries, when one hears of, or see, them in pitiable situations. In sending karuna, the Pali text, "Dukkhā muccantu," can be translated to "May they be free from the present miseries". The wish to free the poor from sufferings so that they may be well and happy is karunā. The wish to shorten the time of suffering so that the sufferer "may die quickly" is not karuna; it is malice and evil. Karunā is genuine only if it is aimed at the sufferer. Verbally saying, "dukkhā muccantu," alone cannot be true karunā.

Method of sending mudità

Mudità is the kind of delight and gladness that arises when one sees, or hears of, the wellbeing of someone, accompanied by the wish that he or she does not lose the prosperity already in hand. So, in sending mudità, one would say, "*yathāladdha sampattito māvigaccantu*" in Pali, or "Let the good health and wealth now in possession be there firm and fast in all his life" in one's own language. Only if it is sent with true gladness upon seeing, or hearing of, the person of good health and wealth, the mudità is genuine. Saying verbally alone, "yathāladdha sampattito māvigaccantu," would not make mudità.

Method of sending upekkhā

In sending upekkhā, one says "kammassakā" in Pali, or "Kamma is the only property one ever owns: fortune and misfortune are the results of one's kamma." The basic thinking is that even if one sends mettā for the other person's wellbeing, the latter would be well, only as a result of kusala kamma. One may send to someone karunā, the latter would be free of troubles only if that person had kusala kamma. Although one is glad about someone else's wellbeing, also wishing the latter to be able to hold onto his or her fortunes, only good kamma would maintain his or her wellbeing and longevity. So, one needs not worry. It is only up to "kammassakā".

Summary

Thus, these four categories of brahmacora are different by way of different modes of attention given to the beings. Mettā is attendant on the love of beings; Karunā on the pitiable situation; mudità on the gladness for fortunate ones; upekkhā on leaving fateful affairs to the result of kamma (wholesome/unwholesome).Thus it is impossible to send to individuals or group of individuals all the 4 categories at one and same time. Therefore, when one sending mettā, say in full gusto of mettā the 4 lines (either in Pali or one's own language), starting with "averāhontu" through "sukhiatthānam paraharantu,"

Similarly, one says the respective lines in Pali or one's own language for Karunā, mudità and upekkhā. If recitals are only a matter of lip-service, saying what one has learnt by heart, but not for the real original purpose, then there is no need of any more comment. Since there are nowadays so many so-called Buddhists perfunctory in their religious habits, it is incumbent on up-coming new generations to set up a systematic reform programme in this respect.

11. THE THREE ABSTENTIONS (VIRATI)

sammāvacā, sammākammanta, sammāājiva

Before we study these 3 abstentions of *virati*[127], first the ten articles of *duccarita*[128] must be understood. [*Duccarita*[129] will not be studied in this book,) The articles are divided into two divisions, namely that concerning vocational matters, and that non-vocational. Killing for purposes such as robbery, assignment to kill by other people, professional jobs like fishery and butchery, are vocationally aligned physical duccarita. Killing by way of hate or impulse, without expectation of any material gain, is vocationally non-aligned physical duccarita. Other duccaritas should be similarly divided.

Giving false evidence at a court of law for material gains, unlawful advocacy by lawyers, telling false tales and make-up stories by story-tellers are vocational verbal duccaritas. Giving false evidence without expecting any material gain, inciting animosity between two people, saying abusive language, and telling false tales and stories, free of charge, are non-vocational verbal duccaritas.

Virati

Refraining from physical and verbal duccarita is *virati*. Although occasioned to talk falsehood, one purposely avoids telling it: if that is not to do with livelihood, it is *sammāvācā virati*; in cases of livelihood, it is *sammāājiva virati*. On occasions to kill, one purposely avoids killing: if that is not to do with livelihood, it is sammākammanta *virati*; in cases of livelihood, it is *sammāājiva virati*.

Where there is no involvement of virati

With no involvement or need of virati, saying wholesome words and making vows to keep precepts can be said to be *sammāvācā* (right speech). They are kusala cetanās (wholesome volitions). In doing blameless deeds such as offering donations, going on a pilgrimage, etc., they need no restraint and barring, and are called *sammākammanta* (right efforts). They are kusala cetanas. Earning a living by traditional agriculture and blameless commerce, not needing any restraint, can be said as *sammāājiva*.

---

127. The 3 deliberate abstentions from wrongful deeds the manner of verbiage, body action and livelihood
128. Evil conduct, moral misconducts, consisting of (1) killing, (2)stealing, (3) sexual misconduct, (4) telling lies, (5) slandering, (6) rough language, (7) idle speech, (8) envy, (9) malice, (10) wrong views
129. See Appendix A on "Duccarita" and "Sucarita"

As there is no involvement of avoidance or restraint, sammāvācā and sammākammanta must not be noted as virati cetasikas. Note only that they are ordinary kusala cetanās (wholesome volitions).

Samādāna, sampatta and samuccheda

Each of the three viratis of sammāvācā, sammākammanta and sammāājiva has three branch viratis, namely samādāna virati, sampatta virati and samuccheda virati. Out of the three, refraining from duccarita by making vows is samādāna virati. On arrival of a cattle to be butchered, the man thinks, "No, I will not kill," and if he promises, "*pānātipātāverā -mani sikkhāpadam samādiyāmi* (I will keep the promise of restraint from killing)," then samādāna virati is effective at the time of making the vow.

Once upon a time, a devotee, after taking precepts from a bhikkhu, went out looking for his lost oxen. On climbing a hill, a python caught him and coiled round his leg. Preparing to cut the snake with his machete, he suddenly remembered the precepts he had taken and decided not to kill. The snake released the man. In this story, the man kept sila (moral conduct) and refrained from killing, and so the cetasika was samādāna virati. At the time of keeping the precepts, as well as thereafter, keeping oneself away from the act of duccarita is *samādāna virati*. [Samādāna = keeping sila, virati = refraining from duccaritas]

Without keeping precepts, one may not do duccaritas when chances to commit them arise. That is *sampatta* virati. Once upon a time, a Singhalese devotee by the name of Cakkana, when he was young, went out into a wood in search of a rabbit for fresh medicinal meat for his sick mother. He caught a small rabbit coming down for paddy sprouts, thought of killing it, but he felt pity towards it and so released it. On getting back home, he told his mother all about it. He then said an oath of truth, "Since I came of age to understand things, I have never killed any thing willfully." On account of the power of the oath of truth, the mother was completely cured. In this story, without keeping vows, the avoidance of duccarita was spontaneous, and so it was *sampatta virati*. [Sampatta = occasioned (sudden encounter) duccarita, virati = avoidance from wrong deeds]

When magga is attained, reactions to defilements are avoided for their complete extinction, and the virati in the magga ñāna is *samuccheda virati*. [samuccheda = cutting out all defilements to the subtlest element, virati = avoidance] Thus, each of the 3 original virati cetasikas, such as sammāvācā, is multiplied by 3 branch viratis, such as samādāna,

Conclusion

This ends the chapter on the cetasikas that influence the mind to be wholesome, noted to be good for practical application. Now, the reader understands the wholesome factors of influence on the mind, and those of unwholesome influence (Chapter Two). This being so, one should consider "which of the two sides of wholesome and unwholesome cetasikas arise in one rather too often."

In studying the wholesome cetasikas, there are such falsehoods as "false saddhā, false sati, and false hiri-ottappa" and so on. In studying the unwholesome cetsikas, we have studied them by themselves, unmixed. That much of analysis should be enough to cause one to think, "There are too few wholesome cetasikas, but rather too many mixed wholesome-unwholesome and totally unwholesome cetasikas, occurring in the continuum of our consciousness."

Samsāra is long on account of these various, unwholesome cetasikas. Even in this knowledgeable world, if the evil influences take place overwhelmingly too often, then however much one may wish and pray for Nibbāna, certainly, Nibbāna will be no where near, but rather too far away. Thus, anyone wishing to be listed as an upright person and to enter Nibbāna in the shortest possible time must be prepared, whole-heartedly and self-convincingly, to be a righteous person, rather than to impart a good impression on other people. As for my part, I wish to be a person of integrity in every existence now and hereafter, with a wholesome and sharp mind, perfect in nature, untainted with deceit, māyā and sātheya. May all my associates, young and old, be established as genuinely upright persons.

> Having presented these factors of the mind,
> May I, with power of my past merits, help
> people embrace these precious, noble minds;
> May I be righteous always,
> As I travel, step by step, to Nibbāna;
> And my associates, old and young,
> Cultivate, likewise, the proper minds,
> And reach, without fail,
> The Eternity of Nibbāna.

Here ends the chapter on the mind-associates that influence a character to be blameless and wholesome

CHAPTER FOUR

MIXED FACTORS

1. phassa (defined below)	*6. jivitindariya*	*11. viriya*
2. vedanā	*7. manasikāra*	*12. piti*
3. saññā	*8. vitakka*	*13 chanda*
4. cetanā	*9. vicāra*	
5. ekaggatā	*10. adhimokkha*	

[Summary] - Contact or touch is ***phassa***; sensation, ***vedanā***; cognition, ***saññā***; volition, ***cetanā***; one-pointedness (of mind), ***ekaggatā***; mind-matter continuum, ***jivitindariya***; attention, ***manasikāra***; attention, ***vitakka***; hanging on and considering the senses, ***vicāra***; making decisions, ***adhimokkha***; effort-making, ***viriya***; rapture, ***piti***; a mere wish, ***chanda*** - these are the thirteen mixed factors of the mind.

1. PHASSA (SENSE IMPRESSION)

The sensorial contact with sense objects (*āramana*[130]) is *phassa*. In saying "contact", it does not mean physical contact or the impact of one object with another. It is a matter of meeting of the mind with objects in the nature of elements (*dhātu*)[131] as they come into contact with each other. Such elemental contacts or impacts are almost as clear as directly observed evidence of physical contacts or impacts.

When a man, recovering from a recent illness, sees someone chewing a citrus fruit, an excessive desire for the fruit is roused and his mouth waters. A man susceptible to fright has his knees trembling in seeing a fist-fight. A girl in puberty may feel some strange sensation in her bosom when she sees or hears a young man of her age and same social status; the same thing can also happen to a young man seeing or hearing a girl. In these instances, the mind makes a dhātu (elemental) contact with the fruit, etc., arousing a

130. Ārammana paccaya (P), meaning objects in contact with the mind, and cognized.
    (Ārun or āyon is most often used in the Myanmar vernacular.)
131. *Dhātu* (P) means 'elements', the ultimate constituents of mind and matter.

sensation which causes mouth-watering, trembling, strange stirring in the chest, etc. The nature of phassa is thus the phenominal dhātu (elemental) touch, contact, or impact.

Phassa is involved in contact with wholesome and unwholesome objects (āramana paccayas), playing their roles in both noble and evil minds. For instance, salt imparts its taste in good as well as bad dishes. Cetanā and like cetasikas to be shown later are also involved in both noble and evil minds. [In the cases of vipāka and kariyā that are neither wholesome nor unwholesome, phassa also plays its role in cognizing the arammanas.]

2. VEDANĀ (SENSATION)

Sensation arising out of an ārammana is *vedanā*. The six ārammanas have been shown earlier. They can be categorized in three, each as *itthārammana*, *atitthārammana* and *itthamajjhattārammana*. The ārammanas people desire and seek are called **itthārammana** (itthā=desirable + ārammana=object). They include beautiful looks, pleasant voices and sounds, sweet smells, good tastes, pleasurable touch, fame, comfortable living and so on. What people do not desire or want are called **anitth-ārammanas** (anitthā=undesirable = ārammana=object). They include ugly looks, unpleasant voices and sounds, rotten smells, bad tastes, unpleasant touch, infamy, ruined buildings. The āruna objects that are neither good nor bad, all of middle class quality, are **ittha-majjhatt-ārammana**. They include looks, neither beautiful nor ugly, and so on.

There are 5 kinds of vedanā, namely sukha. dukkha, somanassa, domanassa and upekkhā. Itthārammanas are composed of desirable tastes and sensations. Taking pleasure of the sense objects is called **sukha vedanā** (sukha=happy + vedanā=sensation. feeling). While taking such pleasures, a sense of happiness arises in the mind; this happiness is called **somanassa vedanā** (somanassa=happy, satisfied + vedanā=feeling). Those vedanās called sukha and somanassa are evident when taking pleasures in kāmaguna[132] ārammanas such as rupārammanas (sights), sotārammanas (sounds), etc., and also when being completely happy while in devotion to the Buddha, dhamma and sanghā.

Anitthārammanas are composed of unwanted tastes and sensations. Feeling of such unpleasant tastes or sensations is called **dukkha vedanā** (feeling of unpleasantness), and the resultant feeling of unhappiness,

---

132. Plain sensuality in the subjective sense, cords or strands of sensuality in the objective sense

domanassa vedanā (unhappiness or aversion). How these dukkha and domanassa vedanas, named as soka, parideva, dukkha, domanassa, upayāsa, have come about has been shown in connection with dosa cetasika. [The mind's wellbeing or otherwise due to physical contact is known as sukha and dukkha, whereas that due to sight, sound, smell, taste and thoughts is somanassa and domanassa.]

In itthamajjhattārunas, neither good nor bad feelings are clearly present. Such neutral feelings are called *upekkhā vedanā*. Because the ārammanas bear no clear definition, one cannot know if one is sensing them. But then, in our daily life, we find so many of such neutral ārammanas along with all other sensorial ārammanas.

Upekkhā vedanā also takes the sensations of both kusala (wholesome) and akasula (unwholesome) ārammanas. Because this vedana can take both wholesome and unwholesome ārammanas, it means exactly the nature of taking up this duality when we say, "Just as sensual pleasures can be enjoyed so also can be the import of Dhamma,"

3. SAÑÑĀ (PERCEPTION)

Perception or cognition is *saññā*. It is more clearly recognizable in persons of low intelligence and little knowledge. Relatives tell a small child, "this person is father, and this mother. The child noted them as "father, mother." Upon seeing an aeroplane for the first time, "which are wings, which tail, and which the main body," are noted. All unfamiliar things are noted when visiting a strange place. Thus, there are many things for saññā to take note of.

The two effects of saññā
Saññā brings forth two effects. When the relatives teach the child," This man is father," the child's saññā noted and gets to know him as its father at that instant. Then, later on, upon seeing him, it remembers the person to be its father.

Perceiving what is right and what is not
Saññā, like paññā, does not only know the right, but also takes wrong notes. A person, susceptible to fright of ghosts, thinks the stump of a dead palm tree in the dark of night as a ghost; that is perception contrary to the right image... Wrong views include ditthi as well as this kind of wrong notation. It is very difficult to reform a person who is already deeply rooted in a saññā of wrong views and notations.

The wide province of saññā

The saññā that takes on wrong views as right has a very wide sphere of influence. For most people, samsāra is extremely long. It is due not only to avijjā and tanhā but also to this misleading saññā. Let us get it clear: although human beings see the excrements as horrible, the maggots take it as food. Similarly, vultures think of the rotting corpse of a dog as good food.

The Buddha and aranhantas think rightly of all sensual objects as horrible. "*Hino*, all are mean and base; *gammo*, they are the laity's property; *puthujjaniko*, the property of impure, unclean folks; *anariyo*, not the property of the saintly person; *anatthasamhito*, nothing of benefits," said the Buddha in clear contempt. But a great many people, not paying attention to such noble words, are pursuing those sensual objects in all might and main. Thus, samsāra is an extremely long march because of those wrong kinds of saññā.

Saññā in pretence of sati

In reminiscences of wholesome deeds, sati (un-forgetfulness) plays a role. Wholesome saññā also plays a role. Genuine sati applies only to wholesome deeds. Such sayings as "Love since tender age is remembered for a hundred years; marriage since youth holds fast for ten thousand years," are concerned with unwholesome remembering, and so not true sati but saññā in the form of a memory as sharp as sati. Look over in Section on Sati.

4. CETANĀ (VOLITION)

Volition or will that urges the mind and its factors, all bound up together, to be or do something is *cetanā*. When the mind takes on an object, phassa makes the contact. Vedanā feels the sensation. Saññā perceives the contact and the sensation. Similarly, ekaggatā, jivintindariya and manasikāra, to be shown later, appear together with the mind in doing their respective duties. The unwholesome principles of lobha, dosa, etc., and the wholesome principles of saddhā, sati, etc. play their roles as the mind takes on sense objects.

When the mind together with its factors takes on an ārammana, no one associate factor is left out. No one factor is allowed to neglect its duty. All the associate factors together with the mind are caused to be closely bound up. The mental factor that causes the sense objects, the mind and other mental factors to be bound together is no principle other than this cetanā. So, it is said, "Cetanā is volition."

There is more. When the mind is taking up sense objects together with all matching factors (cetasikas), leaving none out, the mind and its factors arising together can be considered an association (a team). In that association, the mind leads as chairman, and cetanā is executive member. In ordinary associations, the executive member is very busy. He must urge other team members not to be lax in carrying out their duties, and he himself very diligent in performing the business functions of the team.

In an association, the executive member is somewhat twice as busy as other members. Likewise, cetanā is busy organizing and urging the mind and other associates to be thorough and not to be negligent in their respective functions. It also carries out its own duties. Notice how the captain is busy in fighting a battle. So, if cetanā is poor, the mind lacks eagerness. Other cetasikas also become poor. If cetanā is sharp and vigorous, the mind and other associates are likewise, sharp and vigorous. As the mind and the associates are sharp and vigorous, the body becomes alert and fast. Thus, in every case of taking on an ārammana, whatever the ārammana, cetanā plays the supreme role.

Cetanā is kamma

Suppose a case in which a group of people gang-beat a man. Every body but one was hitting the man so lightly that the man did not suffer a scratch. But the exceptional man was hitting twice as hard as the other men such that the victim was killed. In that murder case, the true culprit was the man who did the hitting to actually cause the death. Likewise, cetanā is the most capable and the most assertive agent in the combination of mind and its associates, and so, the attributes of cetanā are etched out in the consciousness continuum of the one doing the kamma. So, in seeking out the doer of kamma (the culprit), it all comes down on to cetanā. Therefore, cetanā is named "kamma, the accused, the culprit." The Buddha had said, "Oh bhikkhus, I call cetanā kamma". As per this saying, note, "If cetanā is sharp, kamma is huge and strong. If cetanā is poor, kamma is little and weak."

5. EKAGGATĀ (CONCENTRATION)

Tranquility and quietness is the nature of *ekaggatā*. Ekaggatā is also called samādhi (concentration), often translated as one-pointedness of the mind. The ability of ekaggatā or samādhi is such that when the mind is taking on a sense object, it can hold the object in the mind for some length of time. Samādhi can be maintained on an object in complete stillness and quietness, like the motionless candle flame in a windless place.

In gathering attention on a certain object, if the attention can be held repeatedly, again and again, for a long period of time, then it is usually said, "Samādhi has been established or samādhi has come on strong." The person in strong samādhi is calm, quiet and graceful in his or her way of life and manners of talk and walk. In human relationships, the person would be straight and honest, but can be riveted to a certain topic and object of interest.

6. JIVITINDARIYA (LIFE OF NĀMA)

The mind (citta) together with the associated mental factors (cetasikas) are called *nāma*. The life of those nāma elements is *jivitindariya*. Whatever the mind and its associates are, they have life (*jivita*). Therefore, all citta-cetsikas are alive, not dead. Because they are alive, they can know sense objects (ārammanas). If they had no life, if all of them were dead, then they would not be able to carry out any functional duties. Briefly stated, only on account of the life element called jivitindariya, citta-cetasika continuum carries on without interruption. That life would last for as long as kamma may allow. So, it is said, "Not to part with the life of nāma, jivita carries on without interruption." Just as nāma elements have nāma-life, so also matter (rupa) elements have rupa-life. These two elements of jivita, the nāma- and rupa-life, are called the life of beings. Apart from these categories of *rupajivita* and *nāma-jivita*, there are no other entities of life such as a being called life, soul or self (*atta*) in the physical bodies of all beings.

7. MANASIKĀRA (GIVING ATTENTION)

Putting into the heart[133] is called *manasikāra*. In saying, "Putting into heart," the heart means the mind (citta). Putting a sensorial object into

133. Heart or *hadaya vatthu* in the Buddha's Teaching is the housing where the mind most of the time dwells, so, alternatively, it is a house for mental activities. So putting into heart would directly mean thinking or giving attention.

the heart so that its image appears (as if it were actually emplaced there) is said to be "putting into the heart." Actually, manasikāra cannot pull a sensorial object into the mind. But because of the powerful influence of manasikāra, the mind gets some object for its attention all the time. It is a metaphorical term suggesting that manasikāra fetches and carries the object into the mind.

Mind and 7 attached associates

For a mind to arise, from contact "phassa" to attention "manasikāra", 7 cetasikas play their roles. Lobha, dosa, saddhā, etc. come into play only when their matching objects are called into attention. Out of the 7 perennially attached cetasikas, when some sensation arises, *vedanā* is evident; when cognizing, it is *saññā*; when committing some kamma, *cetanā*; when in concentration, *ekaggatā* called samādhi; the rest, namely *phassa*, *jivitindariya* and *manasikāra* are not so clearly apparent.

8. VITAKKA (THOUGHT INITIATION)

Thought-conception is *vitakka*. It is also called "thinking, contemplation." There are 3 unwholesome vitakkas, namely *kāma vitakka*, *vyāpāda vitakka* and *vihiṁsā vitakka*; and 3 wholesome vitakkas, namely *nikkhamma vitakka*, *avyāpāda vitakka* and *avihiṁsā vitakka*. Thus there are 6 types of vitakka.

Kāma and nikkhama vitakkas

Contemplations of objects of sensual sphere (*kāmaguṇa*) such as sight (rupā-rammana), sound (*sotā rammana*), etc., and that of objects in connection with lobha such as seeking wealth, are called "*kāma vitakka*". Contemplations of objects, free from lobha-tanhā, such as renunciation, donations, keeping of moral precepts, and meditation are called "*nikkhama vitakka*".

Vyāpāda and avyāpāda vitakkas

Vyāpāda is dosa, the desire to destroy and kill some other person. Contemplation in connection with that dosa is called "*vyāpāda vitakka*". *Avyāpāda* is the opposite of vyāpāda - it is *mettā*. Contemplations of objects in connection with *mettā* (the wish for wellbeing of all beings and the thought to do something about it) are called "*avyāpāda vitakka*".

Vihimsā and avihimsā vitakkas

Vihimsā is dosa, the desire to ill-treat or torment other people. Contemplation to beat up and kill, or somehow cause trouble to, other people is called "*vihimsā vitakka*". *Avihimsā* is the opposite of vihimsā (dosa) - it is *karunā*. Contemplation, in connection with that karunā, to save beings from suffering, or to do something about it somehow, is called "*avihimsā vitakka*". Avoid the evil vitakkas, and be in the habit of the virtuous vitakkas.

9. VICĀRA (SUSTAINED ATTENTION)

Repeated and sustained application of the mind is *vicāra*. Vitakka contemplates to draw the mind onto an idea or an ārammana, but it does not hold on there for long. Contemplation moves onto other ārammanas. *Vicāra*, on the other hand, attends over and over to the ārammana that vitakka has pulled onto the mind so that the attention stays on the ārammana - it is like rubbing an object against another repeatedly, and over and over. Keeping attention (mind or consciousness) thus on an ārammana again and again, and over and over, like rubbing each other repeatedly, is the function of *vicāra*.

10. ADHIMOKKHA (DECISION MAKING)

Making decisions is "*adhimokkha*". When some business is to be done, or when the right or wrong of an idea is to be resolved, *adhimokkha* takes up the role of decision making. Evil deeds such as killing and noble deeds such as giving in charity are accomplished after the decision by *adhimokkha*. Believing in lies of other people is not saddhā but adhimokkha that makes wrong decisions.

11. VIRIYA (EFFORT-MAKING)

Most people understand that making efforts is "*viriya*". Considering the nature of making efforts with diligence, there is an element of courage and freedom from fear. So, "Where courage is, there is *viriya*" it is said. The maxim speaks of the truth. One without diligence is called "a lazy one". The lazy man, in fear of having to work, would give excuses like, "it is too early; too late in the night; too cold; too hot; not too well in eating; not too well, having eaten too much; too weak after recent illness; got to go somewhere; just gotten back from a trip out; and so on," for not doing any work in hand. Such lazy mood is not wholesome. It is only excessive *thina-middha*, an *akusala citta*, an unwholesome mind.

The diligent person, however, regardless of the heat and the cold, would not even care a whit about sacrificing his own life in cases of emergency and extreme importance, and would face anything and do the job courageously with might and main. In the jataka[134] story of Mahājanakka, when the large sail boat was about to capsize and be destroyed in a storm, the 700 merchants on board relaxed on their diligence and made devotional offerings to their traditional spirits and prayed, although there appeared no saviour, and soon became food for sharks. But the Bhodisatta, taking no refuge in any spirit, infusing repeatedly into himself bravery, courage and diligence, even keeping Sabbath, swam across the sea. That was the nature of courage and freedom from fear in the application of viriya.

Health

Benefits of viriya are clearly very evident. It is essential to keep fit by doing regular exercises and walking - walk around and about one's own home if walking far is not practicable, eating at regular times, not restraining from bowel-waste discharges for whatever reason, bathing at proper times, eating dietary food and drugs as indicated and prescribed, and so on. All of that cannot be accomplished without viriya, and laziness is not permissible. So, only those with viriya can perform these various fitness regimens.

Entrepreneurship

In doing business, those who are afraid of heat and cold, etc., would fall behind others with viriya who will be selling their wares earlier, and the lazy lot would only end up with the proverbial "cow dung and sand". The record of weakness in, if not lack of, viriya is probably established by Myanmar men. Foreigners rise early in the morning, set and lay out wares for sale in neat and tidy manners, keep the shops in good shape, bathe and change clothes, and already begin to drink tea and attend to their business, when the Myanmar men have not risen from beds yet. When it is time to rise, they would roll from side to side, yawn and blow out the hang-around sleepiness before reluctantly rising. Then, they would sit for some length of time on the beds with disgraceful looks, dull and dumb. How can such lazy people ever raise their standard of business acumen and build a fortune?

---

134. Stories retelling Bhodisatta's former lives

The gift of women

Myanmar women personally run the commercial business. A great many bazaar sellers in Myanmar are women. Myanmar men of their age are either students at schools or simply unemployed, living as dependents of their parents and sisters. If only Myanmar women are home-bound, then the country would be more degrading and further left behind. Status quo[135] owes its maintenance to these ladies.

If both sides work hard

If all men work as hard as women, if men do some business in towns, this would become a progressive little country, full of many graces, bright and fresh like the new moon in the sky.

Education

Men are a poor lot not only in business activities, but they are also not so good in education: looking at the examination results, those passing with honours and flying colours are too few; besides, there are fewer Myanmar men than foreigners in the pursuit of higher education. That comes about, probably not due to their mothers' birth-faults. The reason seems to lie, to a large extent, in the laziness and indulgences of those who pay no attention and regards to the huge expenses that incur for their education in the universities, showing little consideration and appreciation of the financial support given by their parents, brothers and sisters.

When they enter the universities, they are close to 20 years of age. There had been people like Tabin Shwehti, Bayint Naung, Minye Kyawswa and so on, who were not that old, and yet brought about the grace and honour of our people. Why are our present youth so lazy, so dull and dumb? Shouldn't they be men of courage, and pride?

It is not only the laity who are poor in education. It is also in the Sāsanā, scholarly standard is low. That is true. The monks of olden days were benefactors not only to the general citizenry, but also to the royalty and the nobility. If we could change with time in our education, we can probably keep abreast with time and be the benefactors of the people in the present era. But, there has been no reformation, and so, we are sliding down; in many village monasteries, there are no alms-gathering youngsters[136]. This indicated the poor state of affairs in the life of the Sāsanā in Myanmar. To explain the root cause of this low impression, it

135. Time was pre- and post WWII and immediately around 1948. The writer made no reference to country folks who tilled the land.
136. These are the children from the age of six to teens or older, acquiring monastic education, provided with boarding and lodging.

would require "untying the bundle and exposing its contents"; I would not like to do that. All I want to say here is that our health, business and education qualities are less than adequate because of the lack of viriya and the prevalence of lethargy.

Buddhahood due to viriya

Our Refuge, Lord Buddha, became a Buddha by personally fulfilling the viriya parami (perfection in diligence). After the attainment of Buddhahood, He worked all His life time in the delivery of His teaching, non-stop. In every line of dhamma that the Lord had exhorted, knowledge comes first, and then work with diligence must follow in accordance with the knowledge so learned: "True men should work with diligence, and be wise not to be lazy."[137]

Let us reform

As Myanmars, professing to take refuge in the Buddha and to observe His Teaching, calling themselves Buddhists, have actually hung up the Teaching in some hidden corner while people of other religions, in line with the Buddhist teaching, pursue worldly affairs in earnest and become great men of wisdom. The Myanmar Buddhists take great pride in sitting under the golden umbrellas when ordained into young novices, high-minded as if they were in Tāvatimsā[138]. And yet, they have not come out of the bush. So, as we have said before like "We, father and daughter, change the way we sit," now too, we should do something about removing the lethargy and get viriya out in our lap.

"For one who possesses viriya, there is nothing that cannot be accomplished."[139]

[Although it is an urging to have viriya in earnest, it does not mean the sort of viriya that entails in no benefits, like the way the proverbial blind elephant pushes its way in the wood. It only means viriya applied with intelligence.]

12. PITI (RAPTURE)

Contentment and joy about a sense object is *piti*. Piti is not like sukha vedanā that is to do with feeling. It is not the liking or satisfaction. When a thirsty man sees the sight or hears the sound of water, he is happy, full

---

137. Pali text: "*vāyametheva puriso na nibbindeya pantito.*"
138. The abode of a class of heavenly beings in the sensuous sphere
139. Pali text: "*viriyavato kinnāma na sijjhati.*""

of *piti*. When one gets to drinking it, one feels satisfied, full of *sukha vedanā*.

When one sees one's love, talks to each other or hears the other sing, or when one hears a dhamma-talk, one is completely happy even to the point of having gooseflesh. Such happiness is piti. A long time ago, as the story says, a heavily pregnant woman was unable to go to a pagoda festival on a hill, and so she paid homage to the hill-top pagoda from where she was, repeatedly and over and over. In so doing, she soon became so absorbed in the image that she rose and dropped to the forecourt of the pagoda, without her knowing what was happening, it is said[140].

While doing some meritorious deed (charity), by looking at the offertories or by watching people eating proffered food, the donor can have piti. Sometimes, such piti is so intense that it can become somanassa; then the face is lighted up with a smile, and the whole body activated, ready for some action. Those in pursuit of body fitness, education or commerce with strong viriya are bound to reap the benefits as desired. Then one would have piti, looking back at one's own performance.

Even the Exulted One, after standing up from the seat under the Bodhi Tree, walked a distance and looked back to watch the Pillar of Bodhiñāna (the Tree) without blinking the eye-lashes for a whole week with a joyous look and in great piti. The yogis in meditation can be drawn under the influence of piti in such a way that they do not want to rise from their seats. Thus there are a great many opportunities for the viriya-owners to have and dwell in piti.

Chanda (Wish, Will to do)

The wish to get hold an ārammana of something is *chanda*. "Wanting to do, or wanting to have" is not the same as lobha that clings to, and is stuck with, the object. It is merely a desire to do or have something, no more and no less.

So, it is said that chanda is "a mere wish to dwell on the ārammana of an object." The nature of this chanda is very clearly evident in all beings. A child extends its hands, being urged by a wish, to change hands from its father to mother. That is chanda. Wishing to go from place to place; to see, hear, or kiss someone; and to eat, hold, touch, and know something; these are all mere wishes or chanda.

---

140. From a Singhalese story

A wish for Nibbāna; a wish to be aggasāvaka[141], mahāsāvaka, Buddha, king, millionaire, heavenly god, brahma, hermit or monk; a wish to do charitable works, keep Sabbath, or have the benefits of some wholesome work; these are all chandas. A small wish is a weak chanda whereas a wish to get something big by might and main is a big wish, a strong chanda. Founded on this kind of chanda, the Bodhisatta worked to accomplish all the perfections (*pāramis*) with unremitting viriya, to attain Enlightenment that He had aimed for.

If there is as yet not even a basic chanda, no one would have put up a strong viriya and accomplished anything to get to the top. Thus, there must first be a chanda to get something of benefit. This chanda is also called desire. Then, since one gets nowhere by only desiring (making a mere wish) alone, one must put up all untiring efforts (viriya) to achieve success. For instance, the desire to go from Mandalay to Yangon is chanda. With that chanda alone, one cannot reach Yangon. One must have sufficient amount of money for train or air fare. One must work so as to make that amount. That work to make some money is viriya. Likewise, to enter Nibbāna, one must work (fulfill paramis) adequately as befits the virtues of sāvakas[142] and the Buddha as the case may be.

Those lay people and monks who are now in higher echelons of society, capable of achieving anything they desire, are not god-sends. Most of them have put up their viriya equal to their desires. Human life is hard to come by. Only by virtue of the past wholesome kamma, human life-form is attained. If one is devoid of a desire for progress, then one's life is not different from that of an animal. I urge people, each and every one, to cultivate strong desires to work for some progress in this life and also for access to the Path of Magga in the samsāra.

"For one who has chanda, there is nothing that cannot be achieved.

"*Āsā phalavati sukhā* = Desire, if worked hard and followed by resultant benefits, is the way for happiness."

Conclusion

Thus has concluded the chapter on cetasikas that, like salt in all dishes, influence the mind in both wholesome as well as unwholesome ways. For this wholesome work of writing to explain those cetasikas, I wish readers to have strong desires, and work with diligence, keeping keen volition in

---

141. Aggasāvaka and Mahāsāvaka are graded positions of the Buddha's disciples in His lifetime.
142. Sāvakas are disciples of the Buddha or followers of His teaching.

carrying out wholesome affairs. As for me, I wish I spend all my time in all the lives to come in doing wholesome deeds with proper chanda and viriya. As for my associates, old and young, I wish they, like me, work with diligence and keen volition in pursuit of perfections (pāramis).

> May one and all benefit
> From what I have written
> On the cetasikas
> That influence the mind
> In both good and evil ways;
> For me I wish to be gracious
> In the way of chanda,
> To be complete with viriya,
> And keen in cetanā,
> To do more meritorious works;
> May my associates,
> Like me, breed noble minds,
> And work, to head
> Straight into Nibbāna.

This ends the chapter on cetasikas that influence the mind in both wholesome and unwholesome ways

CHAPTER FIVE

CHARACTERS AND TEMPERAMENTS

What has been shown in the last four chapters should be sufficient to enable one to understand how cetasikas work. The various mind types, wholesome and unwholesome, are not just what pop up in the present life; they are actually connected with habits and traits of previous lives. Good traits in the past lives are likely to be deposited in this present life. Evil traits in the past lives are hardly likely to make a good character in this life.

A "reformed mind" due to the influence of association with good and noble people, like the "sealing wax away from heat", is likely to slide back to its original evil state once those good people are not close by. The crooked tail of a dog, dipped in oil and kept in a straight hollow of a bamboo stick for 12 years, is still crooked when taken out of the bamboo sheathing.

Just as a well-fed dog, with a full stomach, satisfies itself by kissing the old rag of a leather when it sees one, so also a man, inborn with evil and foolish elements in his mind, is likely to be holding those habits even if learned and in a high position. So, people should, first of all, understand the assessment criteria so as to check and see "how these traits and inclinations come about" in them as well as in their associates.

Carita
Carita is character that is particularly distinct and more pronounced than the normal human nature. It is categorized into six types, namely rāga, dosa, moha, saddhā, buddhi and vitakka.

[Lobha is also called rāga; paññā is buddhi. These have been shown as cetasikas earlier.]

[Each individual is likely to have one, or more, or mixed in two or three, of these characters.]

How to evaluate a character

To evaluate a man as to "how his carita would be like", one must keep watch of his physical and verbal manners, way of life, kind of food he likes, and frequently recurring attitudes and other behaviours. Among the various types of characters, similarities can be discerned in the styles and manners of movement, work, eating and so on, which would characterize rāga and saddhā, dosa and buddhi, moha and vitakka.

Rāga and saddhā characters

A person with rāga carita and another with saddhā are both polite and civil in the manners of body movement and posture. They are good in housekeeping and laundry works. They like good clothing and well-prepared food, sweet in taste and pleasant in flavour. The difference lies in the facts that the one with rāga is extremely fond of sensual pleasures, full of feints and deceits (māyā), wicked and pretentious (sātheya). The person is also proud and greedy. The other one with saddhā is characterized by lack of māyā, sātheya, lobha and māna. Besides, this one is charitable, devoted to the Buddha and Sangha, and happy to listen to dhamma talks.

[By body movement is meant the four ways of body culture, "*iriyāpatha*", namely walking, standing, sitting and reclining (lying down).]

[**Maxim**]
The person with rāga is cultured
In four-way iriyāpatha,
Neat and tidy in household affairs,
Fond of food sweet-bitter-sour
And sensual pleasures,
Deceitful, pretentious,
Proud, and greedy;
The person with saddhā is free
From deceit and pretensions,
Glad that he should give charity,
Devoted to the Buddha and the Sangha,
And to the dhamma he listens,
'Tis the way
Of a noble, generous man.

Dosa and buddhi characters

Both characters have rough and tough manners of body movement and postures. They are not neat and tidy in laundry work, sweeping or house-keeping; they may like sour, salty, bitter and spicy tastes in food.

Encountered with obtrusive sights and sounds, they can hardly bear them and may swear, shout or be rough with impatience. These manners are natural to both types (as long as they do not reform their minds).

The difference between them is that the person with dosa carita is characterized by the habits of grudge, revengefulness, malice, jealousy, slander, ingratitude, ostentation, vying for supremacy and unreasonableness, whereas the other one with buddhi caritta is characterized by the person's habits of amity and magnanimity, reasonableness, balanced eating, and wise vision of the future and the samsāra - this character is accustomed to charitable and other wholesome deeds of merit as a matter of fulfilling perfections (pāramis).

> [**Maxim**] - The dosa character is rough in the four postures,
> Not proper in other affairs, choosy in food sour, hot and bitter
> Taking delight in all sensual pleasures, but like gun powder on fire
> Blew out anger with a temper, as ugly sights and sounds appear;
> Grudge and revenge, envy, malice and slander,
> Ingratitude and ostentation,
> Unreasonableness that one would entertain;
>> Whereas, the one with buddhi carita
>> With the same fore characters,
>> But unlike the remainder, he is proper
>> In his habits of eating, reason and wisdom,
>> A noble person
>> With vision of the future and the samsāra,
>> Destined proper to a life hereafter.

Moha and Vitakka characters

The character with moha carita is negligent and forgetful. His personal affairs are chaotic and in shambles. He does not have liking for any particular type of food. He cannot see reasons and distinguish between the good and the evil. He may praise those whom other people praise, and dispraise those others dispraise. Lacking attentiveness and learning, he is always dull, sluggish, lazy and scatter-brained.

The character with vitakka is not much different from that of moha carita. In the affairs he is involved in, he is usually talkative, getting nowhere as he talks. He is little capable of doing anything worthwhile, lazing away his time. He enjoys associating and talking with people of his kind, playboys, handsome but with no ability; they are men of no substance, burdensome on mankind, full of plans with no work done.

[**Maxim**] - Moha character, inattentive and confused ,
Is chaotic in all his affairs diffused,
Not consistent in his habit of eating,
What is right and wrong not knowing,
Nor the good from evil.
Always scatter-brained and lazy,
In all cases, a follower of others;
Like him is the vitakka character,
Always mixed and talking with men
Of his kind, playboys and idle men,
Full of plans,
And yet getting nowhere in terms
Beneficial and wholesome,
That is the way of leisure and pleasure
Played by the men
Of idleness and extra-burden.

The root of carita

We should consider the question as to "why people, being of the same human race, are different in caritta?" If kusala kamma (wholesome deeds) were done in the past lives with the aim of luxuries of life (indulgences and material wealth), then, as a result, the person is likely to have rāga (sensuous) caritta in this present life. If those deeds were done with accompanying dosa, the likely result is dosa carita; if done unknowingly and with no reasoning or consciousness, it is moha carita. If wholesome deeds in connection with learning and education, or deeds full of wisdom or with a desire to be wise were done in the past, then the kammic effect in this life would likely be buddhi caritta; Similarly, the deeds of charity, generosity and magnanimity (saddhā) done in the past would likely result in saddhā caritta in the present lifetime. If kāma vitakka (sensual desires) were the root, then the result would likely be kāma vitakka. Thus, since the various characters in the present life are the result of the past kamma, in order not to have evil characters in future lives, we should all try to do kusala kamma (wholesome deeds) in this life, surrounding ourselves with saddhā and paññā.

Vāsanā[143] accompanies lives in continuum

In all unwholesome affairs, *vāsanā* (trait, inclination) is the property of kilesā (defilements). The vāsanā in wholesome affairs is sammā chandda (wholesome desire). Vāsanā is thus part of the consciousness continuum in all beings. If rāga caritta was very strong in the past lives, that rāga trait clings to the person's conscious continuum to persist into the present life. This calls for suppression of such habits now, in this life, fairly well so that they do not persist into the next lives. Dosa and moha vitakkas should also be minded in the same manner. A man with paññā vāsanā should attempt to fulfill his paññā parami as far as he can and save it in this life so that he will be a solid lump of knowledge and wisdom in the lives to follow through the samsāra. If one is determined to be a Buddha, paññā is the main theme; for a sāvaka[144], like Ashin Sāriputtarā, one has to be good at paññā so that the trait (vāsanā) will be continuous and cumulative in all of one's lives to come. So, the serious consideration to be given is to eliminate all the bad habits and set up, successfully, some good habits in this life.

One with rāga caritta must meditate on *asubha kammathana*[145] for all ārammanas that appear, so that rāga (lust) may be kept to a minimum, and finally eliminated. One with dosa caritta will attempt at mettā bhāvanā[146]. The element of mettā, by virtue of its very nature of calmness and peacefulness, would extinguish the fire of dosa that is, by nature, unbearably hot and disturbing. One with moha caritta will have to consult the men of much learning and the wisdom, and practice in-breath/out-breath kammatthāna. As enquiries multiply, so also will the knowledge, thereby eliminating the moha trait. The one with the good carittas of saddhā and paññā must try to keep up with the good habits so that saddhā and paññā would grow, and grow.

Hereby the subject of caritta vāsanā has been fully treated. For the meritorious deed of writing this article, may a great many people fall in line with wholesome caritta. May all my associates also be able to avoid all the evil habits and get into good habits from this life onwards.

For me who has been writing and teaching the literature every day, may the paññā habit be firmly established, indestructible and over and above mediocrity, in my consciousness continuum. May that good habit

143. Vāsanā is the trait or inclination of a character towards certain tendencies, a property of the consciousness continuum from existence to existence, identifying itself of a caritta in the past life.
144. Savaka is disciple and the protégé of the Buddha.
145. Meditation with attention on the sense of unpleasantness of the body, also called cemetery meditation
146. Sending or extending mettā to one and all (mettā kammatthāna).

be able to cultivate saddhā that enables belief in the truth and disables wrongful views.

> For this noble practice of writing and teaching,
> May everyone get into good habits in their living;
> May I be devoid of rāga, dosa, moha, vitak' caritas,
> full of clean cetanā, bright saddhā and shining ñāna;
> Let my associates, likewise, be able to uphold caritas,
> Pure and proper, till they enter the Entity called Nibbāna.

CHAPTER SIX

[In this chapter, the reader should come to understand the 10 articles of *Ducarta*[147], the 10 articles of *Sucarita* and the 10 articles of *Poññakariya vatthu*. Out of the three categories, the articles of *Ducarita*[148] and *Sucarita*[149] have been fully dealt with in 'Ratana Gonyi'[150] and many other books; only the articles of *Poññakariya vatthu* will be described in full in this book.]

THE TEN WHOLESOME DEEDS

By "*poñña*" is meant purifying factors of the mind; in the vernacular, it is translated as noble, wholesome deeds. Because these factors are what one should abide by, doing all routines according to them, they are termed "*kariya*" in Pali meaning "what should be done". "*Vatthu*" means seat of benefits. Thus, wholesome deeds worthy of doing, the seat of all virtues and great benefits, are called the articles of "*poññakariyavatthu*." They number ten, namely

1. *dāna* (Giving, charity)
2. *sila* (Keeping precepts)
3. *bhāvanā* (Meditation)
4. *apacāyana* (Due respect)
5. *Veyyāvicca* (service)
6. *pattidāna* (Sharing one's merits with others)
7. *pattānumodana* (Taking a share in others' merits)
8. *dhammasavana* (Listening to talks on dhamma)
9. *Dhammadesanā* (Discussing dhamma)
10. *Ditthijukamma* (Holding right views)

---

147. The 10 *ducaritas* and *the 10 sucarita* - for details please see Appendix A
148. The ten misconducts:- (1) killing of life, (2) taking what has not been given, (3) amoral sexual conduct, (4) telling falsehood, (5) slandering, (6) using rough language, (7) frivolous speech, (8) envy,
(9) malice, (10) holding wrong views
149. The ten virtuous, moral conducts: - the opposite of the ten misconducts (above).
150. A companion volume of this book

1. DĀNA (CHARITABLE DEEDS)

Giving possessions away in charity is "*dāna*". There are two kinds of dāna namely cetanā dāna and vatthu dāna. Donation of food, robes, monastic buildings and so on are called "vatthu dāna". When doing such dāna, there comes about willful benevolence (cetanā) in the donor's heart; this is called "cetanā dāna". The benefits resulting from these donations are due to this cetanā dāna, not the food, robes, monastic buildings and so on. The materials of donation are only object articles (ārammanas) that prompt the cetanā. So, if materials of charity bear lofty status, cetanā can also be high and noble.

Carried a bit further, in donating food to the Sanghā, seeing the alms food being proffered and the monks eating the food, the donor's heart is continually filled with an abundance of cetanā. Although the cetanā that appears disappears, it does not vanish completely; it disappears only after leaving its impact in the consciousness continuum to take effect for benefits in some future time.

[The kmrmic property-continuum will be explained in the chapter on Kamma. Now consider how many times the cetanā would have appeared and multiplied in (say) 3 hours of the alms-food donation service - a piece of the mind can pop up and out a million-million times in the flicker of a moment.]

How dāna material and recipients can help make cetanā strong

Although dāna materials such as food by themselves, and recipients such as the Sanghā cannot carry and give benefits to the donor in his/her next life, they can help in making the donor's cetanā strong. The perfunctory type of cooking and offering food to the Sanghā does not arouse much cetanā. But the ārammana of special cooking for dāna brings about a very sharp and strong cetanā. In offering food to a mediocre type of person does not cause strong cetanā, whereas donating food to highly venerable monks arouse in the donor a very sharp and strong cetanā. That is how the type of alms material and the recipients' image can make the difference in the quality of the donor's cetanā

Small and big donations

In the matter of efforts in putting up material donations, big and small, the quality and measure of effort differ. It takes only a short time in the effort of small donations. It takes correspondingly longer time in the cases of bigger donations. While gathering materials for donation before the actual deed of it, a lot of cetanā is taking place. Therefore, it is quite obvious in comparing big and small types of donation that more cetanā is involved in larger donations. While in the process of donation also the person with big donation has a lot of grand cetanā depending on the attention given in accord with the size of donation. After the donation proceedings also, reflection upon the proceedings gives rise to a retrospective cetanā that would be grander and bigger for a grander and bigger donation than minor efforts. Thus, the cetanā is strong before, during and after the actual charitable deed.

Importance of gladness with cetanā

Some people are not particularly glad about their great donations; neither is their cetanā strong, doing it only as a matter of functional duty. For such people, the cetanā cannot be said to be sharp and well developed. When King Dutthagāmani Abaya[151] was at his death door, he was contemplating the gladness of a simple kusala kamma in offering a meal to an arahanta in the jungle while he was a fugitive, instead of his grand donation of the Great Ceti - on account of that simple dāna, when he died he was reborn in Tusita deva realm. In short, cetanā is more important than the material dāna.

How dāna is like putting a seed to ground

Recipients are like the farms, while the donor is the farmer;
Dāna is the seed to bring forth the fruit to be picked later.

The Peta Vatthu Pali gives a parable, "The recipients of donation are like a farm while the donors, male and female alike, are farmers. The material articles of donation are similar to the seeds. The benefits enjoyed in future samsāric lives are like the growth of plants from those seeds that bear fruit." Giving proper consideration to this parable, one may find in the industry of a farm:

1. Just as quality of the plants and fruit depends on the quality of the soil they are grounded in, so also the benefits due to certain dāna are dependent on the moral (sila) quality of the recipients;

2. Just as there is a difference between qualities of the seeds, so also the benefits due to a certain dāna differ from others, depending on whether the material articles of dāna are gained in all fairness or not;

---

151. A king of ancient Singhaladipa or Ceylon

3. Just as the differences in quantity and quality of the plants and crop produced depend on the amount of work and effort as well as the know-how put into the farm work, so also the quantity and quality of benefits accruing from an act of charity would depend on whether the donor is knowledgeable and glad about his/her dāna (*munca cetanā*)

4. Just as the plants and the crop depend on the preparatory work done before seeding, so also the benefits depend on the cetanā prior to the deed of the dāna (*pubba cetanā*);

5. Just as development of the plants and crop depend on watering and weeding, etc., after the seeding, so also the benefits depend on whether there is remembering, contemplation and feeling of joy about the dāna after doing it (*apara cetanā*);

6. Just as one destroys the farm in a fit of one's bad mood, so also if one regrets doing the dāna (if there is a lack of apara cetanā), the benefits from the dāna already done would not come about (or, would be very little, if any);

7. Just as the plants and crops are well developed and good when the farm and the seeds are ready and put to ground at an appropriate time, so also the dāna would bring forth commensurate benefits only if the dāna is done at an appropriate time even though the recipients and the alms are ready for proffering beforehand.

Thus as Petavatthu Pali is given serious consideration, what has been indicated above become clearly defined. Therefore, in doing dāna, one should choose recipients, donating only where required. One should be happy about the occasion. The dāna cetanā should be pure and not mixed with any desire for worldly riches, greed and lust.

Benefits dependent on the recipient's personality

"Dāna recipients are like the farming ground," we have said. Thus, just as the farm soil quality can be classed as first, second or third, so also, there are different classes of the alms recipients. Just as the cropping plants grow strong and healthy if the farm is free of weed and grass, so also the donor's benefits are great if the recipients are low in lust, anger and ignorance (the lower of these, the better). Just as the farm must get a good feeding of manure and water for a good crop, so also the benefits to the donor are great, if the recipients are noble and great, the nobler and greater the better, in their sila, samādhi an paññā.

Sanghika dāna (donation to the Sanghā)

"*Sangha*" in Pali means congregation or the Order of Monks; in Myanmar it is "*Sanghā*"). The dāna intended for the sangha is called sanghika dāna. A membership fee of 1 kyat belongs to all members (the poor as well as the rich) of an association. Likewise, in the case of a bowl of food or a robe donated in the name of the Sangha, intended for the Order, the material becomes common concern of the Sangha as a group (including the arahantas and the lowly putthujjhana monk). There is no need to go round and distribute the material so intended for dāna to all the sanghās of the world. Just as the membership fee of a kyat belongs to, and can be used by, all members of the club, so also the sanghika dāna material can be distributed for use among all members of the Sangha around and about the monastery.

Sanghika dāna only if so inclined

In donating materials as Sanghika dāna, it can be effective, true to the letter, only if the donors are so inclined in their mind. Whilst saying, "This is donated to the Sangha," the real intention is directed to the monks in the monastery or the monk they particularly revere, then the dāna cannot be true Sanghika. Truly aiming for the Sangha in general, the dāna offered on the monks' daily alms round[152], or a morning meal to a particular monk at home can be a true Sanghika dāna.

Sanghika dāna offered in monks' daily alms rounds

In contemplation of prosperity and longevity of the Sāsanā that was founded by the Buddha whom we adore and worship, and carried down and brought forward by generations of the Sangha, all lay men and women, dispelling the ideas of "my abbot", "my monk" and so on, should prepare the food items, saying by word of mouth, "This food we are preparing and offering is for the Sangha," with mindful attention on the Order of the Sangha in general. Only such willful act of offering in the monks' daily alms rounds can be called true Sanghika dāna. Offerings to personalities and the particular monasteries cannot be Sanghika dāna. It can only be an act of dāna intended for a person (or a particular group of persons).

Sanghika dāna in offering food to monks in a home

To offer food to Sangha in a home, the donor must go to the monastery nearby, and make a request to the head monk by saying, "Sayadaw phaya, kindly bless us at home with a monk (2, 3 or more as the donor wishes) for

152. Every morning in Myanmar devotees offer rice, dishes and other eatables as monks, with bowls in their folded arms, appear in the streets or stand at the gates of homes. .

101

our food dāna at 6 o'clock tomorrow morning." [Never say ". . . together
with Sayadaw phaya."] After the invitation, in preparing the dishes for the
purpose, every now and then, think in mind and say by word of mouth,
"Sanghassa demi; Sanghassa demi." When a monk comes as invited, and
if the monk is mediocre, never minding, offer the food to the monk with
due respect as for a proper Sangha, and be mindful, "I am not offering food
to him; it is for Sangha." Do not be too glad if Sayadaw himself comes: be
mindful, "I am not offering food to Sayadaw; it is for Sangha." Such kind
of offering, with the mind inclined towards the Sangha (the whole Order),
even to a single monk, is genuine Sanghika dāna.

A donor's correct thought

Once upon a time, a devotee requested the Sangha to send him a monk
for alms food; he received a notorious *dussila*[153] monk, regarded corrupt by
people. But the donor was not disappointed. He prepared a seat properly
laid out under a perfumed canopy. When the monk came he personally
washed the monk's feet and offered the articles of his dāna the way he
would have if it were for the Buddha Himself. The reason why he could
attach so much importance in that dāna was because he considered it to
be one for the Sangha. So, even though it was a dussila monk who received
his dāna, the donor's was a true Sanghika dāna.

There is more to tell. Because he was treated so deferentially, the dussila
monk was much impressed and thought, "The donor revered me." In the
evening, he came to the donor to take a loan of a hoe for use in repairing
his monastery. The donor lifted the hoe with one foot and gave it to him
saying, "Take." Neighbours saw what took place. Being curious, they asked
the donor why he behaved so differently. "In the morning, it was respect
for the Sangha, not for the monk. Now it was disrespect for him," said
the donor. In consideration of this story, it would be well for donors to be
inclined towards the Sangha so as to make their offering a true Sanghika
dāna.

Differences in resultant benefits

Where dāna is aimed for selected monks, numbering 1, 2, 3 and so
on, or (say) even where the dāna-recipients number over a thousand, it is
only a *puggalika* (personal) dāna. According to scriptural texts, Sanghika
dāna is more beneficial for the donor than puggalika dāna, with the
exception of the dāna towards a Buddha or a paccekabuddha. Logically,

153. Of corrupt character

the term Sanghika includes all saintly arahantas; in the selected few, however, such inclusion is improbable; even if inclusive, the benefits would not be as much as that for a Sanghika dāna. Sanghika dāna also amounts to donation towards the most saintly persons. In puggalika dāna, it calls for some knowledge in the search for proper personalities. So, it carries more weight in terms of benefits to do a Sanghika dāna than a puggalika dāna.

Dāna intended for the Buddha

People could donate offertories directly to the Buddha during His life-time. But as the Buddha is no more, we should learn from the scripture as to how to offer dāna to the Buddha as if He were alive. If one wants to offer food to the real Buddha, prepare food as for a bhikkhu, sufficient for one, and place it in front of a Buddha image, or if there is no image in the vicinity, present it to an imagined Buddha statue. A person originally doing such chores as house-keeping in the service of the Buddha is entitled to eat the food so offered, afterwards. If there is no such person around, the one (a monk or a lay person) now doing the service is entitled to eat the food. In the case of a Sabbath-keeper, he or she may take the food before noon, and give service after the meal. In offering food to the Sangha headed by the Buddha, food for the Buddha should be prepared and presented in the same manner.

The robes offered to the Buddha may also be worn by members of the Sangha. Lay attendants of a Buddha shrine may exchange the robes for other materials to be used for whatever may be necessary in the service of the shrine. The present-day manner of offering flowers, lights and joss sticks are proper. But offering water to splash around and wet everywhere, flowers in rubbish heaps, and lights with wax and oil dirtying all around are not proper manners of veneration (just as landlords and abbots may not like such manners in their households and monasteries). Therefore, it is a blameless, clean and tidy veneration, good for now and in the lives hereafter, if the water, flowers and lights are offered in a clean and tidy manner in front of the Buddha images.

Devotional offering from a distance

Nowadays, since not everyone can visit a pagoda and a Buddha image every time one wishes to, people offered flowers, etc., aiming for the Buddha at home. Whether that is of good benefits or not has been considered long before. It all depends on the cetanā of the devotees. If it is real cetanā in one's heart in offering such materials, why can't one be endowed with benefits? Absolutely, benefits would certainly be forthcoming.

In the past 118th kappa (world), counted from this present world, there appeared a Buddha by the name of Atthadassi. One day, a man saw the Buddha accompanied by bhikkhus, traveling in the sky. Then he offered flowers, incense, etc., to the Buddha, already gone quite far away. For that wholesome deed, he was devoid of *duggati* (lowly destinations), and became the famed arahanta by the name of "Desapujaka Mathera" in the life-time of our Lord.

2. PUBBA, MUNCA AND APARA CETANĀS

Pubba cetanā

Three kinds of cetanā are involved in the process of a dāna, namely *pubbacetanā, muncacetanā* and *aparacetana*. From the time materials for dāna are sourced and gathered up to the point immediately before actual offering, the wholesome thoughts that took place in the heart of the donors are termed "pubbacetanā". In the domain of pubbacetanā, there should be no thoughts of self-importance, self-praise and fame, and boastfulness on the part of the donors. Besides, while sourcing and gathering dāna materials there should be no akusala kammas such as quarrelling among family members, show of anger, pride and so on; there should only be gladness for the forthcoming dāna, and no backward thinking to abandon the idea of the dāna for any reason. If the dāna can be managed gladly and satisfactorily in all aspects, then it is certainly "full of very pure pubba cetanās".

Munca cetanā

By "munca" is meant "disowning, dispossessing". So *"munca cetanā"* is the cetanā that pops up at the time of releasing one's own materials for dāna (in food donation, the cetanā at the moment of proffering food, or at the moment of saying "I donate this food" if not personally proffering the items). At the moment of this munca cetanā also, the aforesaid unwholesome thoughts must be voided; one should note that, as it is an act of dāna out of sheer generosity, " it is really a pure munca cetanā" where there involves absolutely no clinging (tanhā-lobha) of the donor to the recipient of the dāna, and no expectation of return of favour from any quarter.

Apara cetanā

All thoughts in connection with, and after, the completion of the acts of dāna is called "*apara cetanā.*" Therefore, after an accomplishment of a wholesome donation, every time that dāna is thought of, it is something for the donor to be glad about, something considered worthwhile as "having done a good dāna and wanting to do more of it," and so the domain of apara cetanā expands. If, after an act of dāna, the donor's possessions are ruined, or after donation of a monastery, some disappointment arises as to the behaviour of the abbot, one may come to regret the dāna already done - such disappointment or regret about one's dāna already done is dosa, an akusala kamma.

Caution

There are grandiose acts of dāna such as donation of a monastery and a pagoda. On lesser scales, there are acts of dāna such as offering food, robes, medicines, etc. to the monks, and some charitable works towards the poor. In the cases of grandiose donations, there may occur regrets and disappointments due to either the unbecoming behaviour of the alms-recipients, or interference from other people. These are the cases in which many donors, not capable of correct thinking, may find their cetanās tending to go sour. So, in giving such great acts of charity, people should not only think as properly as they possibly can, but also they should seek good advice from friends and learned Sayadaws in the matter of choosing personalities to be involved in their dāna proceedings. For small donations, it is not important to choose recipients, as it is of great merits even for feeding domestic animals. In some cases it is important to make it a Sanghika dāna, and in others the dāna materials should be given away with complete detachment. One should try to be a *muttacāgi* (donor with absolute detachment). It means "the donor with no clinging either to the recipient of the dāna or the dāna materials, and with no forethought on, and wish for, a good life hereafter, but only aiming for attainment of Nibbāna."

The difference between dvihetu and tihetu kusalas

Alobha, adosa and amoha are the three articles of "*hetu*", as has been shown in the Chapter on Cetasika. By "hetu" is meant "the source, the root." The root of a tree is the source of support for it to grow with profuse foliage, flower and fruit, and be strong. Likewise, the hetu conditions are the cause of their associate cetasikas to grow profusely and be strong. Therefore it is to be noted that kusala citta (wholesome thoughts) are of two kinds: dvihetu kusalacitta associated with two articles of hetu, and tihetu kusalacitta, three articles of hetu.

Dvihetu kusalacitta

The wholesome thought (kusala citta) associated with alobha (charity) and adosa (mettā or loving kindness) is named dvihetu kusalacitta. In the 10 articles of *sucaritta*[154], the view that "all kammic actions result in corresponding effects," is "*kammasakatā ñāna.*" A child or a savage may not know the principle of kamma and its effects, but he may be glad with a kusalacitta when giving something to someone. But there involves no knowledge of kammasakatā ñāna or *amoha*, that "the present kusalakamma remains in one's consciousness continuum, and this will entail in wholesome benefits later on". It consists only of alobha and adosa hetus." That kind of kusalacitta is called "dvihetu kusalacitta."

A great many Buddhists nowadays give away charities just like any body else, without really understanding the principle of kamma and its results. Theirs is also dvihetu kusalacitta. A person, although knowledgeable, may have done an act of charity as a matter of course, and so it also dvihetu kusalacitta. In short, it is all dvihetu kusalacitta at the moment of the deed if it is done without the wisdom called kammasakatā ñāna.

Tihetu kusalacitta

The kusalacitta associated with alobha, adosa and amoha, the three articles of hetu, is called "tihetu kusalacitta." It is tihetu kusalacitta if, at the moment of doing the charitable deed, the donor knowingly thinks of the principle of kamma and its effects, the kammasakatā ñāna. Nowadays, men and women of some intelligence are serving in the affairs of the Buddha, Dhamma, Sangha, parents and elders with pure cetanā. The kusalacitta is the tihetu type since it has the understanding of kammic effects in the samsāra. For one who practises insight meditation and contemplates, at the moment of doing the dāna, that "this material that I am giving away now is only a compounded kalāpa (the tiniest) units of rupa that are subject to change, miseries and beyond anyone's control," it is, indeed, the best type of tihetu kusalacitta. There is no need of saying more. Therefore, parents and teachers should educate the younger generations about the principle of kamma and its possible effects, as well as the three characteristics of *anicca, dukkha and anatta*[155].

---

154. For Duccaritta and sucaritta, see Appendix
155. impermanence, suffering and absence of self or soul

Qualities of kusala kamma

The dvihetu and tihetu kusalacittas, if surrounded by kusalacetanā both before and after the act of dāna (with no akusala citta, but only engaged in kusala citta), are *ukkattha* (noble) kusala kamma. If surrounded by akusalacetanā both before and after the act of dāna, it is *omaka* (inferior) kusalakamma.

When saying "surrounded" by kusalacetanā and akusalacetanā, it means the kusala and akusala kammas in association with kusalacitta and akusalacitta at the moments of pubba- and apara-cetanās. The word "surrounded" cannot be used in cases of independently done kusala and akusala kammas not associated with that kusalacitta. For instance, the donor was angered for failure of a debtor to honour his debts and so a law suit was initiated. It is dosa and lobha akusala. But the mind was set for dāna and the donor was glad about it. His aparacetanā for the dāna is strong. But the anger and greed were there due to the legal affair. Because that affair is nothing to do with the dāna, it cannot interfere to make the dāna less noble.

Summing up, tihetu kusala kamma, strong in pubba and apara cetanās, is "tihetu ukkattha kusalakamma." If either one of pubba or apara cetanās is lacking, then it is "tihetu omaka kusalakamma." If both are lacking, it is more of "tihetu omaka". Similarly, it can be noted of dvihetu omaka. Note similarly dwihetu ukkathta and dwihetu omaka [Sila and other kusalakammas can be classed according as the 3 cetanas of pubba, munca and apara, the two kusalas of tihetu and dvihetu, and the two kusalas of ukkattha and omaka.]

[Maxim]

1. Whilst doing kusalakamma, if knowledge of kamma and its effects are associated with wisdom, the type of kusalakamma is tihetu.
2. Whilst doing kusalakamma, if knowledge of kamma and its effects are not associated with wisdom, it is dvihetu kusalakamma.
3. If prior and after cetanās are associated, it is ukkattha, the lofty kusala.
4. If prior and after cetanās are lacking, it is omaka, the lowly kusala.

One other method of classifying kusalakamma

The three other types of dāna are hina dāna, majjhima dāna and panita dāna. If one donates articles such as food and clothes of some quality lower than those one uses, then it is *hina*(mean) *dāna*; If of the same quality, *majjgima* (moderate) *dāna*; if better, *panita* (noble) *dāna*.

In one other way, there are three others, namely dāsa dāna, sahāya dāna and sāmi dāna. Actually, hina dāna is *dāsa dāna*: it means "a lowly kind of dāna addressed to the slaves." Similarly, majjhima dāna is *sahāya dāna*: it means "a middling type of dāna addressed to friends." Also, panita dāna is here *"sāmi dāna"*: it means "a high-class dāna addressed to one's mentors and benefactors."

In still another way, if the donor's chanda, viriya and saddhā are weak, it is "hina dāna. If those mental qualities are middling, it is "majjhima dāna." If they are strong and sharp, it is "panita dāna."

In still another way, if the donor's dāna is done following up a wish to be titled donor of a pagoda, a monastery or a grand donation, and to be praised as "a very noble person," it would be "hina dāna." If it is a dāna after a wish "to gain some merits in the lives hereafter," it is "majjhima dāna." With only a simple thought of the tradition of noble persons in respect of charitable deeds, one gives dāna irrespective of whether there are merits for one to enjoy in the samsarā; there is only a wish (cetanā) that somebody else may eat or put on the clothes (or robes) that one offers. This type is *"panita dāna."*

Remark: In this method, it should be noted that the dāna done without an expectation of any return benefit is nobler that with some expectation. The cetanā that "it is all well to see someone else get the benefits," regardless of one's own benefit, is the type of high and noble mentality borne out by the great Buddhas-to-be.

Still another way of thinking: The dāna done so that one may be rewarded with the good things of life is "hina dāna." The dāna done with the aim of freeing oneself from the samsara (wishing that this dāna be the basis of magga-phala ñāna) is "majjhima dāna. The dāna parami (perfect dāna) that is built up by bodhisattas, who have the vision of freeing intelligent beings from the samsaric entanglement is the noblest "panita dāna". And this shows how (with proper mental culture) one type of dāna is nobler than the other. [In the cases of sila. etc. also, there can be three degrees of inferior, middle and noble kammas dependent on the three different mental cultures.]

Benefits arising out of *dāna*

There is no need to say much and elaborate on the benefits arising out of dāna. An act of dāna in feeding a little animal to its belly-full once can result, for a hundred existences, in the five benefits of "*āyu* (long life), *vanna* (good looks), *sukha* (physical and mental wellbeing), *bala* (strength), and *patibhāna* (wisdom)". Humans and devas may owe their being born so to other kusala kammas, but those who had done dāna are noblest in the qualities of life amongst them.

During Kassappa Buddha's life-time, there were two monks in close friendship. One gave dāna while the other did not. Both kept precepts well, and so they were reborn as men and devas time and again till the time of our Lord, Gotama Buddha; all along, the man with dāna was always of higher social status than the other. In the present life-time, they met each other in the palace of King Kosala; the one with dāna was a prince while the other was son of a wet nurse. While the former enjoyed a cradle under a white parasol, the other rode a wooden cradle. They were good friends in spite of their differences in social position.

Does dāna stretch the samsarā?

Nowadays, some people wrongly believe that "dāna begets a long samsāra". The man with past dāna in the afore-mentioned story was not late in attaining enlightenment. So, dāna should not be mistaken as the reason for the shortening or lengthening of samsarā. It is only due to impure thoughts in doing dāna that "tiger gets cattle for negligence of owner." In fact, dāna is not the cause of a long samsarā. It is the greed-led wish that aims "for enjoyment of a rich life as a human being or a heavenly god in the next life" that carries the donor down stream in the long river of Samsāra.

Some people with little knowledge think, "The Buddha had to traverse a long road of the samsarā for his great acts of dāna." An uncountable number, a great deal more than the sand grains of the Ganga and the Vālu rivers, of Buddhas with great acts of dāna had come and gone. Are we here, still not being able to break free of the entanglements, because our acts of dāna were greater than those Buddhas? King Vessantarā, the second last rebirth of Gotama Buddha, did great acts of dāna. Why didn't those acts of dāna cause the samsarā for the Bodhisatta any longer?

Therefore, dāna by virtue of its own nature does not stretch the samsarā. It is the greed (tanhā) that stretches the samsarā. The long samsarā for the Bodhisattas are actually due to their original aim for attainment of Sabbaññuta ñāna (Buddhahood) that required fulfillment of the Perfections worthy of such inimitable, incomparable, self-sought omniscience, taking so long to reach maturity. For instance, only mature mangos get ripe in time whereas tender mangos cannot be made truly ripe even if given some warmth under cover of a thick fabric.

Vatta nissita and vivatta nissita

Wishing for a good life of man or deva when doing a kusalakamma, the kamma is called "vatta nissita kusala". [vatta = on round trip through samsarā + nissita = supportive kusala] It is a kusala kamma done with the aim of going round the samsarā, rather than to disentangle from it. A kusalakamma done with the aim for Nibbāna is called "vivatta nissita kusala." [vivatta = vatta-free Nibbāna + nissita = supportive kusala] In these two types of kusalakamma (dāna and sila) vatta nissita stretches the samsāra. If it is truly vivatta nissita, it would be easier to get free of the samsāra as soon as possible according as one originally, truly wishes.

Dāna in support of other paramis

People with dāna parami are well endowed in every existence. If well-endowed, (for good-natured people and those with vivatta nissita dāna) sila is ensured: they can keep Sabbath for days on end. For the poor, however, food being a daily problem, Sabbath is out of the question - it is difficult even to keep the five precepts. Dāna can beget sila easily. It is easy for those with dāna to pursue education. This fact is a familiar sight in modern institutions. Even at some monastic schools that give free education, the well-to-do children are better cared for in the classroom. Dāna, thus, paves easy access to education.

People with dāna, if insulted, find it easy to forbear it either out of nonchalance or forgiving. Poor people, however, would not stand such insults, thinking, "I am insulted for my poverty." The well-endowed people are respected by other people, and in response, they are inclined towards those other people with mettā and kindness. People in poverty receive respect from very few people, and they are ready for quarrel with such non-caring people - there is dosa instead of mettā and kindness, and pride is ready to show up. Following this lead, try to elaborate on how forbearance and metta paramis come easily on account of dāna.

In the world where " promises cannot be kept due to poverty ", dāna is important to assist in the performance of *saccā parami* (perfection in truthfulness). Thus without dāna, there would be hindrances in fulfilling all other paramis. So, all Bodhisattas take care of dāna first and foremost.

Our Lord started out with dāna when he was Sumedhā hermit, and concluded fulfilling all the paramis with dāna in the life of Vessantarā.

The one who does not have to do dāna

There is a type of person who does not need to do dāna. A yogi (meditator) is the type, working to end the rebirth of khandha and achieve the ultimate peace in the present life-time. If that person were giving dāna, it would be time wasted for kammatthāna work. So for a person determined to attain the Ultimate Wisdom today or tomorrow, there is no need of doing any dāna. There was once a dāna-inclined elder bhikkhu from Mandalay, taking kammatthāna training from our mentor, Mahāgandhāyon Sayadaw[156]. One early morning the yogi bhikkhu was picking flowers to offer to the Buddha. Seeing that, Sayadaw pleaded with the yogi, saying, "Kindly offer the flowers later. Now, please work hard at kammatthāna practice."

We do not know if the Mahāgandhāyon Sayadaw ended khandha vatta, but we do know that he worked with unremitting determination in meditation sessions. Although firm with diligence at kammatthāna, Sayadaw managed distribution of the offertories received, and performed the act of dāna after coming out of the cave.

Therefore, there is no need of dāna while in session at kammatthāna training so that the yogi may gain insight, but at other times, the yogi like other people should give dāna every day as he wishes.

Dāna is a happy affair

Giving away dāna is a very delightful affair. With a real cetanā and an earnest interest, based on kindness for the poor and gladness for the well-to-do, with mettā for all beings, the face of the one giving dāna, as a matter of habit, is always clear and peaceable, full of grace, and seemingly very happy.

The dāna-recipients' response is mettā toward the dāna-giver. Moreover the richer the dāna-giver, the gladder (more muditā) the recipients are about the rich donor, thus a single act of dāna develops into all aspects of brahmacora dhamma. So, if the dāna is genuine, a simple dāna readily results in the bhāvanā aspects of mettā, krunā and muditā.

From charity to riches

Just as there are some well-to-do people in this world, there also are only a few who do not have to worry about day-to-day food-clothing-and-

---

156. This is the first Mahāgandhāyon Sayadaw before the writer of this book

shelter situations. Those who are now in the list of poverty and deprivation had not done dāna in their previous existences. Those who are now in the list of the wealthy had given dāna in their previous lives, well enough to be wealthy now in this life. Should those wealthy people be contented with just the riches they own in this life-time? As soon as they close their eyes, the present wealth is finished, and a new life will begin on its own.

Therefore, only if the good-natured people of riches distribute his possessions (after leaving enough for his heirs) among the poor, "wealthy people of previous life are now wealthy, and the wealthy people in this life will again be wealthy in the next life," thus possessors of wealth and property at all times till the time of entry into Nibbāna. Therefore one should consider the present wealth as not "my own", but "something of mine to be shared with the poor", and must of necessity be able to distribute it among the disabled and the unfortunate."

Wealthy people likened to a river, etc.

In the books of *lokaniti*[157], it is said, "Virtuous people of wealth are like rivers, trees and rains." There is water in all rivers, but the rivers do not drink it: they collect water for people and others who need it for drinking, bathing and other uses. Trees also do not eat the fruit they bear; they bear fruit for people and other creatures to eat. Rains do not fall only on lakes, ponds and wells, but fall all over dry lands too.

Likewise, good-natured wealthy people also work, seek and stock up the riches not for their own use alone, but also keep them for distribution among the poor. In giving dāna (the rains), not the only rich people who are like wells full of water (the well-endowed sayadaws), but also the poor people who are like the dry land should also be included.

"All those five great rivers

with their five hundred tributaries together,

do not drink the cool emerald water they gather;

the rich expanse of trees bear fruit they do not eat;

the rain that falls does not fall

only on a particular well alone;

the property, the jewels that belong to the wealthy

are there for the benefits of all and sundry,

that is true as always can be.

(Niti Pyo)

---

157. Ethics and civics

The charity that the wealthy people give out makes mettā, karunā and muditā grow. This imparts clear look on the donor's face. The action is a meritorious one, and this is the impetus for the donor to be wealthy once more in his next life, thus opening up a straight path through the sea of samsāra towards the target of the safe beach called Nibbāna. So, how should anybody afford to forget to do dāna?

If one gives dāna to all and sundry, regardless of their moral (saintly or lowly) character, with the eight precepts[158], ten precepts or ājivatthamakasila kept, wearing clean clothes after a bath, meditating on the three dhamma articles of brahmacariya (mettā. Karunā and muditā), keeping oneself in a steadfast frame of mind with confidence as "by this practice of dāna, aiming for Nibbāna, one will certainly be liberated from aging, diseases and death", how joyful would that be? Wouldn't that be the fast way of ascension to Nibbāna?

Dāna is indispensable

What has been discussed so far is not a complete list of benefits accrued from dāna. A treatise on the subject cannot list all the advantages of dāna. So, dāna should never for any reason be disregarded. Supposing some people discarded dāna as a matter of principle, then there will be no exchange of gifts with blessedness among people, no show of love, nor any kindness. Their world certainly would be drab, dry and desolate. If no dāna is offered to the poor, then how, with what kind of cetanā, could anybody look at them? That is how "Let these people stave and die!" would have to be the order of the day, an utter non-caring world. If that were the case, disregard for dāna would cause the mind rough and harsh. The harsh mind only begets ugly, violent looks (and actions).

Our Lord, since renunciation and leaving his kingdom till the attainment of Buddhahood, He was assisted only by charitable donors. Also after the Enlightenment, depending wholly on the assistance of such donors as Anāthapinnikassa, Visākhā and King Bimbisāra, He was able to found and propagate the Sāsanā. If the time had been full of people devoid of dāna, there would have been no Buddha, and no Sāsanā anywhere near us. Even leaving that alone, the countless number of Buddhas of the immeasurably long Samsāra before our Lord would not have come about without the charity of donors. May the future worlds be free of those who reject dāna.

---

158. For all the precepts, see Appendix.

All powers and advantages of dāna,
This little book cannot list to the end;
But do not be misguided, or confused;
All the Buddhas that had already come
Came on the support of dāna, for the benefit
Of all to hear the new Teaching
And be delivered from miseries of life;
Dāna various shines over all other virtues,
Its light bright,
Highest and noblest of all values;
Look at the troubles that come without dāna
That is to be nurtured and cultured
As nourishment for mankind to be happy
And be free from entanglements of life.

3. *SILA* (KEEPING PRECEPTS[159] OR VIRTUOUS MORA L CONDUCTS)

Normally, one may find it hard to see the truth of the saying that "sila is nobler than dāna." But considered deeply, the saying has good reasons. In all the works in the world, the deeds that serve others so that they may not suffer, and the actions that serve others to assist in their wellbeing are all wholesome, beneficent works (kusala kamma).

Dāna is the kind of work that serves to assist in the wellbeing of others, whereas sila looks after others so that they may not suffer in miseries. [Here sila is meant by the five precepts and the ājivatthamakasila. The 8-precept and 10-precept sila are kept for a different kind of purpose.]

The service of dāna

Supposing a certain person is occasioned to be poor as "a result of his/her own actions". Aiding that poor person by way of gifts and other assistance is the job of dāna. Take also the example of members of the Sangha. These people are not really poor. But they do not have enough food and other life's necessities of their own. In a way, they are poor. Therefore, dāna given to members of the Sangha amounts to helping them in their life's sustenance.

There is another kind of dāna that is addressed to very powerful and rich elder monks. If the items of dāna material are what the monks need (as may befit the monks), it is by nature an assistance to the poor. If the dāna-

159. Precepts are listed in Appendix B.

recipients are the wealthy monks who have every thing they need, the dāna is meant for distribution for use among the needy pupils and beneficiaries, and so it is, in fact, aiding the poor. Therefore, dāna being a wholesome kind of work that looks after one, two, or even all the poor people in the world, it is the one thing that all those who understand the benefits of dāna could and should very much love to do as a way of living.

The vow not to kill (*Pānātipāta virati*)

The purpose of sila is to look after others so that they may not suffer. Supposing many people fail to observe the precepts such as "I promise not to kill", and kill whatever comes in sight, just think how frightful and miserable would it be for the poor *sattavās*[160] being killed. For such failure to keep this sila (*pānātipāta*), see how much suffering would befall on all the fish in the rivers before being killed: and the cattle, buffalos, goats, pigs, chickens and so on in the villages and towns. Also, think of the news of wars between humans, cruelly killing each other, with red blood spilling all over in many parts of the world - consider how much stricken with fright would the people be even upon hearing the coming of battles or wars. Is it not true that failure to observe such a single precept as non-killing causes suffering for one, two or more people, even worldwide?

If the precept of non-killing is kept, it would amount to saving those who would otherwise be shedding tears, suffering excruciating pains under the threat of killing, actual beating, and torture. If one person keeps this sila, one being would be saved; if two or three keep it, two or three would be saved; if people all over the whole world keep it, then the human race would be saved from those miseries, and everybody would get the benefit of mettā, karunā and muditā. Indeed, the world would then be peaceful, a very happy place to live in.

Comparative study

Comparing this sila of non-killing alone with dāna, it is quite obvious that sila is nobler than dāna. Compare gladness of one for receiving a gift from someone else, with the gladness of another who is freed only a moment ago from the threat of being killed. In the instance, everyone capable of reasonable thinking must admit that the happiness of one getting a gift is a thousand times less than that of the one being freed from

---

160. A living being - a deva, a human or an animal, (In Buddhism, the term "creature" is not applicable.)

the jaws of death. Even the gladness of a starving man when someone feeds him cannot match that of the man pardoned from a death sentence.

The vow not to take things not given (*Adinnadāna virati*)

Because of thievery and robbery, owners of properties being robbed are unhappy. Because a country is annexed and looted, the king of the annexed country, his queen, royal lineage and the subjects are intolerably sad and miserable. They are not employed in their country the way they should be. There are no opportunities for them. For them, resources are scarce; they are made poor. Therefore, it is plain that robbery without abatement results in the suppression and oppression of the wealthy people in such a way as not to be able to reinvigorate their enterprises. Therefore, only if the vow of thievery and robbery is observed in general and especial, such miseries would not be found on the face of the earth. So, this vow from taking things not given (*adinnādāna viratisila*) is the kind of sila that paves the way for freedom from poverty, and for enjoyment of physical and mental wellbeing.

The vow not to commit sexual misconduct (*Kāmesumicchācāra virati*)

Because the sensual pleasures are a kind of distinct enjoyment for ordinary people (*puthujjana*), they are attracted more to those objects of pleasure than any other kind. One (if not mad nor handicapped) cannot lend that (highly adorable) kind of object that one owns to anyone else even for a short while, leaving alone giving it away altogether. Often, the other person who robs one of such an object would be considered a great enemy. Robbing one of the highly attached object one owns makes one deeply miserable, more so than being looted of other objects. If capable of a fight, it can become a life-and-death affair. Therefore, avoidance of sexual misconduct (*kāmesumicchācāra virati*) by one is actually conscious abstinence from a behaviour that would cause unhappiness for other people. Thus, general upkeep of this sila is a cause for happiness of many people.

The vow not to tell lies (*Musāvāda virati*)

The feeling of anger and puzzlement when being lied to was like "the very foul smell of soft excrement of a cat," very disquieting. Ruinations as a result of such lies are evident to the naked eye. One can also imagine the extent of damages done as great liars can even trick whole countries. Following up instructions by many teachers from various religions, a great many people have taken wrong paths and suffered enormously. So,

116

here too, restraining from falsehood (*musāvāda virati,* according to the Buddhist view) takes care of suffering of one, two or more people or even the whole of mankind. [Think how some preachers of 'Buddhism' tell falsehoods, and how the less intelligent people are misled.]

The vow not to take alcoholic drinks, etc. (*Surāpāna Virati*)

By merely drinking by oneself, one alone will suffer resultant miseries in the samsāra, not much damage being done to others. But the action would not stop there. When intoxicated, that one would be prone to breaching the other precepts. A very clever man would not commit murder, theft or sexual wrongs, but he would train lackeys thoroughly and get them do the mischief. That clever man (although not doing the mischief himself) is more dreadful than his lackeys. The miseries he so caused are more severe in degree and quantity than those that he might have done personally by himself. Likewise, the drinking habit would gradually grow and when addiction is complete, it can become the cause of sufferings for beings, more than killing, theft and sexual misconduct; and so, more frightful. Therefore, *surāpāna virati* would save one's family, and by extension the world community, from some miseries.

Think similarly of the resultant benefits of other classes of sila such as ājivatthamaka sila. Contemplating thus on the resultant effects, it is quite clear that the world would be a safe place to live in, if the five precepts were kept by every one all over the world. This shows, clearly, how sila is nobler than dāna. Therefore, I wish that every one, self and all others, fully and securely keep the five precepts mindfully, with mettā and karunā for all beings.

The Sabbath sila

Included in the Sabbath precepts are vows such as *Brahmacariya* (the practice of celibacy), *vikālabhojanā* (not eating after noon), etc., are not meant to safeguard others from miseries, but to raise one's own mental capabilities to higher values. This is not the type of Sabbath sila that many people nowadays would keep merely to make a good impression upon neighbours, but the kind that one wholeheartedly keeps in full confidence: it is called "*Ariya* (saintly) Sabbath [161] ". [The various kinds of Sabbaths and their applications have been extensively described in Yatanagonyi.]

The person with ariya Sabbath would have to keep up with an ārammana in meditation such as the Buddha-guna[162], dhamma-guna,

---

161   (P) The Sabbath of the noble and holy ones (*ariya-puggala*)
162   *Guna* = (P) property or quality

sangha-guna, one's own sila-guna, or dāna-guna. As meditation proceeds, there occur less and less of lobha, dosa, māna, and etc., in the mind while it develops into higher, purer levels. Thus, Sabbath sila is not a mere fast, but, in fact, associated with meditation, and, being an extension of the basic precepts of *pānātipāta*[163], etc., they are higher and nobler than the five basic precepts.

4. *BHĀVANĀ* (MEDITATION)

"Bhāvanā" is translated in Myanmar as "repetitive application of, and infusion with, a scent, an idea, a thought, an ārammana) ". It is the working of the mind (*mano kamma*) to purify and make it noble. So, truly wishing every living being that one sees to be well, happy, and to prosper is *mettā bhāvanā*. It is "making mettā to infuse and grow in one's consciousness continuum". The habitual meditator in that mode is filled with metta at all times; one's whole body seems impregnated with metta.

One who has that mettā in one's heart, when one sees others in poverty, is willing to help them out, and so he is ready for *karunā bhāvanā*. Because one has mettā, one is glad when one sees prosperous people; *muditā bhāvanā* appears in one. These 3 types of bhāvanā can take place in truly good-natured people wherever they are, and at all times.

In taking ārammana of *anussatis*[164] such as Buddhānussati, serious contemplation must be applied in 3 developmental steps, i.e. the beatitude of the Buddha's past kamma (the paramis), the flowering of the Bodhi-ñāna (fruit of labour), and how the Buddha's Wisdom had finally turned into enormous benefits for all beings (fruit for one and all).

The Beatitude of Efforts (the Cause of Wisdom)

The efforts here mean the perfections (*paramis*), the prerequisites of Buddhahood. In fulfilling those perfections, the tasks were not performed perfunctorily as might be expected of any mortal man, but the efforts were superhuman, unrelenting and diligent to the extreme. The Boddhisatta was not doing that all along the long samsāra for his personal benefits, but with the vision of wellbeing for the multitude of human beings, gods and other forms of life. To gain a clear understanding of this, let us take a look at the dāna pārami performed by King Vessantarā, the Bodhisatta (of our Gotama Buddha).

---

163 (P) The precept of non-killing

164. (P) Six objects of Recollections, anussatis: Buddhā-, Dhammā-, Sanghā, silā-, cāgā- and devatā-nussati

When giving dāna, a great many people want to show off their being "donors". They want the recipients to be grateful; even to get a pay-back of the debt of gratitude, if possible. For that charity, they want to enjoy great comforts and riches in the lives hereafter; they might wish for Nibbāna only at the end of all that. But the Bodhisatta Vessantarā was not like that. Soon after his birth, he spread out his little hand, asking for something to give away; he did not know then what prestige was, or the like of it. It was an inborn trait (*patisandhi citta*) that made him want to give.

Being charitable to the extreme, he, as a child, often took off items of jewelry he was wearing and gave them away. After his ascension to the throne, he had a pavilion built where he gave away millions in charity. He was very happy, watching people enjoying themselves, feasting, putting on new clothes and so on in the pavilion. He had no time to think either of his wellbeing in the samsāra, or of the prestige now. It was the extreme desire (*chanda*) to help the poor, with a view to "the noble duty of the wealthy" toward the poor.

He was not thinking of his prestige, or the life's blessings, when he gave away Paccaya, the royal white elephant, to the dismay and noisy protests of his people. He was praying, "May this wholesome act of dāna contribute to the attainment of Buddhahood." Some may think that wishing for Bodhi ñāna is selfish. Actually, that is not so. The Bodhi ñāna was a great burden on the Buddha. For, on account of that Wisdom, the Buddha had no rest, talking and teaching Dhamma, traveling great distances on foot, all through His life as Buddha. Therefore, it is clear that the desire for Buddhahood was not a selfish one, but a wish for the good of all.

Finally, he was able to give away his loved ones - son, daughter and wife - very clearly showing that it was "not for his sake but for the benefits of all beings."[165] To say more of it, for the good life of man or god, the supreme purpose is to live happily with one's good spouse and precious children. Without them, even the fabulous Ruler of the World[166] would not be happy. In the life of King Vessantara, Queen Maddi and their two children were the most important persons in the whole world. So, to give away the most precious children and beloved queen cannot be equated to prestige and a desire for pleasures of life. It was only for the wellbeing of the people in misery that he strived for the *Sabbyiññuta ñāna*[167].

---

165. The purpose of Bodhi ñāna is to bring about benefits of all by way of knowledge and Wisdom. .
166. *Sakkyavade*, the fabulously just and gentle Ruler of the human world as depicted in the Buddhist literature
167. The Ultimate Wisdom, same as Bodhi ñāna.

With this kind of *chanda,* the Bodhisatta risked his life in a great many world-cycles to keep sila, withstand all hardships, and to save others' lives so as to fulfill the ten perfections (*paramis*). These are the good reasons for which the Buddha should be so revered. They are the good reasons for aspiring to be the Buddha.

The Beatitude of Effects (Resultant Benefits)

By "the blessedness of effects" is meant the loftiness of the Buddha's achievements on the bases of the Perfections He had so well fulfilled. These include the sublime looks, the grandeur of wisdom and the enormity of superhuman powers. One may pay homage to these properties in accordance with one's knowledge.

Benefits for the living beings

After getting in possession of all those grand, befitting benefits, the Buddha did not take any rest, but for the great benefits of all sattavas, passed His 45 years of Buddhahood by teaching dhamma, non-stop. Even at the time of proximity to *Parinibbāna* (passing-away), He reminded bhikkhus "to be always mindful, and never to forget" - (*"handa dāni bikkhave, āmantayāmi vo; vayadhammā sankhārā, appamādena sampādetha"*). On account of all those tireless travels and talks of dhamma, countless numbers of sattavas (humans, gods and others) were freed from cyclic entanglements in the samsāra, and delivered to the Ultimate Peace.

When one pays attention with full confidence to these beatitudes of cause and effects of Buddhahood and the tireless works for the benefits of all sattavās, one is overwhelmingly imbued with the thought, "for us, Lord Buddha is our refuge, and there is no other," (*Buddho me saranam aññan natthi*), and the strong saddhā comes about in one's heart. This is a brief description of how one meditates on Buddhānussati. Likewise, Mettā and other anussatis can be practised, and doing so repetitively for as long as one wishes with all one's heart is called "*bhāvanā*". These are some of the bhāvanās that can be done while walking or paying homage to the Buddha. For more common bhāvanās, look up in some relevant books.

5. *APACĀYANA* (PAYING RESPECTS WHERE DUE)

Giving respects is "*apacāyana*". It is giving respects to those who are senior in age or in monkhood, higher in moral (sila), spiritual (samādhi) or intellectual (paññā) prowess; also to parents, uncles and aunties. "Respect" means rising and giving seats to those to whom respect is due; making way when meeting with such person on a path; moving with one's head bowed or waist a little bent forward, not upright, in front of those people; holding one's palms flush together in front of sanghas; and so on. Other customs of taking off hats, giving a salam or salute are also giving respects. Only giving respects with an honest will amounts to apacāyana kusala. Without an honest will, out of fear, or with expectation of some favour, a manner of respect may be performed, but that would be a false one that amounts to deceit, a form of māyā, not a wholesome act.

Food for thought
Bowing down one's head, bending body forward and putting palms together raised to chest or forehead are signs of respect as regarded by many. Some Buddhists with heavy loads on their heads, on seeing approaching monks, put down the loads to sit down on the bare ground and bow down. Others, in the midst of people in movement, take off their slippers and bow down. Giving respects as due is nothing to find fault with. If given in true volition, it is truly beneficial. But in modern terms, it would be sufficiently respectful in such situations, for both men and women, to put palms together and bow their heads down a bit, or to say, "My kowtow, sir," or "May I be excused, sir/madam," on some occasions commonly encountered on overcrowded trains and boats, perhaps with some foreigners sitting on seats at higher places. In such a situation the sayadaws (senior monks) are themselves busy in both mind and body, and so it feels awkward to observe many respectful people sit down and kowtow.

6. *VEYYĀVACCA* (SUNDRY SERVICES)

Assistance by way of running chores in somebody else's meritorious deeds is called "*veyyāvacca*". Therefore, one must give in one's assistance in the chores as may be required in the deeds of dāna with all one's heart and soul, so that the donor would be comfortable in mind and body, and make the dāna performance a success. Helping old and frail people as well as other stronger ones lift and carry loads beyond their capacity is veyyāvacca kusala; so also is helping out in the chores (that are not unwholesome) of relatives and friends senior to one.

Doing such chores would be conducive to merits more than that of the donors, if correct attitude is applied. There was once a vassal king by the name of Pāyāsi who had been converted to Buddhism from wrong views by Ashin Kumārakassapa's teaching. He was continually giving out charity, not by himself personally, but through a lad, by the name of Uttara, on his behalf. In spite of the fact that it was somebody else's show, Uttara wholeheartedly involved himself well in the management of the dāna veyyāvacca. When they both passed away, the donor became a god in the lower Catumahārājabhumi whereas the helper became one in the higher Tavatimsā.

7. *PATTIDĀNA* (WISHING OTHERS TO SHARE MERITS)

To express one's wish to share one's merits with others equally is called "*pattidāna*". [patti = merits due to one + dāna = giving] In doing dāna, there are merits (kusala) for that dāna due and to be received by the donor. The wish that one's merits be shared equally by other beings is really the work of a mind, pure and noble. The wish saying, "I give equal share of the merits for my dāna to all living beings," with that kind of chanda is the real "pattidāna kusala".

Caution
It is difficult to call it a pattidāna, if the wish-saying is perfunctory and said, "Take a share of merits," because it is customary, something of "follow the others" mentality, not knowing one's own orientation. Once upon a time, a well-known donor borrowed money and gave a grand show of charity. There was not as much material and cash return[168] as he had expected. He was mentally balancing his accounts during the libation ceremony ("water dropping" ceremony conducted by a monk). He soon found that a large amount was in the red, and was in complete puzzlement, feeling morose. When a man near him said, "Give out share of merits, give out share of merits," he came to, and called out loud "I am ruined" instead of "Come and share my merits."

No less merits by sharing merits with others
It may be imagined that one may get less by sharing one's merits with others. In performing kusala actions, cetanā is the mind-element that counts. For the dāna kusala that one has done, there has already been the wholesome cetanā in the mind. As one wishes others to get the same merits as one does, it is like "framing emerald in gold", adding pattidāna onto the original dāna. So, upon giving a share of the merits to others, the kusala

---

168. It is customary that relatives and friends contribute to the capital of donation unless the donor explicitly expresses no wish of such contributions.

benefits do not get less, but grow. A match is consumed for lighting the first oil-lamp; it does not get less bright by lighting other lamps with its flame; in fact the light grows all the brighter as other lamps are lit. [Sharing sila kusala and bhāvanā kusala with others is also pattidāna]

8. *PATTĀNUMODANA* (TAKING A SHARE IN OTHERS' MERITS)

In response to the merit-sharing invitation[169] called out by donors, saying, "Very well, very well. very well", with all gladness, is called "*pattānumodana*". [patta = for the kusala due to distributing one's own merits + anumodana = one is glad, calling out *sādhu*, 3 times.] It is a very noble attitude (akin to muditā bhāvanā) to be pleased with the kusala kammas done by others. So, this joy is noted as a kind of kusala kamma. Without this kind of joy, calling out sādhu (with thoughts elsewhere) as a matter of form can hardly be called "pattānumodana". A few others are envious (issa), rather than joyous.

Immediate benefit of pattānumodana kusala

We have a custom of offering food to the Sanga, listening to a dhamma-talk after that, and distribution of the merits to be shared by those who have passed away. In receiving the share of merits by saying out loud "sādhu" gladly, the deceased[170] benefit from the merits at that very moment. According to the canonical literature, answering in sādhu to the calling of merit-sharing in food offering, the hungry beings would receive good food; in the case of clothes-offering, it would receive good clothes. In all cases of dāna acts for the benefit of the deceased, it is very important that the recipients of the dāna should be morally upright. Once upon a time, living relatives offered dāna to a dussila monk (one without sila) for the benefit of a dead relative; despite calling out "Take share, please" 3 times, the deceased (a peta) did not get the share of the merit, and so it shouted, "The dussila is robbing me of all my benefits." When a morally upright monk was invited, offered the dāna, and called out the dāna-sharing invitation, it gets the benefits of the merits. [Uparipannāsa Dakkhina Vibanga Sutta atthakathā]

---

169. Calling out three times "Take a share of my merits", in Myanmar being "amhya, am-hya, amhya yudaw mu gya par kon law" = "Share, share, take share, please". Answer = "Sadhu, sadhu, sadhu".

170. The deceased may be out of reach when this is being done as a new paticchandi may have occurred; but some (as petas or ghosts) still stay at or near home and can see and hear the meritorious deeds and the merit-sharing calls.

Upon this word, in sharing out dāna to the deceased, grieving and weeping must be done away with in the first place. With a purity of dāna kusala, the offering of food, robes, slippers, umbrella, monastery and so on, must be carried out. [Donation of a monastery would offer it (the departed being) some place to live in.] That dāna must be offered to a chosen character of the highest morality [or, make it a Sanghika dāna]. It is better to invite the deceased to come for the dāna occasion beforehand [it would come if it could]. And then call out the name of the deceased, with a voice loud enough for it to hear, and say the merit-sharing invitation.

Practice in currency

Nowadays, there is no choosing of proper personality (of recipient), nor caring to purify one's mind (to make it a good dāna kusala), but only to be free of criticism or to be praised, with grieving and weeping, some material donations (some cash also) are offered to the Sangha at the graveyard, and merit-share-distribution called out. There was no thought given to whether the deceased really receive the share of merits or not. Such offering in anxiety and grief at the graveyard should be replaced with some clarity of the mind and an orderly dāna procedure and merit-sharing at home. If it can be done with little grieving and weeping and with a clear mind, then it would be beneficial. [Cautions regarding this affair are given in "Anargut Sāsanā".]

Recipient of the share of dāna

In giving out the share of dāna, only if the departed one is a peta staying around and about the house, it can receive the benefits of the dāna. If it were a human, a deva, an animal, or a peta in the forests or on the mountains, it cannot respond with sādhu to the call of share-distribution, and so cannot receive the benefits. But then, since there can be some petas who have been one's relatives once, they can get the benefits of the merits, and so calling out share-distribution of merits when someone dies is a good custom.

9. *DHAMMASSAVANA* (LISTENING TO DHAMMA TALKS)

Listening to dhamma talks is known as "*dhammassavana*". There are 5 benefits for the habit of dhammassavana: the listener (1) hears what one has not learned before; (2) understands more clearly what one has heard before; (3) clears away one's doubts about certain things; (4) arrives at sammāditthi, the right view; (5) has clear mind and vision, having developed confidence (saddhā) and wisdom (paññā).

[**Maxim**]   By listening to the word of the wise,
                 One learns new knowledge;
                 Comes to understand
                 Clearer previous knowledge;
                 Clears doubts about some views;
                 And grasps Right Views
                 To have a clear mind with
                 Growing confidence and wisdom.

Pretentious dhammasāvana

It is true kusala kamma if one aims for these benefits in listening to dhamma talks. It so happens that some people go to dhamma gatherings, because they love the dhamma- kathika (teacher), or because they like the comic parts of the talk, or because they do not want to be censured as "too lazy to listen to dhamma", or because they want to be praised, or because they want to evaluate the calibre of the teacher and to censure him if warranted. Thus, in listening to dhamma talks, the caution is against "*wum*"[171], the way a local Chinaman said about a leaking boat.

Once upon a time, a Chinaman traveling by boat was warned by the boatman, "Paukphaw[172], take care sitting. This boat *yo*[173] (leaks)." The Chinaman thought, "Does it matter if the boat yo?" So he sat in the bare hull of the boat, completely abandoned. Soon, he felt kind of cool at his bottom. Looking down, he saw the water and said, "Oh dear, it does not yo. It *wum*s." (He meant it took in water.) Likewise, while listening to dhamma talks, it is something of concern to have unwholesome thoughts "wum", instead of "yo".

Benefits of reading

Today, there are a great many books that can educate and inculcate good moral character upon youths as well as adults. Reading and digesting

---

171. "Wum" (M) as he said was a corruption (Chinese accent) of "win" in Myanmar, meaning "enter".
172. "Paukphaw" (M): Companion by birth (brother), as affectionately addressed to friendly Chinamen
173. "Yo" is Myanmar for leakage of water, for both ingress and egress, but the Chinaman knew only one way, the leakage or seepage of liquids out of pails, drums and pots.

the contents of those books can benefit the reader the same way as listening to dhamma instructions does. So, instead of listening to some of those modernistic dhamma talks, it is better and more beneficial to read, or listen to somebody with clear voice read, those books.

[In case one is not sure of what books to choose for good reading, Jinatthapakasani, Buddvamsa, Samvegavatthu Dipani, 550 Jatakas and other books compiled by ancient Mahātheras can certainly be of great benefits.]

10. DHAMMADESANĀ (GIVING DHAMMA TALKS)

Giving talks on dhamma is called "*dhammadesanā*" kusala. Given in absolute honesty and purity of goodwill, this kind of kusala is "*Sabbadānam dhammadānam jināti*" = "Giving dhamma talks is better than any other dāna kusalas, resultant benefits being better." So, to make it a real dhammadesanā, there should be no expectation of any kind, including material return, fame and prestige. Such expectation would mean lobha that works against the dhammadesanā kusala and belittles the benefits resulting from it. A corresponding parable is the exchange of sandalwood for buttermilk gone bad, as was observed in the story of King Kosala's dreams.

[Maxim]   Some change high-valued sandalwood
            For worthless rotten buttermilk;
            And others
            Swap precious kusala dhamma
            As taught by Lord Buddha
            For gains by way of the four paccayas[174].

A dhamma-teacher's personality

The personality of a dhamma-teacher is not commonplace. He must have the capability of expounding the word of the Buddha in a pleasant, clear voice, and of making the audience comprehend the message of the talk; he is so rare, being "one born from amongst a thousand mothers". That is the truth. It is a very rare chance to find a mother who had given birth to a really gifted dhamma-teacher, just as it is difficult for a thousand cows in a corral to deliver a king bull, tall and mighty, with a majestic hump.

---

174. Food, robes, monastery and medicine are the 4 essentials for monks

Faulting vocal music

So, the dhamma-teacher must think of one's own noble kamma of the past lives, taking great care, in uttering the Lord's dhamma, to avoid making the voice too musical, too short or too long, or in any trilling notes, but with a manly[175] voice, firm and serene. The Lord showed 5 faults in making dhamma-talks musical and pleasant. He had said,

"Bikkhus, there are five faults in stretching out vocal sounds to appear musical in the matter of dhamma-talks, namely (1) enjoyment of one's own pleasant voice, causing tanhā, (2) also causing tanhā to the audience, (3) censure by gentle folks with an accusation, "monks, calling themselves 'sons of the Buddha', sing songs just like us" [now, young people also are making the same accusation], (4) collapse of one's own samādhi during the talk for wanting to make vocal music, (5) young monks in posterity would also think, 'It is proper to give dhamma-talks in a sing-song manner', and try to imitate the musical dhamma-teacher."

[**Maxim**]   Vocal music in dhamma sermons
Is bound to arouse tanhā in speaker-self,
And the audience so addressed infected,
And the wise blame it on the speaker,
It also causes samādhi to disappear,
Inviting the young to copy the manners;
Better note these five faults
So that no one finds faults
In the delivery of the dhamma talks.

The faults as pointed out by the Lord have now been shown sufficiently Coming-up generations are now already learning and imitating strange, new manners of expounding upon the Buddha's teaching, There are too few intelligent gentle folks attending these talk shows. Those intelligent folks who come for one reason or another are actually not interested in the shows. The educated people, although wishing to hear true dhamma, think it is shameful to go to those shows. So, it is quite apparent that musical vocalization of Buddha dhamma is something to be shunned.

---

175. This is an instruction to monks. For lady teachers, the voice would have to be non-appealing to both men and women, not to arouse rāga, keeping in mind that the dhamma-talks are no art shows. (Translator)

Conversation is also a dhamma-desanā

Talking dhamma, addressed publicly in a grand manner, is not the only type of "dhamma-desanā". Talking to one or two devotees on the Buddha dhamma, not with the expectation of any material return but in a pure goodwill, is also "dhamma-desanā". Instructions given by elders to the youth on good manners and way of life, training in blameless vocations, teaching literature, reading out dhamma are all dhamma-desanā. Therefore, modernity demands that not only the public dhamma-speaking but also methods of fruitful conversation, reading and writing should be studied.

Ditthijukamma (Right Thinking)

Right thinking is "*ditthijukamma*". [Ditthi = thinking, view + ujukamma = right, truthful]. If every thing is viewed in the right way, it is *sammaditthi* (Right view). If it is in the wrong direction, it is *micchāditthi* (wrong view). Consider the following points as to what kind of wisdom one is committed to:

wholesome or unwholesome deeds;

resultant effects of those deeds;

Life hereafter, the life resulting from those deeds;

devas (gods), Brahmas (higher heavenly beings);

those in jhāna, abiññāna (absorption, psychic powers), and arahantas (the saints, the liberated) after proper, diligent efforts

If those 5 points are considered deeply and given to the view, "They are quite likely to be true, they ought to be or must be so," then the view is sammāditthi. That sammāditthi is also called "ditthijukamma" or "kammasakatānāna". [kamma = action + saka = one's own + tā = to be + ñāna = knowing: "*kammasakatā ñāna*" is the conviction that only the good and evil actions are one's own properties that accompany one in lives hereafter.]

Regarding those five points, if one holds the view, "They cannot be true and ought not to be," such view is *micchāditthi* (wrong view). Due to such view, animals are not considered to be the resultant effect of their past akusala kammas, and so one may kill them without a whit of conscience. On account of the view that "there is no such thing as kamma and its resultant effects", it is believed that there is no life after this and, that some super-powerful being create the entire animate and inanimate world. Can anybody know such "omnipotent" personality as clearly defined and observed as the way we know of the historically recorded Lord Buddha?

How to become a Buddhist

Ditthijukamma has been defined as the right view. Not every one of those who hold the right view (sammāditthi) is a Buddhist. Hindus also believe in kamma and its resultant effects; but they are not Buddhists. Truly believing in the Buddha, Dhamma and Sangha, and by reciting, *"Buddham saranam gacchāmi, dhammam saranam gacchāmi, sangham saranam gacchāmi"* in Pali, or "I take refuge in the Buddha; I take refuge in the Dhamma; I take refuge in the Sangha" in the vernacular, one becomes a Buddhist, fully established in *Saranaguna* or, more correctly, *saranagamana* (properties of the 3 refuges also known as *Ti-saranagamana*). In so worshipping, with faith in the traditional way, one is a Buddhist even though one may not really know the great values or properties of the refuges[176] (like the way children are). [The virtues and properties of the 3 refuges, their meaning and explanations have been given in "Yatana Gonyi".]

Qualifying points of ditthijukamma

Ditthijukamma, also known as sammāditthi as well as kammasakatāñāna, comes about when one is thinking of kamma and its effects, and of the present life and the next; also when, immediately prior to a deed of charity or promise of moral precepts, one is mindful of the merits to bear fruit in the next life. Also at the very moment of doing dāna and sila kusalas, with full confidence in the kamma and its effects, this ditthijukamma takes place. Done with this ditthijukamma kusala, any wholesome deed (kusala kamma) will result in nobler and better benefits than with others perfunctorily done.

40 articles of Poññakariyā

Not only do such kammas as dāna, as shown, are kusala (meritorious) by doing them in person, but such methods as getting it done by a direct agent, also inspiring others to do likewise, and taking delight in others' kusala kammas, but also these 4 actions amount to the same noble acts. So by multiplying the ten original articles of poññakariyā vatthu by these 4 types of actions, there become 40 articles of poññakariyā vatthu.

[**Maxim**]   The ten articles of wholesome deeds extended
by 4 modes of body, thought and speech:
(1)   Doing a wholesome deed in person,
(2)   Asking others to do it on one's behalf,

---

176 For these Properties, see in the Appendix

(3)   Inspiring others by talking of virtues of it, and

(4)   Being glad of it in contemplation,

thus making up 40 factors of mind purification.

Conclusion

We now come to the conclusion of the articles of poññakariyā vatthu that accompany wholesome citta and cetanā. For the noble deed of writing with certain clarity about them, may the readers of this book find inspiration to carry out the contents of these articles more firmly than ever before. May all my associates also work hard to observe these ten articles, completely happy with the vision of Nibbāna.

For myself, basing on dāna, sila and bhāvanā, every time I do wholesome deeds, may I be able to discard hesitancy and backwardness, and be fully developed in the five *balas*[177] of keen saddhā, viriya, samādhi, sati and paññā

Aiming for the benefits of others
I have written
these articles of wholesome matters,
So that they may be well and happy,
prosperous and powerful, but for me,
I wish to carry these ten articles well
To the lives over yonder;
May my associates also live
This way of life well,
Till the attainment of Nibbāna.

[This ends the ten articles of Poññakariyā Vatthu.]

---

177   (P) Articles of power: (1) physical strength, (2) intellectual prowess, (3) material wealth, (4)morality and integrity, (5) communal influence (or power of association by way of popularity)

CHAPTER SEVEN

GENERAL NOTES ON KAMMA

WHAT IS KAMMA?

Kamma in translation is any volitional action performed. There are three types of action, namely physical, oral and mental. Physical actions are those performed with parts of one's body such as feet and hands, e.g. killing the life of one other living being with one's own hands, giving out dāna in person, and so on.

Oral actions mean utterances by word of mouth, e.g. urging others to "kill that fellow, offer food to monks, etc," telling lies, giving dhamma talk, and so on. Mental actions are to do with thoughts and so exclude all physical and verbal actions, but consist only of thinking, planning and contemplation. For instance, malicious thoughts like, "How great it would be if I get hold of his possessions," feeling kind towards others, wishing the wellbeing of others, wishing to meditate, and so on are mental actions.

Finding the culprit

Those physical, oral and mental actions do not come about on their own free will. In killing life, there is a real culprit that urges one to get hold of a machete and get it on the victim. In a speech too, there is some culprit that persuades one to utter the sounds for each word. While asleep, there happen a great many bits of the mind that arise, but none that is active. This shows there must be something that is quite different from, and more powerful than, the passive mind. Just as the responsible person must be found for any problem in the ordinary sense, so also we must find the real operator that is responsible for our physical, verbal and mental actions[178].

---

178. Mental actions: the active part of thoughts founded on cetanā capable of producing physical and verbal actions

Cetanā is kamma, the one responsible for actions

The instigator of those physical, verbal and mental actions is *cetanā*, a will-predominant cetasika that arises in the consciousness continuum. Therefore, cetanā-cetasika is actually the one that pushes people to perform physical, verbal and mental activities. Just because it causes the "kamma" (actions) to be accomplished, (signifying the causal kamma as the original cetanā) this cetanā-cetasika is called the "kamma dhamma". [How cetanā leads in all the other cetasikas and how it is charged as the real doer of kammas, has been discussed in the section on cetanā-cetasika.]

The less-obvious kinds of citta

Looking at the way citta-events arise in one's own mind, some are quite distinct, while others are not. When asleep, the mind continuum goes on as usual, although it is not distinctly noted in the mind how or what mental events are taking place. While awake also, some sight, sound, smell, and touch come and go scarcely noticed. When thinking haphazardly and gazing out without paying attention, the mind does not know distinctly what is going on. Although wholesome and unwholesome thoughts occur during those non-attentive moments, because nothing is so clearly defined, no action is committed and accomplished. Thus many instances of cetanā come and go without a trace.

DISTINCT KINDS OF AKUSALA CETANĀS

When contemplating to kill a person, dosa-javana-citta-cetanā[179] is very distinct. At this moment the will to kill is very powerful. Also when a thought for sexual action appears, the lobha-javana cetanā, the urge, is so strong that exterior parts of the body are activated for movement. Thus, unwholesome properties of the akusala cetanās from inside push the physical, verbal and mental actions of evil nature to come out in the open; these akusala cetanās are very strong and powerful, unlike the normally indistinct javana citta. The nature of their arising is thus very clearly self-evident.

Distinct kinds of kusala cetanās

At the instants of doing such kusala kammas as charitable deeds (dāna), keeping Sabbath precepts, taking care of old people and parents, hearing and discussing the Teaching, meditating, avoidance of unwholesome habits and urgings, and accommodating all wholesome urgings (kusala cetanās)

179. Dosa-impulsion-led cetanā that drives the mind into action

are also just as strong and sharp. To accomplish those deeds, the will (vyābāra) must be very strong. Because of this powerful will, the physical, verbal and mental actions come about.

How properties of kamma remain in the continuum of khanda

Those self-evident kusala- and akusala-javana cetanās are called "kamma". Although those cetanā-phenomena may disappear, they do not get lost in all totality. Traces of their kamma properties are embedded in the continuum of khandha[180]. What it means is that as thoughts (minds) appear one after another, indistinct cetanās totally disappear, none being left behind; but properties of distinctly strong cetanās are left behind in the continuum of khandha. For instance, while influence of mediocre parents disappears on their death, sharp and powerful parents leave, in clear evidence, their strong influence on their children when they die.

The way kamma properties follow the continuum of khandha

All fruit-bearing trees carry with them an element of *dhātu*[181] that brings about fruiting - it is there in the sprouts and shoots; when a tree is mature with tender buds, stems, branches, leaves and fruit, the whole tree together with the fruit and its seeds carry this element. When the mature seed of the tree is put to ground and nursed, it has the capability to grow another tree and bear fruit. Though not possible to separate and identify "what exactly it is", there certainly is a kind of dhātu by virtue of which the trees bear fruit in perennial continuity. Similarly, in the continuous process of appearing and disappearing of one rupa after another, and one nāma after another, the new rupa and nāma that have arisen are imparted with the dhātu property of the ones that have already disappeared. At the moment of cuti (death), these kammic properties are there. After cuti and at the moment of conception (patisandhi) in a new life also, these kammic properties follow through. And then throughout the whole of the next life, at the moment of death in that life and in the next conception, (not showing themselves in any distinguishable form) the kammic properties that have yet to be discharged as effects continue to be dormant in the present life. [By kammic property is meant the mere qualitative property (of kamma) that has no discernable material form.]

---

180. Khandha (rupa-nāma formations) in continuum, much the same way as consciousness continuum
181. (P) An elemental matter consisting of properties of the 4 fundamental matter and their dependent properties as has been explained elsewhere in this book...

The direct effect of kamma

As discussed above, although beings change from one existence to another, they become as a result of the effects of delusion (avijjā) and craving (tanhā) and kamma in previous lives, and so the one in the present life is no one other than the one before that life. Although the cetanā-kammas (wholesome deeds) of the previous life have disappeared, the influence of those cetanā-kammas linger, and taking a hold, on one's consciousness continuum, follows and looks after one in the next life (like the shadow following a man). Also the influence of unwholesome kammas committed before always follows up to harass one (like the cart-wheels running after the yoked oxen). Some people think, "This body takes punishment in this life; the next body will take punishment in the next life." But the body in the next life belongs to one that is none other than that one turned into a new life form.

Sowing kusala kamma together, reaping benefits together

There are a great many Jātaka stories relating to couples enjoying benefits together as a result of doing wholesome kammas together. Wholesome kammas done together in the past are the source of benefits to enjoy together in the present life. These "shared kammas" include giving charity together, observing precepts together, and, if togetherness is not opportune, being agreeable and glad about a partner's such acts of benevolence (the gladness of a husband, who is away seeking the needs of the household, about his wife's charitable deed at home)[182]. In doing such shared kammas, if they were good and wise, they would listen to each other, agreeable and wanting to be always together (*sammā chanda*), considerate and fulfilling each other's aspirations (*tanhā chanda*). These mixed *chandas* are inevitable in all acts of kusala kammas. When those kusala kammas are opportune to take effect, the two people are likely to be together and enjoy the benefits together. This is called "shared kammas/shared benefits".

Benevolent people of such strong consideration for each other roam the samsarā as couples assisting in the fulfillment of each other's Perfections (Paramis), happy with each other the way the bodhisattas and their spouses had been. For one to believe this, take a look at the life stories of the Buddha and Queen Yasodayā, Ashin Mahākassapa and Mai Baddā, King Mahākappina and Queen Anojā, and more - the stories of Ashins

---

182. "Kam'-tu" in Myanmar, directly translated, would mean "kamma equally shared" or "shared kammas".

Sāriputtarā, Moggalana, Anuruddā, Rāhulā, Khemā Theri, Upalavunna Theri, Queen Gotami and King Suddhodana,

Sowing akusala kamma and harvesting miseries together

In the affairs of unwholesome deeds, if done in agreement between the two, they will share the undesirable resultant effects. Once upon a time, a boat-wracked man and wife landed on a deserted island. There was no food but small birds that they killed and ate. For that evil deed, they suffered in *niraya* (hell). In the lifetime of our Lord Buddha, they became King Utena's son, Bodhi, and his queen. For their kamma of killing and eating the small birds, they were childless. If the wife had not agreed to the killing of the small birds, she could have borne children. If the husband did not agree to the killing, he would have the right to children. But they were of the same mind in the killing and eating, now that shared evil deed entailed in childlessness. Bearing this kind of shared akusala- kamma-resultant effect in mind, one partner should forbid the other for committing evil deeds.

In the proceedings of kusala and akusala kammas,

Not agreeing to the wife as she did, the husband would not get the resultant effect;

Not agreeing to the husband as he did, the wife would not get the resultant effect.

("The Great Verse of Maghadeva")

THE POWER OF KUSALA-KAMMA-RESULTANT EFFECT

There are groups of people such as teachers and students, parents and children, and relatives. The kamma-resultant effects for one are shared equally by the rest of the group to which one belongs. During the reign of King Bhātika in Singhaladipa (Sri Lanka), those who ate beef were punished with fine. Those who could not pay up the fine were punished by having them work as cleaners in the king's palace. One amongst them was a pretty girl. The king saw her, and giving favours, he named her "Sāmā Devi" and kept her in the palace. The king also set her relatives free and helped them to get in good livelihoods. This is how relatives are benefited by the kusala kamma of one of them. [Here, it can be said, "the relatives must also have their own kusala kamma." True, but their kusala kamma had not enough influence without that of Sāmā Devi.]

Side influence of akusala kamma

Akusala-resultant effects also have side-influences like the kusala-kamma. During the lifetime of Kassapa Buddha, a wealthy man had a mentor monk who was morally upright. But he was unable to stand the way his devotee gave respects to a guest monk in his monastery. So, when he was about to leave for the dawn breakfast at the wealthy man's house, he hit the bell lightly with the tip of his finger so that the guest monk would not wake up. When the man asked the monk after the guest, he said, "Oh, your monk sleeps too heavily. I left him as he did not wake up at the sound of the bell." [The speech had the tone of jealousy.]

The tactful devotee suspected the monk's attitude. So, after the monk finished the meal, he put some food in the alms-bowl, saying, "Please offer this food to the guest monk." The monk was disagreeable. On the way back, succumbing to jealousy and for fear of the guest staying on in his monastery, he threw out the food, saying in his mind, "If he gets to eat this kind of good food, he wouldn't leave this monastery." [Here, take note of the heavy offense of throwing out food.]

The guest monk, knowing how the abbot was thinking, had left the monastery earlier by taking to the sky, toward his desired destination. When the abbot could not find the guest, he was regretful and puzzled. His mind was set afire. Withered both in mind and body, he passed away, He fell to niraya as he died.

After rising from that niraya, he was an ogre 500 times, and a dog 500 times, scarcely able to get enough food to eat most of the time. He was conceived in the womb of a fisherwoman in a village of one thousand fishermen in our Lord's time. Since that conception, the villagers caught fewer fish. And not only that, they were criminally charged and punished seven times and there occurred seven cases of fire in the village.

Then some thoughtful elderly men said, "There must be someone with bad kamma, and so let us divide the village into two halves," and divided the village in two halves. The half with the woman had the same problem. The process was repeated until the household of the pregnant woman was isolated. The mother delivered the baby in very poor circumstances. When the child was able to walk, leaving him with a bowl in hand, the mother fled. The child lived by begging and at the age of seven, Ashin Sāriputtarā found him. The Ashin robed the child made him a novice (*sāmanera*) who later became a bhikkhu with the designation of "Losakatissa". The bhikkhu worked hard at meditation and (as he had been a morally upright monk in a previous life) eventually became an arahanta.

In spite of being an arahanta, he never received and ate enough food, not even for a day. On the day he was to enter Parinibbāna (passing away), Ashin Sāriputtarā invited him and, together, they went out on their alms round. On that round, even Ashin Sāriputtarā did not get food. Only after sending the bhikkhu back and going alone by himself, the Ashin received food. The Ashin, after eating the meal at a devotee's house, sent some people with a bowl of food to the bhikkhu. The men on the way somehow forgot their purpose, sat down, and ate the food meant for the Bhikkhu. When Ashin Sāriputtarā came back to learn that the bhikkhu did not get the food, he asked King Koala to donate some *catumadhu*[183], which he received and holding the bowl (fearing loss of the bowl if he let it go), fed the monk from the bowl; the monk passed away after eating the food to his satisfaction.

Remark: In this story, it can be seen very clearly how kamma-resultant effect recurred for the evil deed done by a man at the time of the Kassapa Buddha, on not only the man himself but also the whole village associated with him, and how, as a side-swipe, Ashin Sāriputtarā in association with him (Bhikkhu Losakatissa) could not get food on his alms round. It is evident as to how a man's mischief could result in the misfortunes of others who were associated, but nothing to do, with the mischief. Therefore, those who hope to see the samsarā as a clean line should keep as far away as possible from bad characters, regardless of them being relatives, and even if not totally inalienable, so that good, virtuous people could be free of those corrupt characters in all their lives to come.

How the kamma-resultant blow strikes

Resultant effects of some akusala kammas do not fall on the evil doer directly, but they fall on close associates like parents, teachers. his children, servants and pupil-devotees, if the mischief-doer is so careful as to protect himself well so as not to have the blow fall on him. Such side-swipes of punishment are known as "getting punished for someone else". The akusala-doer is also regretful and miserable. In a way, the culprit also gets some punishment.

"Standing on a base of some past good kamma, the evil-doer frees himself from the present danger, but his companions, even his beasts of burden, may be ruined on account of his mischief."

["The Great Verse of Maghadeva"]

---

183. A medicinal food made from four ingredients, namely honey, molasses, butter and sesame oil.

Partiality in kamma-results

In this world, there are two kinds of people: one is the good kind, spiritually very pure, and the other, a bad lot, naturally very corrupt. When the two of them each committed an ordinary kind of akusala kamma, the miserable effects of that evil kamma, even if minor, may fall on the bad character heavily as he has no dependable good kamma for defense; as the good character has a great many kussala kammas as his safe guard, the evil kamma done once finds no opportunity to cause him any harm. For example, a son of a wealthy man on one particular night stole a chicken from a house. An opium-eater also stole another chicken. The fowl-run owner not only dared not accuse the wealthy man's son of theft, but he had to plead with him for the return of the chicken; with the opium-eater, however, he opened a police case for criminal atonement.

Another example: just as a viss (1.5 kilos) of salt thrown into the Irrawaddy River would not corrupt its water, so also a minor akusala kamma would not affect the person who has a lot of kusala kammas. If that much of salt is added into a pot of water, the whole content of water would go salty. Likewise, the power of minor kusala kammas would be destroyed by some minor akusala kamma.

Thus, in cases of kāmāvacara[184] kusala and akusala kamma, just as "the more fortunate are usually the more favoured", so also minor offenses of akusala kammas cannot disturb the more powerful kusala kammas, although those minor akusala kammas can add to other minor offenses of the same kind. This suggests that, as minor akusalas can disturb minor kusala kammas, good people who have already some klusala kammas should build up a storehouse of many more kusala kammas.

SAMPATTI, VIPATTI

"Sampatti" is the state of being complete with desirable factors in close association. Deviation from this state of affairs is called *"vipatti"*. A great deal of kammas have been committed in uncountable past lives, accumulated in the consciousness continuum of all beings. For as long as these kammas find no opportunity of taking effects on the respective beings, they stay dormant in the khandha-continuum[185]; when sampatti is in effect, resultant effects (benefits) of kusala kammas would be released, whereas when vipatti is in effect, the <u>akusala kammas</u> will take their toll.

184. That belonging to the lower worlds, the humans and the devas (excluding the Brahma realms)
185. Same as consciousness continuum also explained in Paticcasamuppada Sutta.

4 categories of sampatti[186]

1. *Gati sampatti*	Fortunate present existence
2. *Upadhi sampatti*	Good personality
3. *Kāla sampatti*	Fortunate times
4. *Payoga sampatti*	Wisdom, diligence, etc.

4 categories of vipatti[187]

1. *Gati vipatti*	Miserable present life
2. *Upadhi vipatti*	Poor personality
3. *Kāla vipatti*	Unfortunate times
4. *Payoga vipatti*	Absence or deficiency of wisdom, diligence, etc.

Gati sampatti

Human, deva and Brahma realms are called "*gati sampatti*". Living in gati sampatti, many kusala kammas find opportunity to take effect. Although there is dukkha in the human realm, there is almost none of that in the deva and Brahma realms. As kusala kammas are opportune to be effective, there is goodness and wellbeing in all necessities of life such as food, way of living, experience and sense faculties. Beings enjoying the gati sampatti may have akusala kammas, but these kammas find no opportunity to be effectual. Although it can be said that human beings are "not without dukkha", they suffer less compared with those in the 4 lower worlds (apāyas). Because, there are better chances for kusala kammas to take appropriate effects, detestable ārammanas can be avoided and desirable ārammanas more often enjoyed.

Gati Vipatti

The four lowly worlds (apāyas) are called "*gati vipatti*". Living in that gati vipatti, many akusala kammas are opportune to take effect. Those in the nariya (infernal world) and peta (ghostly beings), needless to say, suffer from most severe miseries, torture and scorching heat to no apparent end. The animals suffer relatively less: they may suffer from famine, drought, severe heat, cold, storms and quakes, and dangers from man and other more powerful animals, according as past akusala kammas take effect. Greater effects of akusala kammas befall on small animals and insects as they can be easily killed by crushing hoofs and soles of other bigger animals and human beings. When gati vipatti takes its toll, past kusala kammas have no chance of saving them.

---

186. Fortunate situation, circumstances complete with blessedness
187. deficiency, impairment, misfortune

Upadhi Sampatti

Gati sampatti may be well in order, but it is important to have decent looks (especially for human beings). With *upadhi sampatti*, even if born in a poor family, a person would have opportunities to get on well in the world, respected and well thought of by well-to-do and decent people, wholesome kamma-resultant opportunities being heaped on him. The way kusala kammas of one person can result in benefits of associated people has been shown by the fondness the king had for Sāmādevi for her upadhi sampatti. Was it not for the upadhi sampatti of Mrs. Simpson that King Edward fell in love with her?

This does not apply to the human beings alone. Even animals (gati vipatti), if they possess good looks (upadhi sampatti) - cute and handsome dogs, cows and horses - are fed and bred well by well-to-do people, enjoying the best favours as a result of some past wholesome kammas. Evidently, good looks and comeliness, the properties of upadhi sampatti, are essential qualities in life for prosperity and personal wellbeing.

Upadhi vipatti

It is not remarkable that the animals (gati vipatti) with ugly looks (*upadhi vipatti*) have no chance of past kusala kammas to benefit them. Look at the human beings. Human beings are in gati sampatti: upadhi vipatti can affect them by barring the benefits of past kusala kammas from taking effect, at least not as well as they should without upadhi vipatti; even if in the same social stratum, general acceptance as agreeable persons is hard to come by. The reason why (very beautiful) Princess Pabāvati was disagreeable to the love of the bodhisatta, (very ugly) Prince Kusa, was quite plain. When upadhi vipatti was in effect, past akusala kammas befall on the Bodhisatta, and so he had to work at pottery, mat-weaving and cooking for the princess just to be near and win her love. If man and wife are not equal in looks, the one in upadhi vipatti is often thought of as a servant. Evidently, ugly looks and poor appearance, the properties of upadhi vipatti, are qualities of life badly befitting a person for personal wellbeing and prosperity.

Kāla sampatti

When time is such that human society is blessed with morally correct, decent kings and rulers, such a time period is called "*kāla sampatti*". Kings or leaders of a society who administer the people in such a way as to enjoy general wellbeing, prosperity, proper education and good healthcare are cause for opportunities of kusala kammas to take effect. Because of those opportunities, people are blessed with pleasures of the noble kind. Free from anxieties, whole families and clans, whole villages and communities enjoy general wellbeing.

The upswing period of a *kappa* (a world cycle)[188] is also kāla sampatti. When such a period is in progress, such akusala kammas as to effect dire poverty and starvation have little chance to prevail.

Kāla vipatti

Times in which corrupt kings and leaders rule the world are called "*kāla vipatti*". When a country is in chaos and ruin and over-run by a war, it is said to be in kāla vipatti. Then past akusala kammas are opportune to take effect. A great many people are hungry, being struck with extreme poverty. Even those with a lot of past kusala kammas are hit hard as those kammas can find no opportunity to take effect, and effects of whatever akusala kamma one has ever committed would prevail: people must run away and hide from dangers, and eat less than sufficient; families are separated; because there is no appropriate medicine and proper treatment, and no doctors, untimely deaths are common.

Payoga sampatti

Sati (mindfulness), viriya (energy and diligence) and ñāna (faculty of intelligence) are called "*payoga sampatti*". Ñāna here means not only the blameless paññā (wisdom), but also evil-related artfulness as well as good thoughts related to vitakka (thought-conceptions). So, mindfulness, hard work and diligence, competence, cleverness, perceptiveness, non-forgetfulness in everything one is engaged in are all payoga sampatti. Payoga sampatti is not in evidence in the realms of devas and Brahmas, but its advantages are obvious in the world of man. There few people are advantaged by resultant effects of very heavy akusala kammas: some of these effects may take place depending on whether payoga sampatti is present or not. When payoga sampatti is there, these evil effects are prevalent only subject to the strength of the payoga sampatti.

In brief, people should not leave their chances for benefits to the past kammas, but rather work to take advantage of payoga sampatti that can be activated in this present life. Payoga sampatti channels the past kammas to the point of one's practical advantage. So, with the exception of winning a lottery or finding buried pot of gold, in the case of commercial profit, about 25 % is due to past kammas whereas 75% is due to presence of mind, working hard with diligence and know-how (sati, viriya and ñāna).

---

188. Kappa will be explained later.

How payoga sampatti bars akusala kammas

Akusala kammas can be divided into two types: very heavy and not so heavy. Man cannot be freed from heavy akusala kammas regardless of payoga sampatti.

But then, it can lessen the evil effects. King Ajātasatta committed a very heavy offence of killing his father. For that guilt, he was destined for aviji niraya (the deepest of hells). However good his payoga sampatti might be, he cannot be free from that destiny. But since the father's demise, he was genuinely remorseful and took refuge in and devoted his life to the Buddha; for that payoga sampatti, he fell into ussada niraya, a neighbourly realm of aviji niraya, suffering miseries on a reduced scale. One may note now that very heavy penalties for huge akusala kammas can be rendered lighter.

Lesser kinds of akusala kammas can be barred from taking effect. Take for instance swearing at parents, talking ill of teachers, abusing elders, dispraising persons of higher moral character and social stature; these are the lesser akusala kammas. But if, realizing one's wrongful acts, and fearing the adverse consequences, one offers apologies by word of mouth to the person done wrong either in person, or at the graveyard (in case the person is dead), or, if one can do neither, from a distance, (for that reason of genuine apology) the akusala kammas cannot take effects.

Similarly, strong kusala kammas can eliminate the effects of weaker akkusala kammas. (Notice the examples of favouritism in kammic effects in the cases of stealing chicken and salt.) If monks make amends for breach of discipline as per the Buddha's Rules of the Vinaya, the evil effects of some of the offences can be done away with. Thus somewhat heavy akusala kammas can be eliminated from taking effects by means of payoga sampatti.

Economic status and payoga sampatti

There is no doubt that the so-called "micchāditthi people"[189] have kusala kammas done in their past existences. Their mindfulness, hard work and skills are praise-worthy. Not only do they take care of personal health, but also they attend to the business of preparation to meet any eventuality in case of a conflict with, and an attack from, other nations with forethoughts, hard work and diligence. No Buddhists can say that those works (although the so-called Buddhists consider them to be akusala

---

189. People of other faiths (different from the Four Noble Truths and the Middle Way to attain Nibbāna0

kamma, worthy of disdain) are not good for the progress of loka (mankind) and the growth of mangalā (blessedness of human life).

Foreigners who come to this country in search of riches have great presence of mind. Their hard work and diligence are beyond reproach. Their skills and know-how are exemplary. Their choice of place for commercial gain (*patirupa desa*) tells of their knowledge. As that much of payoga sampatti, certainly, is a boost to the effects of their past kusala kammas that are dormant in their consciousness continuum, they are now blessed with success, prosperity and a blissful life (full of mangalā). Many of the so-called Buddhist Mons and Myanmars who are quick, hardworking and knowledgeable, with foresight and payoga sampatti are also prosperous.

Good health by way of payoga sampatti

People have in their consciousness continuum some kusala kammas for good and some akusalas for ill health. In moving from place to place, eating habits and living styles and so on, people should avoid what is improper or unsuitable; one must sleep, eat, wash, walk regularly, with no waste of time but with zest and keenness, knowing what food to eat in what climate, what time to bathe, what medicine to take, and so on. A daily minimum of six-hour sleep is essential. One must know how to pursue health studies. Such knowledge and practices are correct methods of payoga sampatti for good health. Past Kusala kammas in respect of good health for people in this payoga sampatti now find easy opportunity to take effect.

Because payoga sampatti is the prime enhancement factor for kusala kammas to take effect, a person in payoga sampatti can learn well and be wise; be married to a good spouse; meet many good friends, teachers and mentors; have a growing wealth, rising official and social positions; fulfill basic perfections (paramis) in the present life so as to be noble and virtuous in the next lives to come till Nibbāna is attained. Knowledge and wisdom in every aspect of life is of paramount importance in the affairs of payoga sampatti. And then it is equally important to be mindful. And then diligence is the watch word for every business of life that comes up.

Payoga vipatti

Want of intelligence, dullness, forgetfulness, laziness and sluggishness are all *payoga vipatti*. Besides, too much envy and avarice, impatience and anger in every possible way, and conceit are cause for troubles in business and personal development; they are also identified as payoga vipatti. After heavy burdens of akusala kamma in the consciousness continuum of a person have been discharged as effects, there remain lighter kinds of akusala kamma that would take effect if payoga vipatti is prevalent.

For example, young people of good descent would have proper education and proper livelihoods for fair pursuit of wealth in their adult lives, and keep the 5 precepts, all in the light of blameless living. For them, their akusala kammas cannot prevail, regardless. Some people pursue no studies for proper education while in youth, seek wealth unfairly or else none at all, and occasionally break the five rules of moral conduct; for them, payoga vipatti prevails and the akusala kammas will find their opportunity to take effect one day.

In short, with the exception of great kusala and heavy akusala kammas, whether a great many smaller kusala and akusala kammas will find opportunity to strike depends on the predominance of one type of payoga or the other. With an ever-present payoga sampatti, kusala kammas will prevail, not the akusala kammas. With the predominance of payoga vipatti, (even if enjoying benefits of kusala kamma for a while like "the mad dog lives only till noon") a bad fall would come one day for past akusala kammas. - people ruined in this way can be found in one's neighbourhood, just like in some fairy tales.

Amenability of present situation

Some vipatti situations may be amenable while others are not. The gati existence that is already extant cannot be undone. But that situation of having been born in a very poor village or province or country can be changed by moving away to a *patirupa* (a place suited for one's basic necessities) to start a new life blessed with favourable health, education and business environments. Foreigners coming to Myanmar to seek wealth, ancient up-country men going down to lower Myanmar for business, and young people going to good schools for better education are change of environment to correct the prevailing vipatti situations. But then again, such situational change should suit the character qualities of the individuals. For a well qualified person, it is "No change of village, no change of fortune". For a person of low capabilities, it is "Moving away to another village makes a man smell slave" or "Better stay put or else find you lame".

Personal looks or upadhi cannot be changed much. But as it is said about looking good, "A basket for its edging; a man for his dress ", a person, poor in original looks, dressed decently would present himself well enough. Notice the difference in appearance between provincial and city folks. New-born babies' feet, legs, hands and other parts of body can be straightened out and made well-proportioned. Because mothers do not care for correction, babies who sleep on one side only have their heads misshaped. New-born babies with bent backs can be treated with flat boards placed under their backs, but that is not taken care of. Even some parents are so foolish as to pull up their children to stand on their feet and force the little ones to walk, cheering, "Baby can stand, baby can stand," before it can naturally do so; this thoughtless behaviour results in ugly bow legs,

By habitually lifting a child by the armpits, the child's chest and shoulders are made to grow small and narrow. The habitual holding and lifting of a baby lying flat on its back by its waist can cause a back-ward bent of the child's body above the buttocks. If tender hands, feet and nose of a child look ugly, they can be straightened out by gentle and careful pressing and shaping with adult hands regularly. Failure to feed the child with proper milk and other foods results in prevalence of early diseases and impairment to the looks. These are the results of parents' lack of knowledge on payoga sampatti, enhancing the chance of the past akusala kamma of the child to take effect in this present life - parents should (with proper knowledge, wisdom and hard work) perform corrective actions of payoga sampatti.

For kāla sampatti to prevail it is primarily up to "leaders and rulers"; oneself alone cannot do much about it. But when the situation is so bad as to have ruined the whole country or a region, one can move away to a place where good leaders and kings rule. Neighbourhood elders, educators and monks can do something to create payoga sampatti locally. Judging from the foregoing, it can be seen that, if total amenability of gati, upadhi and kāla is impossible, correction to some measure and value can be achieved by way of knowledge.

It is easy to make amends on payoga. A forgetful person can become a good present-minded one if the person, with a strong will, tries to be mindful at all times. If lazy by nature, by saying, "I am not lazy," and correcting oneself, one can become industrious. If anger is a habit, by closely watching oneself and making deliberate efforts not to be angry, one can become a really peaceable person. If proud, pride can be similarly rendered to naught. If ignorant, one can listen to and learn from knowledgeable people, and find immediate improvement. Skill and knowledge can be learned, not necessarily by way of rote-learning but by hard work, regardless of people saying they cannot remember anything, thinking they are dull and forgetful, and so learning by heart is no way). The one in this habit of acquiring skill and knowledge is clever and wise; this cleverness and wisdom will be brought forward in one's consciousness continuum throughout the samsāra.

The idea of Kamma should not be the Decisive Factor in all Matters, wholesome or unwholesome

Buddhism, Hinduism, Christianity and Mohammedanism are the four great religions of the world. In Christianity and Mohammedanism, the fates of all creatures, whether good or evil, are decided by the Omnipresent God; the believers cling to the idea of God, the Creator. Buddhists and Hindus cling to the work of kamma (volitional actions) done in the past that "manages the good or evil effects in the present life, which are consequences of those actions." As readers of this book could now have guessed the idea of the Creator as a wrong view, there is no need to pursue the matter any further. Clinging to kamma-resultant effects may not be free of such kind of wrong view as *"pubbekata hetuditthi"* that means, "All the present day beings in sight are subject to various kinds of good or evil effects that are only the result of kammas done in the past existences."

Considering macchāditthi, the Buddhists who literally take "it is the work of kamma that we face now, no matter whether that is good or evil" are not free of that pubbekata hetuditthi. Therefore, considering overwhelming influence of the 4 sampatti factors and the 4 vipatti, one must admit that there remain some un-effected kusala and akusala kammas in our consciousness continuum, but the akusala kammas would prevail if various kinds of vipatti are in effect. The kusala kammas, on the other hand, would prevail when various kinds of sampatti are in effect.

There is more to say. Although it is time for akusala kamma to take effect (during the time of misfortune), those in payoga sampatti guard themselves with sati (mindfulness), viriya (energy) and ñāna (wisdom), keeping the past akusala kammas at bay. If they work in this life for perfections in a (in sila, samādhi and paññā, they would certainly be destined to the noble sugati realms in their next lives, never falling in the lowly worlds of apāya. If such gati sampatti is in effect in all the next lives, then the akusala kammas will never get a chance to take their toll till attainment of Nibbāna. Therefore, without thinking of fear for past kammas that one can never really look back and see, one must work hard to improve one's qualities of life such as business and livelihood, now in this life, as well as in the samsāra. For this reason, people are urged to make earnest, purposeful efforts to be in payoga sampatti.

Repayment of debt owed

Either kusala kammas or akusala kammas may be repaid in the same kind equal to the kammic actions performed. One who kills another is prone to being killed in the same way, or to suffer from various diseases, in every future life for the pānātipāta (killing) kamma one had once performed. This has been discussed plainly in "Ratana Gonyi, on the Five Precepts, kamma and its resultant effects."

Merits in accordance with the kind of dāna (charity) given

When giving donations, the cetanā (volitional will) for the recipients to be able to eat and keep well is dāna. For that willful act of dāna the donor, in whichever realm he/she would be, gets the benefit of wellbeing and wealth. But if the donor, when doing the dāna action, is deficient in goodwill for others (if miserly and regretful after the donation) he/she would not feel like enjoying the wellbeing and wealth due to his/her past dāna, and live like the poor lot, lowly and lackluster.

The story of a man of wealth

Before the time of our Lord Buddha and outside of Buddha Sāsanā, a man of wealth, seeing a pacceka-buddha standing for alms at the gate of his house, called out to his servants to give food. He then went away from the place for some business. As he went, he thought, "Oh, it was a mistake to have the food offered to the monk. It would have been better if I had let the servants eat it," feeling regretful about a meritorious deed after having done it, thus showing a lack of good will (apara cetanā).

The resultant effect

For the good deed of offering food to the pacceka-buddha, he became a man of wealth in our Buddha's time. But for the lack of apara-cetanā, he did not feel like living as a man of wealth. He wore clothes, sewed into one from three pieces. made of rough grass fibres, ate boiled broken rice with dishes of sour bean-paste. Having lived a life of extreme poverty, when he died, all his possessions were seized as the king's property.

Comment: This story should be considered seriously. We now find people who do not clothe themselves, eat or live as may befit their worth. If they were the kind who live according to dhamma and give away clothes and food for charity, they cannot be blamed as it is a virtuous way of living.

147

Unlike that, if they are the miserly type, they can be thought as persons suffering from *vatta* (a resultant effect of a past kamma), like the man of wealth, told above.

The best way

Concluding from the above, only if one eats and clothes oneself well, leaves some inheritance for one's own children, and does some charitable deeds worthy of oneself, one can be said to be endowed with benefits in this life as well as in lives throughout the samsāra. So, Depeyin Sayadaw Payagyi had urged his devotees, "Eat well. Leave some for children. Plant the kusala tree of plenty for lives in the samsāra," and composed a verse:

"Whatever eaten is for excrement; leave something before you die. Whatever kusala kamma done is a tree for samsāra. In this good life, eat well, leave well and do merits; that is living in the best spirit."

Merits in accordance with moral conduct

The Sabbath and the five precepts allow wellbeing for all beings, also allowing oneself peace, freedom from anxiety and unhappiness. So when sila brings about fruiting of kusala kammas (though not necessarily of material benefits), one is free from injuries and diseases, healthy and happy with an easy manner of living. So it is often said, "One's wellbeing is accounted for by charity; healthy body and happy mind by proper moral conduct."[190]

Benefits in accordance with meditation

Desiring to meditate, one takes to a forest retreat, away from any human habit, living alone in peace and quiet, absorbed in meditation. For the purpose of jhāna, one must see all the faults of worldly pleasures and delights. For the purpose of magga/phala ñāna, one must see in personal experience the tiresomeness of rupa, nāma, khandha and the whole of samsāra.

"Like the Great Mātanga taking shelter of the forest, I went alone in retreat, completely satisfied and happy, with no body in company". [The Verse of Maghadeva]

When one reaches the realm of Brahmas, one does not seek a partner in life but lives alone in peace, meditating in a mansion in great dignity and quiet composure, with mettā, karunā and muditā for all beings. In the case of those who have attained magga/phala ñāna, as there is natural antipathy of all that is to do with rupa and nāma, there remains none of those rupa

---

190. "*Dānato bhogavā, silato sukhito*" in Pali

and nāma entities, no bhumi or great mansions to live in, but a kind of dhātu-element that has no connection with rupa-nāma and khandha.

Thus as all dāna, sila and bhāvanā bring about consummate benefits, one should make efforts to discard unwholesome thoughts, keeping only wholesome ones, envisioning the future prospects, accordingly taking care of oneself, until the attainment of Nibbāna.

"Keeping in mind the kammasakā[191] of kusala and akusala, that one, being not lazy is one who loves oneself;

> Keeping in the Right View with no laxity, that one with a capital in good kamma and diligence, supported by wisdom, will be man amongst men, above all mediocrity, like a banner in the sky, the noblest and the matchless, the best of all powers that be."
> [The Verse of Maghadeva]

Conclusion

Thus ends the chapter on kamma and its properties, the way kamma entails in resultant effects. For this kusala kamma of mine, this effort of writing about kamma and all noteworthy facts connected with it, may every reader of this book be endowed with a mature sense of kamma sakatā ñāna (belief in kamma and its consequences), and be a Buddhist with true sammāditthi (right view). May I and all my close associates be sammāditthis (believers of the Right View), and exert great efforts for the attainment of Nibbāna.

For this effort of writing on kamma and all the factors connected with it, may all the readers of this book be true sammā-believers endowed with mature kamma sakatā ñāna; may my inner-circle companions be staunch sammāditthis, like me, and be able to reach Nibbāna.

[This ends all noteworthy facts in connection with kamma.]

---

191. The resultant effects

CHAPTER EIGHT
[This chapter deals with near-death situations]

Mental attitudes that should be adopted and the kinds of deeds that should be performed in life have been discussed in previous chapters. Preoccupied thus with various attitudes of the mind, people are facing the inevitable death that would pull them away from their loved ones and material possessions. It will be shown in this chapter how important the near-death situation is for each and every individual.

4 CAUSES OF DEATH (CUTI)

There are 4 causes of death (*cuti*), namely
1. end of normal life-span,
2. end of kammic support,
3. end of life-span and kammic support,
4. attack by *upacchedaka kamma*[192]. Parables: The flame of an oil lamp dies due to (
    1. exhaustion of fuel oil,
    2. wick being burnt out, (3) exhaustion of oil and burning-out of wick simultaneously, (4) strong wind or blowing out on purpose, with some oil and wick still remaining.

1. CUTI DUE TO NORMAL ENDING OF LIFE SPAN

There is a normal life-span (life expectancy) for each and every bhumi (realm of existence). In human existence, on the up-swing of kappa, the span gradually increases to a maximum of *asancheya*[193], before the down-swing, going down to as short as 10 years. In our Lord's time, it was quoted to be a hundred years. Now, it is guessed to be 75[194]. People of average kusala-akusala kamma cannot normally live beyond that limit. Some very

192. Certain extremely serious akusala kamma that tends to bring about violent death
193. Uncountable number of years
194. This book was written a few years after WW II in Burma when general life expectancy was low (unlike the present-day normal life expectancy of 75/100 years).

fortunate people and those with "rasāyana" super-medicine can live beyond the normal life span.

In our Lord's time, Ashin Mahā Kassapa, Ashin Ānandā and the monastery-donor, Lady Visākhā had lived for 120 years. Ashin Bākula lived 160 years. Their fortunes were extraordinary. Death after living to the full 75 years in the designated life-span of 75 years is called "death at end of normal span". It is like death of the flame due to exhaustion of oil in a lamp, with a length of wick still remaining.

2. CUTI DUE TO EXHAUSTION OF KAMMA-SUPPORT

The kamma that fore-plans a life span continually creates conditions of life from the time of conception (*patisandhī*) so that there is no cessation of the life processes (not to cause death) for as long as its properties are extant. There are other kammas in addition to and in support of the original kamma. When that original kamma and the additional ones have their properties end in exhaustion, cuti would certainly come even though the normal life span has not come to its end. In the 75-year life expectancy, if the kammic capacity can carry life to only 50 years, then cuti would certainly come at 50. It is like the flame extinguished due to burning out of wick with oil still remaining in the lamp. This kind of cuti is called "cuti due to expiry of kamma".

3. CUTI DUE TO BOTH CAUSES

For some beings cuti comes as kammic support and life expectancy are both exhausted, like the flame of a lamp extinguished at the exhaustion of both wick and oil in the lamp. So, the kind of death of a person who has lived with a kammic life capacity of 75 and actually lived fully for 75 years is said to be "cuti on account of exhaustion of the life-expectancy and the kammic support." Alternatively, the kind of cuti due to any one of these 3 causes is said to be "*kāla marana* = death on due time ".

4. CUTI DUE TO DESTRUCTIVE (*UPPACCHEDAKA*) KAMMA

For some beings, the normal life-span is still valid, and there still remains that kammic support that looks after such a full stretch of life;

but certain gruesome mischief committed in any one of the past existences, or some time ago in this life, finds its chance to take effect on the culprit, causing a sudden, unexpected death. It is like the flame of a lamp being blown out by a strong wind that appears suddenly, although there still remain some fuel oil and wick in the lamp. Such sudden, often violent, death is called "death due to *upaccedaka kamma*".

Deaths on account of upacchedaka kamma

Ashin Mahāmoggalāna had, in one of his past lives, killed his own mother. In the present life, that kamma found opportunity to strike back, and he was killed by five hundred robbers[195]. King Bimbisāra had walked with his footwear on in the forecourt of a pagoda; in the present life, that kamma found its chance to take its resultant effect: he was killed from injuries on the soles of his feet being incised with a sharp knife[196]. Sāmāvati[197] and her palace companions had, in one of their past lives, set fire to a paccekabuddha (a holy man) in absorption, thinking he was dead. But then, when the holy man stood up at the end of the absorption, they, knowing him now to be alive, tried to set him on fire again so as to cover up their crime. The kamma now bounced back at them, and they met their end by being burnt to death.

There are stories that tell of people being killed in the present life for insulting and injuring holy persons. The Māraputta deva by the name of Dussi, during the time of the Kassapa Buddha threw a stone at the head of the Left-hand Chief Disciple, Aggasāvaka. One deva-rakkhasa[198] by the name of Nanda hit the shaven head of Ashin Sāriputtarā with his knuckles. King Kalabu bullied and tortured a Bodhisatta, a hermit who practised *khanti vāda,* the view and practice of patience and forbearance, to death. For those awful deeds these deva-rakkhasa and king were swallowed by earth in their present lives. Those people who had committed such actions as insulting and injuring parents, teachers and holy personalities are bound to be hit back and killed in violence before reaching the limits of their

---

195. It was a violent death; his whole body was broken up and crushed before presenting himself (by virtue of his psychic powers) to the Buddha in whose presence he took Parinibbāna.
196. Ajātassatta had his father's soles incised so that the father could not stand up and walk. It was during the Lord's life time. The father was King Bimbisāra. Ajātassatta was the first in the chain of sons who killed their own fathers.
197. Sāmavāti and her companions were devotees of Lord Buddha Gotama.
198. A race of Catumaharaja (earth-bound) devas with ugly looks and ferocious nature, mostly man-eating

life-term and kamma-support. This kind of death due to such upaccedaka kamma is called "*akāla marana* = untimely death".

Untimely deaths

In the *santāna* (consciousness continuum) of each and every being, there reside a great many minor akusala kammas. These little kammas by themselves are not capable of killing the being (carrier of the kamma); but where the being is forgetful and dull (lacking capacities of intelligent thinking and foresight), knowing very little of correct ways of eating, moving and living, they can cause harms (to themselves) that may result in death. The character who had once in a previous life purposely subjected someone to starvation, a snake-bite, poisoning, beating with a staff or cutting down with a machete, drowning in water, or burning in fire, and so on, to death can be hit back and killed in the present lifetime in the same manner as he had done to others.

The one who had, in one way or another, tortured and killed someone is likely to have to live, languid and tired, with gastric ulcers, hawking-ups, asthma, leprosy, and general debility and so on till the time of death from any one of these diseases. These past kammas, although they cannot inflict any injury or cause death to those who are intelligent and careful, do not hesitate to take their toll on the ignorant people with these diseases causing death eventually. Hence the ancient sayings, "Wisdom guards one's life"; "A wrong step now, and death the next moment"; "A mouthful of wrong food now, and death the next moment"; "Don't leave your life to fate where tigers roam"{ (attack by a tiger while walking alone on a jungle path is nothing to do with fate or kamma); "Don't walk into a bon fire, leaving it to fate" (any available wholesome kammas will not help).

What are meant by the elders' sayings is that every one of us had in us some akusala kammas, committed in many past lives, which would hit back in cyclic effects at some points in the samsāric journey. But they, if minor, would fade away. They only find opportunity to strike at ignorant people who do not take care of themselves in their manners of movement, in their eating habits and in other affairs of life. The sayings, therefore, are serious reminders for posterity that if health and related full-lifespan living are not taken care of, the little upacchedaka kammas would certainly come from close quarters to strike at any time, before the full-lifespan and kammic support for that span are all exhausted.

In summary, beings die by one of the 4 ways, namely completion of a full life-span, ending of kammic support, the two of them combined together, and upacchedaka kamma. When, from amongst them, upacchedaka kamma gets the upper hand, as opportune by thoughtless and careless modes of living, eating and traveling, untimely deaths come, and they are too frequent nowadays. So, in order to live full-term lives, the sayings urge people to be careful and wise to safeguard their own fruitful living.

The importance of near-death moment

As death is drawing near, (say) during half an hour before the moment of death, it is important to have wholesome thoughts. If those thoughts stay with the person at the moment of death, it is certain to be a good destination (*sugati*). If unwholesome thoughts are there at the moment of death, it is certain to be a lowly destination (*dukkati* or *apāya bhumi*). Thus, just as approaching the final line is most important in horse-racing, so also it is with getting into a decent form of life hereafter as one passes the line of death. That depends on the kind of ārammana (object) that stays in the mind at that moment.

The three types of ārammana that may appear near death

As death approaches, kamma, kamma nimitta[199] and gati nimitta[200] ārammanas may appear in the mind of the dying person. Kamma is wholesome and unwholesome volitions (kusala and akusala cetanās). By "kamma nimitta[201]" is meant object signs of the kinds and forms of materials used in performing past actions. By "gati nimitta" is meant the kinds and forms of materials to be found in life hereafter (*gati bhava*).

Kamma ārammana

A person would have done various kammas many existences and many worlds before, or many days and months ago, or an hour, half an hour, or may be a few seconds before the up-coming death. Those kammas appear as ārammanas in the mind of the dying person as if seeing in advance the person's conception in the up-coming life. If they are wholesome kammas such as dāna, sila, etc., it is that either those kammas are now remembered, or seen as if the person is doing dāna, or keeping Sabbath now, much like in a dream. If they were unwholesome kammas such as killing, it is the bounce-back in memory of the kammas done, or seeing them in a dream, appearing to be doing the killing now at this very moment. Similar reckoning can be extended to cases of other kusala and akusala kammas.

---

199. signs related to past kamma
200. Signs related to gati or the up-coming life after death
201. Nimitta is sign, object, image or object observed.

Kamma nimitta

Amongst those having done unwholesome deeds, if it was killing (*pānātipāta*), the weapons used in the act of the killing such as knives, staves, guns, nets, bows and arrows, spears and so on may appear in the ārammana of the dying person. A slaughter man once had the ārammana of a huge pile of bones left after killing cattle and stripping the meat from them. One may extend the idea to those who committed theft and sexual misconduct.

From amongst those who have done wholesome deeds, those having donated monasteries may see, in their ārammana, monk's robes, alms food and medicine, or anything connected with the monasteries; donors of pagodas may see flowers, lights, joss sticks, or anything in connection with pagodas and other shrines. Those, having done Sabbath routines and meditation, may see, in their ārammanas, objects such as a string of beads (rosary), clean clothes, meditation retreat centres, shady trees and so on, all in connection with Sabbath affairs. They may also see images people of giving respects and homage to elders, monks, etc. (*apacayana*) and carrying out chores at dāna functions (*veyāvecca*).

Gati nimitta

As death is drawing close, objects to be found in the up-coming new life may appear in the mind. If one is going to the realm of devas, for instance, female devas, heavenly mansions, gardens and so on may appear. If one is going to be born again as a human being, the red fluid of mother's womb may appear in the āyun. If one is destined for Niraya, huge fires, Niraya guards, big dogs, etc., come into the ārammana. If one is going to be a peta (ghosts, demons, etc.), deep forests, mountains, rivers, oceans and so on may appear in the ārammana moments before death comes, depending on the kind of country one will be dwelling in.

Guessing destination from facial signs

Notice the look on the face of the person at the death's door. If the look is clear and unconfused, it shows good ārammana and so a sugati can be expected. If the look is tired or violent and harsh, then evil ārammana is evident and duggati (evil destination) is apparent. [Others may be smiling, thinking of sensual pleasures experienced in the past. That smile is not of a good kind.]

Absent-minded talk

Some people, while nearly dead, are not quiet and gentle but talk or make movements absent-mindedly. Once upon a time, the father of Ashin Sona, an arahanta, was a game hunter when young but became a monk when much older. When he was about to die (some minutes away from death), seeing in his ārammana big dogs threatening to get at him, he yelled, "Son, get them away, please get them away."

Ashin Sona thought, "the monk is seeing Niraya nimitta." So, immediately, he looked for some flowers, spread them in the forecourt of a pagoda, moved his father together with the bedstead there. When he said, "Upazingyi[202], revere well, revere well. We have offered flowers to the Lord on your benefit," the older monk came to and began to think of the Buddha, himself offering flowers in thought. Then again he passed out and, seemingly seeing female devas enter the crowd, absently called out, "Oh son, make room for them. Make room for them. Your step mothers are coming." Just when the Ashin was thinking, "it must be deva-gati nimitta," the father passed away, apparently destined for the realm of devas.

One other way of gati nimitta

Some dying people actually see with their natural eyes the materials that they will be finding in the next existence. A woman by the name of Revati was wife of a monastery-donor, one wealthy Nandiya. Just as much as Nandiya was generous, Revati was miserly. She was not a Buddhist really. She swore at the monks. Nandiya died first and became a deva in the heavens. Revati was next, but when she was about to die, two guards from Niraya realm came and pulled her away to the realm of the devas and, after showing her the good life of Nandiya, dragged her down to the Niraya.

In the life time of the Lord, one devotee by the name of Dhammika lived a blameless, virtuous life, leading many other like-minded devotees. When death was close upon him, he listened to dhamma instructions from bhikkhus; while doing that, he saw and heard 6 stage coaches in the sky, sent from the 6 levels of deva bhumi to take him to their respective bhumis, arguing as to which coach Dhammika should take. Not long afterwards, he passed away and was taken in the coach destined for Tusitā[203] devabhumi.

---

202. A form of address to an adult monk in respect (P+Myan.)
203. The highest of the 6 deva bhumis

Those who would be swallowed by the earth feel, before actually passing away, the heat of Aviji Niraya[204], as this heat can reach the home of man. That is how gati nimittas are variously seen, heard and felt. On the other opposite side of the picture nowadays, some people at death's door hear music and smell sweet scents - even those around the dying person may hear the music and smell the flowers. These gati nimittas and, kamma and kamma nimittas are felt mostly as a matter of opportunity occasioned and powered by kamma, not applicable to all people.

Corrective preparation before cuti

For some people who have been unwell and slowly dying with some ease, well-oriented arammanas can be prepared and managed by good mentors and relatives. If the patient is thought not to be able to rise above the present illness, keep the room and every thing in it clean and tidy. In homage to the Buddha, offer fresh, perfumed flowers. During the night, bright candle lights or the like should be offered.

Addressing the patient, say, "we have offered flowers and lights to the Buddha for you (mother or father). Please be glad." Read aloud well such verses as Dhammacakka Pavattana Sutta. This recital must be done well ahead of time (say a few days before the moment). The patient must not be sad or depressed, and the nursing relatives too. The patient so conditioned would be breathing in the sweet scent of flowers and, hearing the calling of the Buddha and the verses of dhamma for several days, so that the mind is well immersed in wholesome thoughts.

Then, when the time is close, if the flowers, perfumes, lights and the sounds of dhamma are still there, if the patient can still see, hear and smell with his or her own senses, cuti would come before those arammanas are lost. Then the wholesome deeds (kusala kammas) of offering those flowers, lights, etc. will certainly bring forth benefits (resultant effects of kamma). It is thus the responsibility of relatives to prepare the patient to stay with those kusala arammanas before and at the time of cuti. The father of Ashin Sona in the story cited, above, on account of the proper preparatory work of the good son, lost niraya nimittas, and gained deva bhumi nimittas at the moment of cuti.

How patisandhi citta comes about

After cuti citta has come and gone, patisandhi citta takes hold in the new life. The cuti citta is immediately linked up with patisandhi citta. There is no time gap in between the two incidents. It is that fast to get

---

204. The lowest of the 8 levels of Niraya realm

into a new life. Whether it is getting from human life into deva realm or into niraya, as cuti takes place, patisandhi citta in the new life takes hold instantly, and a new life form or khandha, that is nāma (consciousness) and rupa (matter) piled together, is established.

Two wrong views

Concerning the transition of one life to another, one must be careful to understand the right view that is free from *sassata dithi* (wrong view that life is eternal) and *uccheda ditthi* (wrong view that death annihilates life). One of the two views is that "there is a live creature made of nāma (soul) and rupa (material), dwelling in the house called khanda. That live creature, upon death, gets transferred to a new khanda in the new life." That is known as *sassata ditthi*. [*sassata* = the live little creature lives, without a break, to eternity; *ditthi* = wrong view] The other view is called *uccheda ditthi* that believes, "All of rupa and nāma (together with the live creature) of the past life is annihilated; there is no new life. When a creature dies, all constituents of the past life are disrupted. If the eternal God wills it, one other creature may be created." [*Uccheda* = once a life ends, all its nāma and rupa are annihilated, with nothing more to continue; *ditthi* = wrong view]

The right view (*Sammā ditthi*)

The behaviour of beings in the light of the three entities of dhamma, namely *avijjā* (delusion), *tanhā* craving) and *kamma* (volitional actions), determines the beginning of a new life immediately after the present. Near the death's door, avijjā hides the pitfalls of rupa, nāma and khandha of the new life that was coming. Tanhā craves for the new life. In spite of the appearance of fearsome gati nimittas (signs), one thinks it will be a life free of those dangers. Thus, with avijjā hiding the dangers and tanhā craving for a good new life, the beginning of rupa-nāma processes known as *patisandhi* (conception) takes place as the power of kamma would have it.

Because of the causal forces of avijjā, tanhā and kamma of the past life, patissandhi of rupa and nāma in the new life takes place, the *uccheda ditthi* that says, "With no connection with the past, a new life appears, thanks to creation by God, etc)," is incorrect. The *sassata ditthi* that says, "The soul of a creature in the past life incarnates into a new life," is wrong too. The entities of rupa and nāma of the past life cannot get transported to the new life; they cannot move from one place to another even in the present life-form, because what rupa and nāma appear disappear just as soon as they appear. There is no such thing as soul (*atta*) of a creature from the very beginning.

Therefore, the two wrong views of sassata ditthi and uccheda ditthi should be discarded. *Sammā ditthi* is the view that the processes of rupa-nāma patissandhi in the new life first appear as a result of avijjā, tanhā and kamma of the past life; and they are new rupa and nāma in one form or another. For instance, the sound of a shout in the vicinity of a mountain hits its walls and bounces back as an echo. That echo is not the voice of the man who has made the original sound, and yet it cannot be there without the original sound. [In lighting a second candle from the first, the second light is not the light of the first, and yet it is not unconnected with the first.]

Thus, if the past kamma was good, the present rupa and nāma would be good; poor past kamma results in poor present rupa and nāma. Please note that "we meet with variously differing good and poor kamma-results in this life due to the past kamma as well as the present ñāna (intelligence) and viriya (energy, diligence)."

Conclusion

This concludes the analytical work concerning near-death situations. Although we say "cuti", it is not finished as yet. For the new life to come into being, the old one has to enter into cuti. It is important for the new life to be of good quality; that is more important than death itself. At the approach of death, one should have the opportunity to prepare oneself to be in a wholesome state of mind that is possible only if one finds it easy to bear with the death-imposing illness; it is important to have good relatives or friends (who know how to prepare conditions conducive to a quiet, easy death). It is usually difficult to get in such a situation when the time is too close. So, to ensure oneself to be well prepared, well ahead of the moment of death, one should live a correct way of life, envisioning a proper way of dying, minding one's destination after this life and attaining holiness in stages, finally ascending to Nibbāna.

For the benefit of the multitude of people to live and die with vision of peace for the long future (in the samsāra), free of anxiety and miseries, I have written this chapter with certain explicitness. May their new lives, with the good old lives left behind, be beautiful. As for me, if death is still far away, with vision of the future, may I wish for Nibbāna, fulfilling and saving perfections, repeating them a great many times over and over. May

U Nyi

my associates do likewise, fulfilling perfections repeating many times over and over, destined for Nibbāna with absolute certainty.

{This ends the Chapter on near-death situations.}

CHAPTER NINE
[This chapter deals with notable facts on *patisandhi*]

PATISANDHI DEFINED

In Chapter Eight, explanations have been given of the very first citta, cetasika and rupa that come into being in the new life as determined by kamma-results of the past life after cuti. Those elements of citta, cetasika and rupa that appear first and foremost after cuti are called "*patisandhi*" (conception as we know it). In the language of Pali, patisandhi means the "linked appearing" at the point of parting (*cuti*) with the old life.

THE FOUR TYPES OF PATISANDHI

Because patisandhi citta, cetasika and rupa come into being as determined by kamma, the patisandhi differs in 4 types, dependent on various kinds of past kamma, as *opapātika, samsedaja, antaja and jalābhuja* patisandhis.

Opapātika patisandhi (Adulthood at Birth)
This type has distinct *khandhākāya* (bodies). Devas (gods), Brahmas (higher gods in Jhāna), beings in niraya (hellish realm), petas (ghosts) and those in asurā (demons) belong to this type of patisadhi, not needing to be borne in a mother's womb. As soon as the citta and cetasika patisandhi appears, they take the life forms of those beings, large distinct physical forms of normal and natural sizes, in *bimānas* (luxurious mansions), forests and mountains, in rivers and oceans and on beaches. The first human beings (at the very beginning of a world cycle) also appeared in this form of birth.

Samsedaja patlsaudhi (Extraneous conception)
Conception in the form of attachment to something attachable is samsedaja patisandhi. In this type of patisandhi the beings grow slowly from the tiny forms. It includes the larvae attached to rotten materials such as animal excrements and bad fish. Queen Padumavati was conceived in a padumā lily. Queen Veluvati was conceived inside a bamboo tube. The

161

accuser of the Buddha, Cinjamāna was conceived in a tamarind tree. There were many people of such patisandhi.

Antaja patisandhi (Conception in eggs)

Conception in the shell of an egg inside the womb of a mother, such as fowls and other birds, is antaja patisandhi. In some jataka stories some human beings had lived with female dragons (reptiles with some super natural powers), giving offspring of human beings by way of antaja patisandhi.

Jalābuja patisandhi (Conception in a mother's womb)

Conception of human beings, horses, buffalos, cattle, etc. in the wombs of their mothers is jalābuja patisandhi. Some of the earth-bound, lower gods (devas) and tree-dwelling gods are also conceived by way of jalābuja patisandhi. [The antaja and jalābuja patisandhi are also called *gabbhaseyaka* patisandhi. *Gabbha* = inside the belly of mother + *seyaka* = dweller].

The 3 factors influencing conception

Those who are born of samsedaja and opapātika patisandhi are conceived not in direct connection with the parents, but purely on account of their past kammas, requiring no searching for any other reason. Gambaseyaka beings are conceived inside their mothers' bellies, and so the question arises as to "what factors come together so that they can be so conceived". The answer: (1) The expectant mother has just finished her menstrual period so that the womb is clean; (2) the father and mother to-be have conjugated; (3) the child to-be has passed away (cuti) from its previous life. Only when these three factors come together conception can take place. According to literature, conception can be effective within 7 to 15 days of conjugation of the couple. This is the normal way of conception nowadays.

SOME VERY STRANGE WAY OF CONCEPTION

Although the father and mother to-be have not in effect conjugated, patisandhi can take place. The Bodhisatta Suvannasāma's mother had just started her menstrual period when the father felt her navel with his hand, and Suvannasāma was conceived. Mother of King Cantapajjota, when her period had just come, felt joy when a scorpion crawled on her, and she conceived. Byine-out, a grey species of the heron family, feels the southerly winds of early Monsoon with joy to conceive. During the time of our Lord, a bhikkhuni[205] conceived a child as she had sucked the semen gathered on the undergarment of a male monk (formerly her husband). A boy by the name of Isisinga was born to a deer which had drunk the semen in the urine of a hermit. Those incidents are strange and their occurrences rare.

The *kālāla* liquid

There are infinitesimally tiny pieces of rupa matter that come with patisandhi citta and cetasika. Those materials are called "clear *kālāla* liquid". It is said that the kālāla liquid has the size of an oil droplet stuck to the tip of a strand of hair of a lady of the North Island[206], which has been dipped in a very clear type of oil. It is not the semen of the parents; the semen[207] only gives nourishment to the kālāla liquid.

The way the parents' fluids assist patissandhi

It is now comprehensible that kālāla liquid (patissandhi) appears in the mother's womb as a result of past kamma of the being to be conceived, and that the parents' semen comes in to serve as its urgently needed life-supporting material. The kālāla liquid is like the seed of a plant. The parents' semen is like soil and water. The past kamma that is the source of the kālāla liquid is like the planter of the seed. Therefore, for the kālāla liquid to be conceived, the clean womb of a mother and faultless, disease-free, proper semen are urgently required. Why is that so? If the womb and the semen are not clean and disease-free, the fetus is not likely to grow well.

Besides, just as the colour of a monitor lizard is red or black depending on the colour of the hole in which it dwells, so also the infant that clings to the semen carries the physical characteristics of the parents, making them somewhat look-alikes. The hands, the feet and other parts may also look alike. The children may also take after the parents in their mind-sets, intellect, courage, and thoughts.

This mental link-up is probably due to the parents' *cittaja paccaya* (mind source) and *utujarupa* (heat-dependent matter) inherited since conception. It may probably be due to familiarity with, and imitation of, the parents' mental make up and related behaviours. So, it is apparent that good and intelligent children can come of good and intelligent parents

205. A female 'monk' properly ordained to be reckoned as a member of the Sangha
206. Scriptural geography where the ladies' hair is so fine
207. This is only a particular form of a monk's speech, perhaps meaning the fluids in the womb as well as the father's semen, not necessarily an exact scientific term. (The Buddha knew all.)

while children of low mentality and intelligence may come of parents of the same kind. That is the reason why the two parents must be of good descent so as to bring forth children of especially decent character.

[Note: Some ancient books say, "lineage from parents to children, generation-wise, grows banana trees." The proverb was originally meant for royal affairs where cut banana trees were planted as decoration.[208] So, it is not used here for quotes.]

4 DIFFERENT KINDS OF PEOPLE

Some people are conceived (patisandhi) in apāya. They are called duggati ahetuka, meaning miserable, rootless persons (*duggati ahetuka*). [*duggati* = miserable life + *ahetuka* = none of alobha, adosa and amoha minds is present in the patisandhi.] Some human beings and minor gods on earth are also of such ahetuka kind. They are called *sugati ahetuka* persons. [*sugati* = good life + *ahetuka* = none of the 3 hetuka minds are present] Dvi hetuka and ti hetuka kinds will be shown later.

Sugati ahetuka human beings

The above-mentioned "sugati ahetuka" human beings owe their life to very poor kusala kammas to become the blind, the dumb, the invalid, the deaf, the idiotic (who do not know how to orient themselves in the four cardinal directions, how to count small denominations of money, and so on), *napantuka* (persons with incomplete sex organs), *ubatobyi* (persons with both male and female sex organs), and so on, who have only subhuman capacities and qualities of life.

Sugati ahetuka gods

They become gods (devas) due to their past minor kusala kammas. They are devas only in name, having no supernatural powers or separate housing, living in the vicinity of, and dependent on, the mansions of greater earth-bound and tree-dwelling gods. Without access to proper food, they pick up bits and pieces of remnant food, like the way ghosts (petas) do. Sometimes, they frighten and, enter into the body of, weak women and children to eat ghosts' food given in fright. They belong in type to *catumahārāja devas*[209].

208. In ancient times, royal shows and pavilions, and no others, are decorated with upright banana trees. The writer Sayadaw here seemed to show his awareness of the common misinterpretation of the proverb.
209. They are the lowest of the 6 deva realms, closest to the human realm.

Just as there are wise people among the poor, so also there are *dvi hetuka* and *ti hetuka* devas (to be shown below) among the poor lot of the devas. In our Lord's time, some poor gods did attain magga/phala ñāna.

Dvi hetuka persons

In the chapter on dāna, dvi hetuka ukkatha kusala and ti hetuka omaka kusala have been dealt with. Due to those kusala kammas, they become human beings or devas. But there are only two kinds of hetuka, the alobha and adosa, in the patisandhi citta, because they had not applied their wisdom called amoha while doing the kusala; or, in spite of application of the wisdom, there was no proper cetanā; or even with some strong cetanā, there was disappointment on the act of the kusala after the act has been done.

Because the seed called patisandhi was of the poor kind, there is no opportunity for the aforementioned two types of ahetuka and this type of dvi hetuka persons to attain jhāna or magga/phala ñāna in the present life. But if they devote their energy to meditation, they can become ti-hetuka persons; that habit, being a significant kusala kamma, carried in their consciousness continuum, is conducive to jhāna or magga/phala ñāna in their next lives, if not in this life. So there should be an awareness of the necessity to work harder for that purpose.

Ti hetuka persons

When reborn in human or deva realm, the person is a resultant aftermath of conception with *ti hetuka patisandhi citta* (alobha, adosa and amoha) on account of the ti hetuka *okkatha kusala kamma citta* of the past life, as mentioned in the chapter on dāna, That kind of person is knowledgeable and wise. If diligent, the person can attain jhāna, as well as magga/phala ñāna. Nowadays, there are so many ti hetuka people. They have not gained any insight only because they have not made any effort systematically in that direction. There are thus the 4 different types of persons according as their differences in the mindset as to duggati ahetuka, sugati ahetuka, dvi hetuka and ti hetuka cittas.

The eight holy (*ariya*) people

If that ti hetuka puthujana (common person) works hard at insight meditation, and attains sotāpatti magga,

1. the person would become *sotāpatti maggattha puggala*[210] (person);

210.Sighting Nibbāna in a fleeting moment for the first time, commonly referred to as magga ñāna.

2. f sotāpatti *phala*[211] is attained, the person would become *sotāpatti phalattha person* or "*sotāpana puggala*". Similarly, if higher levels of maga and phala are attained,
3. sagadāgāmi maggattha puggala,
4. sagadāgāmi phalattha puggala;
5. anāgāmi maggattha puggala.
6. anāāgmi phalattha puggala;
7. arahatta maggattha puggala,
8 arahatta phallatha puggala.

[The No.8 person is called "*rahantā*"[212]. Paccekabuddhas and the Buddha are also rahamtās with omniscient wisdom.]

Kamma is mother and father of all beings

The kamma that one had committed and done is not only the creator of one's unique patisandhi citta, but also it predetermines the looks and appearances, lineage (family, clans, etc) and the levels of material wellbeing. To make it clearer, suppose some one does his or her kusala kamma with all his or her heart, as wisdom guides him or her. Someone else does not do any kusala kamma, or, if anything, does it with little willful intent. When the two of them take to human patisandhi, the former is conceived in the womb of a well-to-do mother; the mother is intelligent and knows how to take good care of wellbeing of the infant in her womb and is very careful in her movement and eats only proper foods, avoiding items like chilies and others that are too hot or too cold.

The latter with little kusala kamma takes to the womb of a poor mother who is ignorant. Even if she is intelligent, she is in no position to take good care of the pregnancy or avoid what should be avoided as circumstances would not allow her. If the mother takes in chilies or hot food the infant in her womb would be in hellish fire. If she takes in very cold food, the infant would be in a hellish ice-field. The infant is either stretched or bumped in great pain if she sits down or rise suddenly. [These are only some pains and discomforts the child suffers according to the books. Because of the poor kamma of the child, the mother also suffers in carrying and delivering it.]

Thus there are differences as to poverty or affluence since the time the child is in the mother's womb. And then, the child of good kamma is delivered with the assistance of good midwives, coming out as comfortably

211. Results, benefits, fruit of magga ñāna upon reflective contemplation
212. "Rahantā" is a Myanmar version of the Pali term "Arahanta".

as can be, wrapped in soft flannel cloth and nursed properly. The child of poor kamma, however, comes out with extreme difficulties and without the assistance of good midwives, very much like the way a tiny little rat comes out of a tiny little hole, strained and consumed with exhaustion. And then, the child, wrapped and handled in rough fabrics, is not properly nursed, its tender body hurt the way tender wounds are hurt by pricking it with the pointed end of a feather.

That is not all. The baby of good kamma gets not only enough breast milk from the mother but also other nutrients and medicines under the care of good doctors, and all that contributes to its good health. It also gets love and warmth from grandparents and aunties, old and young, making the child a very happy one. The baby of poor kamma, however, does not get the mother's milk, good medicine or the care of good doctors; it does not get the love and tenderness of grand parents either. Even though the mother does not want to get away from the child, she feeds it to its fill and immediately gets busy with her bazaar-selling or some menial work for a living, leaving the infant child to its fate.

Conclusion

In this way the children since infancy, long before working for a living using resources of intelligence and diligence, find themselves in differences of material wellbeing and happiness, these being dependent on the differences of past kammas. That being so, one should not find fault with the well-to-do people for their affluence, but face life with a thought on the nature of the world simply as "'Big Face' takes the best."[213] One must blame one's own poor kamma committed in one's many past lives, while at the same time try to make oneself a big-faced noble kind of person.

If people fail to live blameless lives, and yet, are jealous of the big-faced people, they would find themselves in deeper troubles in the lives hereafter. So, I wish readers of this book and my associates, good patisandhis, doing noble kammas now, in this life.

For the benefit of many people,
To get in good patisandhi I scribble;
But for me,
I try to live a blameless way
So that in all lives to come I may
Not be born of poor patisandhi,

---

213. In the Myanmar proverb, it is "All pieces of meat in the dish go to the 'big face'" (in feasting on a traditional round table meal). 'Big face' is the man of influence.

But industrious
And intelligent I try to be,
Better and better in lives hereafter
Till Nibbāna thereafter;
Likewise,
May my good associates be
Reborn well, till Nibbāna for eternity.

[This ends the Chapter on Patisandhi]

CHAPTER TEN

RUPA (CORPOREALITY)

[Because a material body called clear kālaāla liquid is involved at conception; the phenomenal events of the material body (called rupa khandhā) should very well be understood. In this chapter, all there is to know about rupa will be shown.]

What is rupa?

The Pali word *"rupa"* means matter, material body, corporeality, meaning "the unstable, ever-changing nature." There are many causes, such as heat, cold, etc, for such ever-changing nature. How cold may cause changes in matter can be seen in cracked dry skin in the cool season; darkened skin in extreme cold; sneezing cold with fever; breaking up into pieces of bodies of those in Lokantaritta Niraya (cold hell); and so on. How heat may cause changes in matter can be seen in red skin when walking in the sun; darkened skin when sun-burnt; heat stroke with fever; deaths due to extreme heat in deserts; and so on. Apart from them, people suffer from rashes and other inflammations; injuries from bites of scorpion or snakes and death there-from; extreme thinness and deaths due to starvation. These are the destructive effects on matter (rupa) of the ever-changing nature of physical conditions (rupa). Rupa is thus always in a flux of change.

Maxim: Because of heat and cold, poisons of snakes and insects, thirst and hunger, and many other causes, matter always is in a state of change; that, indeed, is rupa.

[Although there are 28 kinds of rupa, only the more important 19 will be shown here.]

THE 4 CATEGORIES OF MAHĀBHUTA DHĀTU (PRIMARY ELEMENTS)

1. *pathavi dhātu*
   (the earth element)
2. *āpo dhātu*
   (water element)
3. *tejo dhātu*
   (heat element)
4. *vāyo dhātu*
   (air element)

The 5 categories of pasāda rupa (sensors or sense receptors)
5. *cakkhu pasāda* (sight sensor)
6. *sota pasāda* (sound sensor)
7. *ghāna pasāda* (smell sensor)
8. *jivhā pasāda* (taste sensor)
9. *kāya pasāda* (touch sensor)

The 5 categories of ārammana (sense objects)
10. *rupa ārammana* (sight object)
11. *saddā ārammana* (sound object)
12. *ganda ārammana* (smell object)
13. *rasa ārammana* (taste object)

The 4th (13th in the series) is phutthabba ārammana (touch objects) [the 3 mahābhuta elements, namely pathavi, tejo and vāyo, are classed here as a kind of sense object called *phutthabba ārammana*], that consist of:
14. *itthibhāva* (nature of females)}
15. *purisabhāva* (nature of males) - two kinds of bhāva rupa 14 and the 15.
16. *hadayavatthu* (the heart)
17. *jivita* (life, vitality - physical and mental)
18. *ojā* (*āhāra* or nutriments)
19. *ākāsa dhātu* (sky, space element)

The 4 Primary Elements Pathavi dhātu (The earth element)
Just as the earth in its original, natural state is strong and tough enough to bear the loads of materials on it, so also the stiff dhātu or element that can carry groups of co-nascent rupa (corporeal) elements is called *pathavi dhātu* (the earth element). The earth planet and rocks, metals and so on are the kinds of rupa aggregates that have the distinct properties of pathavi dhātu.

Āpo dhātu (The water element)
Just as water in its original, natural state soaks up and collects dust particles into a lump of some form, so also the property of rupa that collects and combines co-nascent rupa particles is called *āpo dhātu*. When liquidity is overwhelming, it has the property of carrying all co-nascent rupa particles in the form of a flow. So, the original natural water, urine, spittle, mucus and so on are flow-evident group of rupa elements.

Tejo dhātu (The fire element)

Just as heat radiation from the sun and fires in its original state dries up the wet and sticky materials, so also the rupa element that dries up only enough to hold and keep material particles together in some form or another is called *tejo dhātu* (fire element). In summer months, there is coolness in the bodies of healthy people. That coolness is also tejo dhātu. So, it should be noted that there are two types of tejo dhātu, the hotness or warmness being called *u-nha tejo* and the coldness, *sita tejo*.

The tejo element is also called *u-tu*. Sita tejo (sita u-tu) covers over all animate bodies as well as inanimate world in the cold season, whereas in summer months they are enveloped in u-nha tejo (u-nha u-tu). This element keeps good health as adapts the hot or cold seasons. If the body u-nha tejo is over and above the normal, the body will fall sick, severity of the fever depending on the degree of the rise in the u-nha tejo. In extreme cases, death is the result. Similarly, the excessive sita tejo would cause certain ailments.

Therefore those who cannot stand changes in tejo should be very careful about traveling and eating very hot food during very hot seasons, and also traveling and eating very cold food during very cold seasons so that they may be healthy and lead a long life. The sun and the fires are groups of rupa at extreme heat whereas the water and ice are groups of rupa at coldness of varying degrees.

Heat in the stomach

There is, under the new-food compartment of the stomach, a kind of fire called "*pāsaka* fire" that digests all food-intakes. That heat digests all intakes of food. If that pāsaka tejo is weak, digestion is incomplete. When that happens, good health is maintained by eating soft food that is easily digestible.

Vāyo dhātu (The air element)

Just as the natural air can push and exert pressure against whatever is in contact, so also there is a kind of rupa called *vāyo dhātu* that pushes and presses against each and every one of co-nascent, adjacent groups of rupa. There are 6 types:

1. *Uddhangama* air[214] - This is the air that rises and pushes up. When that air is in excess due to surfeit, such ailments as

---

214. By air here in modern terms can be interpreted as fluids (mixture of gas and liquids) that exert both types of pneumatic and hydraulic **pressure**, the fundamental property of elemental air.

pressure in chest, hiccups, belching, sneezing, coughing, and so on may result. While in talking, this air is playing its role, and so those with heartburn and similar maladies should be especially careful with their talking. When the stomach is empty, there is more likelihood of a rise in volume of this stomach gas.

2. *Adhogama* air - This is the air that pushes down. When this air is in excess, it may cause excessive bowel discharge.
3. *Kucchittha air* - This is the air that circulates in the abdomen, excluding the colon and the intestines.
4. *Kotthāsaya* air - This is the air that circulates in the colon and the intestines. This air caries incoming new food from the upper part of the stomach into the lower part from where it enters the colon from which the waste material is pushed out of the system.
5. *Angamangānusāri* air - This is the air circulating in all the limbs. If this air does not circulate well, then sickness may result. There are minute nerves and blood vessels in the body. As air[215] circulates in them, those who sit in a bent or prostrate posture or with arms folded. for long periods of time, would have restricted or stopped this air from flowing (like water in a kinked rubber pipe). The air gets collected at some points in the body. So, the blood that flows by virtue of air pressure also collects at some point, possibly causing one malady or another or a rise in severity of the malady that one already has. So, in order to let this air flow freely, people are urged not to sit with tightly pressed crossed legs for long periods of time and to take a walk every now and then to stretch the legs and arms out.
6. *Assāsa passāsa* air - This is the air extant in the in- and out-breathing. It is also called *ānāpāna*.

Thus there are 6 kinds of air.

THE FUNDAMENTAL AND DEPENDENT RUPAS

These 4 mahābhuta elements of pathavi, āpo, tejo and vāyo are basic to all other rupa elements. The rupa elements to be shown now are those dependent and conditional on them. The mahābhuta elements are in hard

---

215. Again this would mean fluids (including blood) in modern terms.

material forms, and the larger their piling up the larger their material body. The broad expanse of land, the huge rocky mountain, the great ocean, the giant flame, the enormous power of a storm and so on are examples of inanimate monstrosities. Big man, big god, huge fish, huge turtle and so on are living examples of living hugeness. They are huge collections of the 4 mahābhuta elements.

For *cakkhu, sota, rupa,* etc. that are to be explained now, the material forms are not remarkably big. For instance, the sweet smell of toilet soap may be enhanced without increase in the size of the soap; conversely quality of the scent may be reduced without reduction in the size of the soap. Therefore, pathavi and other mahābhuta elements should be noted for their basic properties with evident mass and forms.

THE FIVE FORMS OF PASĀDA RUPA

We now have audio and photo receiver gadgets. So also we are fitted with sensors in our body to receive the signals of co-nascent sense objects. Those sensors[216] are called "*pasāda*" in Pali.

Cakkhu pasāda (sight sensors)

The sensors in our eyes, enabling us to see, is called *cakkhu pasāda.* These sight sensors fill the middle portion of the iris. As various forms and colours (*rupāramana* or sight objects) are caught in the sight sensors, consciousness of the sight called *cakkhu viññāna* arises.

Sota pasāda (sound sensors)

These sound sensors, a great many of them, called "*sota pasāda*" are situated in the ring-shaped area inside the pit of ear. When various sounds (*sotāramana* or sound objects) are received in those sensors, consciousness of the sounds called *sota viññāna* arises.

Ghāna pasāda (scent sensors)

These sensors, a great many of them, called "*ghāna pasāda*" are situated inside the nose in the area, shaped like the hoof of a goat. When various scents (*ghandāramana* or scent objects) are received in those sensors, consciousness of the scents called *ghāna viññāna* arises.

---

216. It is "sensual element" in the original text

Jinvhā pasāda (taste sensors)

These taste sensors, a great many of them, called "*jinvhā pasāda*" are situated in water lily-shaped area in the mid-point of the tongue. When tastes (*rasāramana* or taste objects) from various kinds of food are received in those sensors, consciousness of the tastes called *jinvhā viññāna* arises.

Kāya pasāda (body sensors)

Leaving out the dry part of the skin, every other part of the body is filled with body sensors, a great many of them, called "*kāya pasāda*". When all senses of touch, bumps and contact (*photthabbāramana* or touch objects)) are received on the body sensors, consciousness of the sense of touch called *kāya viññāna* arises.

Thus there are 5 kinds of sensors.

The five kinds of ārammana
Ārammana (sense objects)

The Pali word "*ārammana*"[217] is translated in Myanmar as "ārun or āyon"[218], meaning "the mind's natural habitat". The mind cannot exist without an ārammana. Only with the presence of a sense object the mind can exist. Therefore, all sense objects are the natural habitat of the mind. Amongst those objects, the rupa formations such as the looks and lights, the sight objects, are called *rupārammana*; the sound objects, *saddhārammana*; the smell objects, *gandhārammana*; the taste objects, *rasārammana*; and the touch objects, *photthabbārammnana*.

["*Dhammārammana*", however, is not rupa (matter) alone; they are composed of some rupa, citta, cetasika and Nibbāna-paññatti[219].]

Kāmaguna (Pleasures)

These objects include such desirable ones as pleasant sights, sounds, smells, tastes and touch, and they are called "kāmaguna". [kāma = pleasurable + guna = yoke, tether] By the five kāmaguna ārammanas is meant the five objects of sights, sounds, etc... So, the sights, voices and smell of women, the tastes of the food they cook, and their body-touch are the best kāmagunas men enjoy. In the same way, sights, etc. of men are also the most desirable kāmagunas for women.

---

217. Sense objects, objects that have impacts on the 6 sense organs to produce sense perceptions.
218. Ārun is pronounced as "aryon", the phonetics not easily recognizable as a Pali derivative.
219. The Nibbāna designated.

Bhāvarupa (Gender forms)

At the first instant of conception, the past kammas determine a rupa material that has distinct properties to be that of a male or a female. That rupa is spread throughout the body matter. The rupa that is to become a female is called *itthibhāva rupa*, and that for a male to-be is called *purisabhāva rupa*. Just as branches and twigs come out of a tree stem on the basis of the seed, so also itthibhāva rupa produces a woman's form, organs and behavioural charactors; so also the purisabhāva rupa produces a male's form, organs and manly behaviours.

Hadayavatthu (The heart)

Filled with blood, this rupa situates at the mid point in the depression area in between the two breasts, inside the chest. Quite a great many minds have their origin here. [This word is translated as "hadaya-heart" in Myanmar language. But its location is not the same as the doctors say.]

Jivitarupa (The life of rupa)

Called the life of all nāma formations, there is such a thing as *jivitindare* cetasika. Similarly, there is "life" in rupa formations, called *jivitarupa*. This jivitarupa life, however, is not included in the rupas that have their origin in citta, utu and āhāra, but only in the rupas having their origin in kamma. In all beings *nāmajivita* and *rupajivita* are essential for their existence. Without these two jivitas, it is death. The rupa-matters in the body do not get decomposed on account of this jivita-rupa called life. A dead body has no jvita-rupa, and so it gets decomposed. This jivitarupa is extant everywhere in the body.

Ojārupa (The nutrients)

In rice, there is starchy nutrient. That nutrient is called "*ojā*" as well as "*āhāra*". In the body also there are those nutrients. The six tastes, namely sweet, sour, hot, acrid, salty and bitter, are called *rasā* (*rasārupa*). Ojā is the essence of nutrients contained in that *rasā*. The essential nutrients enhance new rupas to multiply and grow.

[This will be explained in some detail later.]

Ākāsadhātu

Ākāsa means "space in-between". Rupa materials do not exist by themselves: a minimum of 8 or 9 materials exist in combination. A unit rupa materials so grouped is called a "calāpa". (Manner of calāpa formation will be shown later,) There is space between two closed fingers. Likewise, although the body is completely filled with calāpas, there is space between any two of them. That space is called "*ākāsa dhātu*", taken as a kind of rupa. Actually, it is not a true rupa by clear evidence. Only in grouping two rupa calāpas, it becomes evident by designation.

Calāpa, calāp and club[220]

Nowadays in big towns, some people organize themselves into associations called "clubs". Club is a noun for a socially organized group. The rupas discussed above do not exist in separate, individually divided, entities either. Those rupas that can so associate may only form a group. Thus the co-nascent individual rupas existing in a group is noted as a unit of "calāpa".

The 8 rupas in constant association

The four primary (mahābhuta) elements, namely pathavi, āpo, tejo, and vāyo always associate with 4 other elements, namely vanna (looks), gandha (smell), rasa (taste) and oja (nutrient). Everywhere and anywhere these 8 rupa elements are never apart. All the infinitesimally small particles of the earth are only combinations of these elements. The earth has looks or appearance (vanna). It issues some smell. There is taste in chewing it. You can touch it. Not only in earth, but in water also these 8 rupas are there. It is the same with air. In the heat and light of a fire and the sun, all show properties of these 8 rupa elements in combination.

The size of a calāpa

A calāpa is infinitesimally small in size. The smallest imaginable size of a dust particle has an uncountable number of different kinds of calāpas, invisible to the naked eye. A bacterium that can only be seen under the most powerful, high-resolution microscope is composed of a great number of rupa-calāpas, predetermined by kamma, citta, utu and āhāra; this fact indicates the impossibility of saying "how small" the size of a calāpa might be. [Look in the books of Sangaha for details of names and types of the calāpas.]

The 4 factors influencing predetermination

Here we must explain the grouping of the 4 primary elements and the roles kamma, citta, utu and āhaāra play in their formations. First, imagine <u>a human form ma</u>de out of clay (earth). Would the human form be possible

220. In the language of Myanmar, calāpa is calāp, very close in phonetics to "club".

176

with the clay dust alone? No. it cannot be. The clay dust will be blown away by wind. So, it must be wetted with water to resist being blown away.

Even with clay and water together, even leaving out the human form, there is no solidarity and no organized form yet. So, the clay and water must be solidified. That is no human form as yet. The wetted clay must be given a sun-bath so that it becomes solidified enough to keep in human form. Thus there is air that supports the combination of clay and water in shape by virtue of internal and external pressure, the heat to dry it to a state of solidity and plasticity sufficient to put it in a form, and the artist who sculptures the lump into a human image. This is only a parable to nāma-rupa formations.

The role of kamma

In the same manner, it is impossible to build an organic body with pathavi element alone. For the particles of pathavi dhātu (earth) not to fall apart, āpo dhātu (water) must wet them for collection in a mass. And then to reduce to and maintain certain solidity, the mass must be subject to tejo dhātu (heat). And then vāyo dhātu (air) assists in keeping the individual groups (calāpas) together in a solid, cohesive mass by way of pressure in the inter-spaces in between them and from outside. The elements of vanna, gandha, rasa and ojā are inalienable parts of the 4 primary elements. Gathering in firm combination, as shown in the parable above, rupa calāpas come into being in a state of association as accorded by past kamma in a "human body".

Kamma predetermines whether a human being is to be born a man or a woman, the gender being dependent on the person's volition when committing actions. It also predetermines destinations as to the type of niraya (infernal world), or the world of petas (ghosts and demons), as appropriate to their akusala kammas. It also predetermines whether the individual is reborn in beautiful or not-so-beautiful form, depending on wholesomeness or unwholesomeness of the individual's deeds. An animal reborn as such on account of some akusala kamma may be good-looking and lovable to be fed well as its previous kusala kammas may find opportunity to show up. Good kamma may have predestined a human person, but akusala kamma gives rise to ugliness, dislike and repugnance so much so that few people are generous and kind towards that person. In this way kamma is the determinant of this organic body from the very beginning of conception in the mother's womb.

The role of citta

The kamma-determined rupa is again manipulated by citta. Sitting, lying, standing and walking are all activated according to the will of the mind. When the will to walk arises, *cittajarupas* (citta-caused rupas) are stimulated and activated throughout the body. In those cittajarupas, vāyo dhātu exerts its force stronger than any other time. Due to flexing of vāyo dhātu, the whole body becomes activated and poised for action. When the volume of vāyo-activated rupa materials grows, they move and move bit by bit as if walking. In so moving bit by bit, the rupas move not on their own but as commanded by the mind.

Here the expression, "move and move bit by bit", must better be explained. In moviemaking, many single frames of a man in walking movement are made so the action appears on the screen. First frame shows the man, standing; the second and third frames may show no difference. After several frames, a foot appears to rise. The lifting of the foot becomes clear after many more frames. In this way, a great many frames of a strip of the film must be passed in succession for the full action of a walk. It is the passing of a connected series of individual frames of the man's portrait which make him appear to walk on the screen   Thus, in saying, "a man walks," the will to walk does not cause the first rupas, although affected by the will, to move, and the whole body is still in standing position. But due to the energy of the vāyo dhātu extant in the first rupa calāpa, restlessness is apparent in the manner. So the second group of rupas has moved forward to a spot ahead of the first group... In this way, the successive groups of rupas move forward to new spots, affecting the movement pattern of the man in the briefest of a moment (because citta arises more than a hundred-thousand times in that time interval, cittaja rupas[221] also arise just as fast in succession).

Moreover, as the saying of "young mind begets young body" goes, a happy man has clear cittaja rupas, while a man talking in endearment and pleasantries has a clear affable face. A reasonably good health can result from a clear, blameless mind. It says, "The mind beats up and the body gets crushed": an unhappy mind begets a tired look. When disturbed after a disagreement, the sweet face suddenly turns sullen.

Just as a house on fire begets other fires in its vicinity, so also withered cittaja rupas begets withering up of associated kammaja, utuja and āhāra rupas. So, an extremely distressed person looks so old as not to befit his/her age. With the sorrow heightening, the person may die, broken-

---

221. Cittaja rupas are the rupas caused and aroused by citta.

hearted. In this way the mind also influences the welfare of the body since conception.

The role of utu

Utu[222] also plays a role in the formation of rupa. Living in a pleasant climate is conducive to clear mind and good health. One who sleeps on a clean bed and wears clean clothes is in contact with good utu of the bed and clothes, generating clean *utuja rupas* that results in good health. So, the constant use of clean beds and clothes is a truly proper way for good health. The use of dirty beds and clothes would generate bad utuja rupas and so results in poor health conditions. Trees in forests and hills thrive and multiply well due to proper utu in rainy seasons. In dry summer months, the utu is so bad the trees wither and dry up. This is the way also with utu in a mother's womb where the child is being bourne. Thus we must reflect upon the way trees are transformed in accordance with climatic conditions as we take note of changes in utuja rupas due to changes in utu conditions of our bodies.

The role of āhāra

The ojā in all things taken as food, including water, can influence rupa. Only if one takes food and medicines that are suitable for one, good rupas grow, making the body properly built, clear in the looks, radiant and healthy. If the food and medicines taken are not appropriate, bad rupas grow, making one tired and dry, and susceptible to diseases. It is clearly evident that those people who take proper food and medicines live long, free of diseases.

While in the mother's womb, since the time the body anatomy is complete, the child is fed through the system with whatever food the mother eats. Then this food gives nutriments to the child's rupas to thrive and grow. So every mother who wishes her child to be healthy must, since the time of conception, avoid eating food that is inappropriate for the child. The mother eats certain food; the child in her womb has to be content with whatever food she has taken. It says in the books that the nutriments from the mother's system seep into that of the child through the umbilicus. Nowadays, following doctor's instructions, mothers begin to take wholesome food since the child's conception, must not walk or move too roughly, visit the doctor regularly, and sleep and eat well. Only if the mother takes care of herself to be disease-free, she will deliver healthy

---

222. Utu literally means climate, weather.

babies. So, mothers must personally take care in the matter of the child's nutrients since the time of conception.

Conclusion

I have now shown all that should be known about the rupa elements. For the noble deed of compiling these articles on the phenomena of rupa, may all those who read this book live in good health in this life, and do wholesome kammas to have good health and good looks in all upcoming lives hereafter in the samsāra before attainment of Nibbāna. May my associates and myself, in whichever life, nurturing kusala-kamma pāramis before reaching Nibbāna, have good health and clean looks that help putting up good efforts in achieving all wholesome noble deeds as willed.

For the sake of good rupa, now and in future, I have compiled facts of rupas in their true nature; for this kusala kamma, may readers of this book, envisioning good health and good looks in future, do wholesome, noble deeds; for me and my associates, may we be in good health and good rupa, able to make good efforts to reach Nibbāna without fail.

(End of Chapter 10 on rupa)

CHAPTER ELEVEN
The Thirty-one Realms

[This chapter contains notable facts on Bhumis or realms of existence]

BHUMI (REALM, OR HOMELAND)

The realm or home land where beings live is called a "*bhumi*" in Pali, or simply "bhom" in Myanmar. There are 4 *apāya*, 7 *kāma sugati*[223], and 20 *Brahma* bhumis, to a total of 31 bhumis. The 4 apāya bhumis consist of *niraya* (infernal worlds or hell), *tiricchanta* (the world of animals), *petas* (ghosts) and *asurakāya* (the titans). The kāma sugati bhumis are 1 human (*manussatta*) world and 6 worlds of heavenly gods (*devas*). The 6 deva worlds are *catumahārāja, tavatimsā, sāmā, tusitā, nimmānarati,* and *paranimmita-vasavatti.* The worlds of the Brahmas consist of 16 *rupa-Brahma* and 4 *arupa-Brahma* bhumis.

NIRAYA

[The Infernal Worlds]

Just as the human world has prisons for criminals, so also right inside this earth on which human beings live, there exist *niraya* prisons for those who had committed various kinds of akusala ducaritta[224]. Those niraya prisons have their origin in past kammas of beings, and they exist as *utajarupas*[225] conditional to kamma. There are various types of niraya prisons, the variety depending on the types of akusala kamma committed. According to literature, *lohakumbhi* niraya exists under the crust of the earth, contiguous with the human habitat. In this book, only the more commonly talked-about 8 levels of niraya will be described. They are; (1)

---

223. Kāma sugati = the good destinations where sensuous pleasure is the object. Apāya bhumis are also kāma bhumis (but undesirable destinations called *duggati*).
224. This can be considered equivalent to crimes against living beings.
225. *Kammapaccaya utaja rupas* - utu-related rupas conditional to past kammas- (*utu* = heat or cold)

181

Sincova niraya, (2) *kālasutta* niraya. (3) *samghāta* niraya, (4) *roruva* niraya, (5) *mahāroruva* niraya, (6) *tāpana* niraya, (7) *mahātāpana* niraya and (8) *avici* niraya. Each and every one of those nirayas is walled in by 5 other nirayas, namely (1) excrement niraya, (2) hot-ash niraya, (3) letpantaw (spikes) niraya, (4) dagger-forest niraya, (5) *vettarani* or "river of molten iron" niraya. Combined, these 5 nirayas are called *ussada niraya*.

Yamamin (King of nirayas)

Included in the Catumahārāja devas, King of Vemānika petas is also called *"Yamamin"*. The king enjoys the pleasures and luxuries of devas sometimes and suffer from akusala kammas the same way all petas do at other times. There are more than one Yamamin. Like the way government officials of the human world have their offices, Yamamins have their offices at 4 gates of the niraya bhumi, and ask questions and make enquiries on the past conducts of new arrivals.

But not all that come are interrogated. Those whose akusala kammas are evidently serious fall directly into niraya. Those with minor akusala kammas are allowed to be asked questions to see if they can be pardoned. So, the Yamamins' enquiries do not aim for punishment, but rather to free those who should be freed. He is much like justices of appellate courts of today. So, note that Yamamins are kings, just and noble, looking after the rule of law in their domain.

[Uparipannāsa, Devaduta Sutta]

Guards of Niraya

These niraya guards are demonic gods, included in the type of catumahāhārja devas. Their job:

They send the convicts with minor offenses to Yamamin, but, like executioners, drag and cruelly beat up those already fallen to niraya. [Dangers such as burning by "hell fire" are kamma-caused utuja rupas (heat) so that only niraya-convicts suffer the burns, not the guards.]

Yamamin's book of records

For general knowledge, an abridged version of Yamanin's book of records is extracted from "Devaduta Sutta" Pali and given here. The 5 kinds of persons in the human world, namely the child, the old man, the sick person, the dead person and the prisoner, are called *"Devaduta"*, although they are not really messengers sent out by Yamamin. [deva = of Yamamin + duta = messenger.] Yamamin questions the niraya prisoners while showing him those 5 persons of Devaduta.

Yamamin -   When you were in the human world, have you ever seen a poor baby like that one there, unable to take care of itself, rolling in the pools of urine and stool?

Niraya prisoner - Yes, I have.

Yamamin -   When you grew up and came of age, while looking at the little baby, have you ever thought, "To be an ignorant baby like that one there, I will have to be conceived again. I cannot escape rebirth. From now on, I better watch my mind and live accordingly"? (Yamamin asked very kindly.)

Prisoner -   I was forgetful, never interested to do meritorious deeds.

Yamamin -   Your relatives, parents and teachers did not do those meritorious deeds for you. You yourself have forgotten, and so, as usual for forgetful people, you are bound to take punishments as suit your kammas.

.In this way, the prisoner was asked for the second time, showing an old man; for the third time, showing a sick man; again for the fourth time, showing a dead body; and finally for the fifth time, showing a prisoner. In spite of the five questions, if the niraya prisoner did not remember any meritorious deeds, Yamamin thinks, "While in the human world, had he ever called Yamamin out to take a share in his meritorious deeds?"[226] If something is remembered, Yamamin tells him of the good deeds. Either for being told or remembered by himself, as soon as the prisoner remembers some meritorious deeds done in the previous life he is free and immediately ascends to deva bhumi. In such a situation, refuge in kusala kamma (meritorious deeds) is clearly evident. If Yamamin does not remember, he says nothing. Then the niraya prisoner is taken away and beaten cruelly by the guards.

Sincova Niraya

"*Sincova*" in Pali is transliterated "Theinso" in Myanmar. Prisoners suffer excruciating pains alive repeatedly in all nirayas. In this niraya

226. In consideration of this point, Yamamin is called out to take share of the meritorious deeds being done.

guards cut the prisoners into pieces. They should die as they are cut up. But they do not die for as long as their akusala kammas are in effect, suffering gravely in the hands of the guards until and unless the effects of akusala kmmas are exhausted. The horrible effects of akusala kamma are clearly evident in this niraya.

Kālasutta Niraya

The ruler line drawn and used by carpenters in hewing up logs is called "*kālasutta*" in Pali, or "karlathote" in Myanmar. The beings that fall into that niraya are chased by niraya guards, like the way hunting dogs chase game animals. When the victims tire out and can run no more, guards force them to lie on their backs, and then methodically draw ruler lines on them and cut them up; and again they repeat their action on the reclining positions on both left and right sides; and then on the back; on the front again, and so on in various postures. It is pretty much like the way carpenters hew up a log. But for as long as their akusala kammas are not exhausted, they cannot escape, but live on.

Samghāta Niraya

The niraya where punishment is meted out by way of heavy crushing and pulverization is called "*samghāta niraya*". It has a flaming iron floor, 9 yojanās[227] thick. The prisoners in this niraya are buried to their waists in this ground, like half-buried stumps of palm trunks. A huge iron mountain rolls from east to west, making thunder-like noises, on top of and over the stumps of the prisoners. And one other iron mountain similarly rolls down over them from south to north. And the mountain in the west rolls back down on them. So also the one in the north returns to south. In this way the two mountains roll forward and backward, repeating alternately over and over. The prisoners suffer, but not dying, for as long as the effects of their akusala kamma lasts, their upper bodies popping up after the crush, only to be crushed again, ... popping up and getting crushed, popping up and getting crushed, over and over.

Roruva Niraya

By the Pali word, "*roruva,*" is meant "weeping in extreme sorrow." The flames of that niraya rage in high intensity. The flames forcefully enter and burn the 9 dvāras[228] of the prisoners, making them scream

---

227. A unit of yojanā is a distance of about 12 miles (or 7 miles in some quotes),
228. These are the 9 openings (dvāras) in the body, namely, the 2 eyes, the 2 ears, the 2 nostrils, the mouth, the anus and the urinal tract

incessantly in excruciating pain. Denoting burning with flames, it is also called "*jalaroruva*".

Mahāroruva Niraya

In this niraya, it is not the flames that inflict injuries and pains but smokes that fill the entire world of it. Smokes soak through all prisoners and cook them to complete tenderness. And yet the male and female prisoners do not die; they can only cry out in extreme pain and weakness. It is also called "*dhumaroruva niraya*".

Tāpana Niraya

The word "*tāpana*" means "causing burns". Those who fall into this niraya are impaled and transfixed on large round flaming iron stakes that burn them. And they live on until and unless the effects of their past akusala kammas are exhausted.

Mahā Tāpana

The niraya that is hotter than tāpana niraya is called "*mahā tāpana*" or "*patāpana*". In that niraya, there is a flaming mountain of iron, with impaling stakes erected at its base. The guards forced the prisoners to climb the mountain. On the mountain, as the past kamma has its way, storms arise and blow the prisoners down onto the stakes that caught and pierce them at the pointed tips. They carried on living, the same cycle of suffering repeated over and over. They live on until and unless the effects of their past akusala kammas are exhausted.

Avici Niraya

In avici niraya, there is no break in the expanse of fire with high flames: the flames are spread out without a gap. The prisoners too are tightly packed, like the way custard seeds are packed in the hollow of a bamboo. There is no relief from suffering and no escape either. Thus there is no break in all three categories: the fire, the prisoners and the suffering. And so, this niraya is called "*avici*". [*a* = non + *vici* = gap, break]

No end to niraya dhukkhas

Beyond these 8 major nirayas, there are many other kinds of suffering in such minor niraya as excrement niraya that is one of the 5 ussada nirayas, mentioned previously. There is also a niraya called "*lohākumbhi*" or hot molten-iron-in-cauldron niraya where the four sons of wealthy parents, who yelled out the proverbial "du - sa - na - so"[229] had taken residence - the Tapodā River near Rājagaha flows out from the border between two lohakumbhi nirayas. This shows that there are many minor nirayas contiguous with our human habitat. It is said that to describe and discuss the types of suffering in all the nirayas would not end even if the Buddha told them in all the months and years available. "Oh Bikkhus, it would not be easy to tell to the end all the suffering in the nirayas. The nirayas are the places of suffering beyond description."

My Advice

One who has some thoughts many times over the suffering in the nirayas should not be sorrowful on account of the akusala kammas already done, but take care not to commit any more of them, and make earnest efforts to sow and grow kusala kammas. Once upon a time, a young bhikkhu was learning this Devaduta Sutta, when he asked his teacher, "Sir, please hold on. Kindly give me some kamatthāna instructions," and began to meditate. Very soon, he attained Sotāpana magga and then carried on learning the Sutta. There were countless number of bhikkhus who attained arahanntaship upon meditation at the end of this Devaduta Sutta. All the Buddhas had delivered this Deveduta Sutta.

[Tiricchanāna, peta and asurakāya bhumis have been described briefly in "Ratanagunyi".]

The Death of a Kappa[230]

The principle of anicca says that whatever material mass that has arisen must certainly perish one day. Therefore, this world or *kappa* too is in the domain of anicca and so will not be here forever: one day it will certainly come to an end and die. The causes of this end are threefold: fire, flood waters and storms. There appear two suns around the world that is about to be destroyed by fire. The regular sun arises during day time, and the new sun in the night, so that there is no night. Due to the heat of the new sun, waters in small creeks and rivers dry up. And then there appears the third sun, heating and drying up the large rivers. When the 4th sun appears, the 7 large lakes in the Himalayas dry up.

---

229. These were the initial sounds of the words the 4 men wanted to say each time one of them popped out of the pool of molten metal for only long enough to utter a mono-syllabic sound before sinking down again. They were the four oft-quoted wanton adulterous young men together in their previous life.
230. This and subsequent paragraphs are descriptions of a model. Present tense is used in recounting.

On the appearance of the 5th sun, the oceanic waters dry up. When the 6th sun arises, there is no moisture left on the earth. With the 7th sun in the sky, a monstrous conflagration takes sway, which could burn a hundred thousand earths like this one. After some periods of time, the flames reach and burn the world of Brahmas in their first absorption (jhāna); the Himalayas, Mt Meru[231], the mountains of the universe and all the precious metals, jewels and the giant celestial palaces and mansions become fuels in the great conflagration, not even leaving any remnant ash. Then the destruction of the kappa or the world is complete. [In the cases of destruction of kappa by flood waters and winds, consider how corrosive oceanic waters eat away all matter, and how stormy winds could crush and pulverize every thing in their track.]

When is the Doom's Day?

It is inestimable when the end of a kappa will come. In deed, it is a very, very long time. The life span of human beings on a kappa begins at 10 years. This span increases gradually to *asankhyeya* (time not countable by years). From that span on, it slides back gradually to 10 years. The complete pair of these ups and downs of life spans is known as *anantara kappa* (in-between kappa). It is said that the time for destruction of a kappa *loka*[232] by fire is due at the end of 64 of these anantara kappas. After the destruction is complete, just like the way a house stays un-rebuilt for a while after it has been destroyed by fire, the destroyed state stays put for a time span equivalent to 64 antara kappas before a new kappa begins to appear.

Every One in Brahma Bhumi

During that period of kappa being destroyed and before reformation, all beings have moved to upper Brahma Bhumi. Hearing the prophesy by devas a hundred-thousand years ahead of the doom's day, beings remember and begin to nurture and make kusala kammas grow; they attain jhana, to be "reborn" in Brahma Bhumi, when the end of the world is drawing close. So, all the beings, with the exception of those holding *niyata micchāditthi*[233], have once been in Brahma Bhumi. [Those with niyata micchāditthi moved

---

231. This immense mountain (Myinmo'r in Myanmar) in Buddhist cosmology situates in the centre of the cosmic system, surrounded by four great islands occupying its cardinal points.

232. Kappa loka includes the earth and all the worlds of beings, except the highest Brahma Bhumi

233. Views with fixed destiny, namely views of "no cause, no effect" and "nihilism" of existence...

to one other kappa in existence, if their niraya terms have not yet been exhausted.]

THE BIRTH OF A KAPPA

After the destruction of a kappa, there comes a great kappa-forming rain, first starting with a drizzle. The size of the rain drops grow slowly and gradually to the size of a house and then to that of a mountain, filling all the destroyed places, the level finally reaching the Brahma Bhumi. A great many years pass and the waters recede, drying up in the places of previous Brahma and Deva bhumis, reforming those realms again. Gradually, the water recession reaches the former earth, the realm of man, where the receding of waters stops, forming mountains, hills in high places, rivers and valleys down below them, and flat plains that have a viscous surface (like the cream over milk) that gradually, after some long time, solidifies into rocks and loamy earth.

That earth is two hundred and forty-thousand yojanās thick. The water below it is very cold, apparently in frozen state. The mass of the water is four hundred and eighty thousand yojanas thick, able to support the earth with ease. That mass of water is supported on a mass of atmosphere nine hundred and sixty thousand yojanas thick. Below that atmosphere is an endless space of openness, it is said.

This complete group of air, water, earth, human habitat, deva bhumi and Brahma bhumi is not the only one of its kind, but there are countless others like it. Therefore, we often talk of *ananta cakkāvalā* (endless number of universes), among which a hundred-thousand cakkavalās are destroyed together and reformed together. To mark borders between any two cakkāvalās, a great rocky mountain stands like a huge wall.

Lokantaritta Niraya

Where three cakkāvalās come together, like the way three round trays are placed in contact, there is a free space, free of the three, in which there is no sun or moon light, and so always dark. That free space is called "*lokantaritta niraya*". This is the habitat of petas and asurās[234] who, when they were human beings, had insulted their parents or the holy people - they have now nothing to eat or drink, seeing nothing, clinging to the cakkāvalā walls like bats hanging on trees, groping in the dark. When they meet each other, they fight and try to eat each other, and then losing

---

234. Petas are hungry ghosts; asurās demons and titans.

handholds, fall into the abyss to hit the water below, breaking up into pieces.

Mt Meru[235]

In the middle of the cakkāvalā-kappa system (loka) stands Mt.Meru, a hundred and sixty eight thousand yojanās high. [Since eighty four thousand yojanās of that total lie below oceanic waters, only the upper half is reckoned as its height, and we say, "the eighty four thousand yojanā high Mt. Meru." A river called "Sitā" flows round the great mountain. Outside of River Sitā stands Ugandhhora mountain; its height is half that of Mt Meru above sea level and that much below sea level. Outside of the Ugandhora flows another Sitā. On the other side of the Sitā stands the mountain of Sindhora. In this way, Mt. Meru is circled by 7 sitās and 7 mountains.

Major and Minor Islands

Outside of those mountains lie the great expanse of an ocean, extending right to the walls of the cakkāvalā. There arise major and minor islands in the middle of the ocean. The islands on the East of Mt. Meru is called the East Island, and similarly those in the other cardinal directions, the South Island, the West Island and the North Island respectively.

The Realms of Devas and Brahmas

On Ugandhora, half as high as Mt. Meru, the realm of *Catumahārājā devas* is situated. The sun, the moon and the stars that we see now are quoted in the Buddhist literature as bhumi mansions in the realm of Catumahārājā devas. In the celestial space at the same level as Mt. Meru situates the home of Tāvatimsā devas.

Literature has it that Sudassana, the celestial city of the king of devas is situated on the top of Mt. Meru. , the other five deva bhumis, namely Yāmā, Tusitā, Nimmānarati and Paranimmitavasavatti are situated in higher planes, having no connection with the earth. Similar are the Brahma bhumis. [See Sangaha Tīkā Vithimutta for more details.]

How Mankind Appeared

When human habitat (*manussatta bhumi*), deva bhumi and Brahma bhumi were all reestablished, some of the Brahmas, having lived out their kamma-resultant full life spans, expired. Some of them became Brahmas in the lower Brahma bhumi levels, some others, devas in the 6 deva bhumi levels; the rest, human beings. Those first, primeval human beings had no

235. Myinmo Taung in Myanmar language.

parents. They appeared in visible human forms as the power of past kamma would dictate in the same way devas appear in their realms. They had no sex organs to distinguish man from woman. They could live without food or water. There was no sun or moon or stars. With body lights of their own, they roamed the sky the way they were used to as Brahmas in their previous life.

The First Food

While roaming in the sky in their own radiant lights, they saw on the surface of the earth creamy, milk-like, yellowish substance. Some one with playful hands, thinking, "It looks good. How would it taste?," poked at the material with a finger and tasted it. It tasted so good that the action could not be stopped. Other beings, seeing the scene, followed suit, digging at the "cream", taking fistfuls and eating it with relish. Then there grew in them the heat of desire and passion (*tanhā*), with the result that the radiance from their bodies disappeared. A complete darkness reigned.

The Sun and the Moon

As the first primeval human beings were very afraid of darkness, and in accordance with their past kamma, the mansion of heat and light called "Suriya" (the sun), 50-yojanās wide, signifying courage to them, appeared in the eastern horizon. The sun lights the day, and when it hides behind a mountain, they wished for some more light. In answer to that wish there appeared the 49-yujanā-wide mansion of the moon. [Because the moon appeared to satisfy their wish, it was named "Chanda", later transmuted to "Canda". With the sun and the moon, stars also appeared. The date on which the sun, the moon and the stars began to make their first round in the sky, according to majjimadesa[236] calendars, was the last (waning) day of Tabaumg (March). So, the new moon of the world is Tangoo[237] (April), marked with a notation of "Tangoo, the month the world began".

The First Rice-meal

As they went on eating away the cream of the earth at the whim of *rasa tanhā*[238], the stock of that food went down and so, they ate bedded creamy crust, When those beds were exhausted, they could only find and eat pieces of sweet stalks of the same staff in fissures of the earth's crust, called sweet vines. When those vines disappeared, a kind of fragrant rice without husk appeared. The rice was put in a pot and cooked on a boulder

236. The region in India where the Buddha roamed and taught.
237. Tangoo is normally pronounced Tagoo.
238. Greed and passion (akusala citta) born out of the good taste of the earth-cream

called "Jotipāsāna" that provided heat that died automatically as the rice was cooked.

The First Men and Women

When the earth cream, cream beds and sweet vines were eaten, flesh and fat grew in the body, and only small pieces of waste material remained. These pieces were burnt out by the heat in the stomach. But when the fragrant rice was eaten, all could not be burnt in the stomach, thereby leaving some liquid and solid waste matter un-burnt. The first human beings had no ducts and holes in their system to pass solid or liquid waste out of the body. Now the vāyo dhātu (pneumatic energy) exerts pressure on those liquids and solids. Thus the urinal and stool tracts were formed. *Itthibhāva* rupa (female organs) appeared in those who were women, and *purisabhāva* rupa (male organs) in those who were men, before going to Brahma bhumi when the last kappa met its doom.

The First Marriages

The first men and women became curious about the differences in each other. Looking at each other, passions arose and welled up. Unable to restrain themselves, some people began to copulate. Other wiser people condemned such acts and tried to forbid them but to no avail. They threw stones and staves at the misbehaving couples, who from then on had to hide away from public view, built houses and began to establish the first households. [This ancient tradition of the primeval people has come down to the present-day custom of throwing stones at the house of the couples on their first wedding nights]²³⁹

Thus, human life began, followed by that of animals in a variety of forms as accorded by their past kammas. A new world had thus emerged.

DEVA BHUMI

[The Realm of Heavenly Gods]

How niraya people in the new kappa thus established suffer untold miseries has been shown earlier. Some of the sufferings of animals and petas are known by personal observation or by hearsay. Mankind's dukkhas are known by experience, and so no elaboration here is deemed necessary.

239. Nowadays it is a custom, acted out on the wedding day, of barring the couple in their track with a gold chain by close friends who "demand" to be compensated or else. . . It is a friendly game. (In the villages, it is pay-up a "stone price" or else, get stones in the night).

But most people would like to know something about the good life of the gods. Therefore, compiling facts from literature, I will endeavour to tell a brief account of the way devas live.

Palaces and Mansions of Deva Bhumi

Luxuries and comfort in the realm of devas are a great deal better in every aspect of life than those of human beings. The difference is as much as that between a globule of dew at the tip of a grass blade and the waters of an ocean. The capital city of Tāvatimsā devas is Sudassana, situated at the top of Mt Meru, in an area ten thousand yojanās wide. The Nandana garden on the East of the city is so pleasant that those devas who are very sad about their approaching cuti, forget about it when they are in the garden.

Emerald green, the garden is full of young flower plants in the midst of which roam couples of devas, filling the garden with grace and beauty. Midway between the city and the garden, there lie two lakes by the names of Mahānandā and Culanandā, very beautiful, properly laid out and full of crystal-clear water. To sit on and view them all from, there are bejeweled seats and benches along the shorelines. It is a scene of grandeur. On the South, West and North of the city, the scenes are similar and just as grand.

Male and Female Devas

The mansions devas possess and live in are full of wonders. Devas (males) are young, 20 years old in human terms, and devis (females) younger at 16. There is no one with broken teeth, grey hair, deafness, poor eyesight or wrinkly skin; their original youth and beauty holds out for the whole lifetime. As they live on the highly nutritious devā-ojā[240] only, their bowels do not produce urine, stool or any other waste; devis are free of menstrual discharge[241]. Some other qualities of life: (1) in all the 6 deva bhumis, their enjoyment of sexual pleasure is not different from that of human beings, but they achieve complete joy by mere movement of blood and flesh, without production of any waste; (2) females are no instrument of reproduction; (3) sayadaws are "born" as sons and daughters, in instant appearance either in the parents' laps or in beds. Besides those adult devas, devis and children, there are also male and female devas in servitude, evidently giving rise to a kind that do not own personal homes. Like in

---

240. An exclusive kind of food for devas
241. For questions by Manle Sayadaw and answers by Minkon Ale Tawya Sayadaw on this subject, please see Appendix D

the human world, there is courtship among the youth. Pancasikha, the famed artist deva, was involved in a love story. He was very much in love with Suriyavacchasā, daughter of King Timbaru Deva. In courting the young devi, he played a harp, singing pleasant love songs. The following is one of them:

> I have done some meritorious deeds towards the most venerable arahantas who are not disturbed by vicissitudes of life, unperplexed and righteous, worthy of worship for merits, now by me alone without you as my partner. Oh devi, blessed with goodness and graciousness, may the good deeds of mine thus done be merits, most beneficial, shared between my loved devi and me, your loving deva.[242]

In spite of this passionate love of Pancasikha, Suriyavacchasā Devi was devoted to Sikhanti Deva, son of King Mātali Deva. But King Timbaru, as a matter of paying back much gratitude he owed, married his daughter, Suriyavecchasā, to Pancasikha. Some devis have their own homes, bored and very much disillusioned, having no male partners who would take them in their possession. As quality of mansions and personal looks vary with quality of past kammas, jealousy of the more fortunate is bound to arise.

In each mansion of devas,
There goes on a festival of galas,
Untiringly joyous at all times,
With music and dancing divine;
Affable, lovable and happy,
Carefree are all divine ladies,
Without a slip couples enjoy life,
Like a love
Newly found in all their lives,
It is love from heart truly acquisitive,
The love that is mutually responsive.
[Maghadeva Lankā]

Thus this bhumi is the best of all realms for sensual pleasures and where seekers enjoy them to their utmost satisfaction. Bur for the ariya

---

242. Original Pali: *yam me atthi katam puññam, arahantesu tādisu; tam me sabbangakalayani, tayā saddhim vipaccati.*

devas who have attained anāgāmi magga/phala and arahanta magga/ phala, the place is disgusting; the anāgāmi ariyas move to Brahma bhumi and the aranhantas enter parinibbāna. So, do not expect deva bhumi to be danger-free for those who want to begin practicing meditation there. That dream may only come true for those who had done their utmost as human beings, and for those who had heard the Buddha's teaching during His lifetime. Perfunctory meditation practitioners will have dropped and lost their insignificant bits of dhamma at the entrance gate to the Nandana Garden.

In deva bhumi, it is very difficult not to breach Sabbath. To hold on to good concentration and meditate is far more difficult. On the caressing of devis, sila breaks down. One only has to remember how often kings, such as King Campeya, of naga realm[243] often breached Sabbath, and how kings of devas, as in Vidhura Jataka, had to visit the human realm to take and keep Sabbath. Bodhisattas took premature cuti from the deva realm, because they found no opportunity to practise perfections (paramis) there - they made up their minds for premature cuti. They fulfilled paramis only on earth.

There, however, is a meagre hope for the noble sort in deva bhumi. That hope is signified by Culāmani Ceti and Sudhammā Hall. Culāmani Ceti[244] is a yojana high emerald monolith, inside which the hair and right eyetooth relics of the Bodhisatta are enshrined. Couples of devas and devis with generous hearts (saddhā) and clarity of minds spent most of their very long lives in the vicinity of the ceti (unlike other couples who spend their time in celebrations in the gardens), preparing and offering flowers and other alms, kowtowing and saying noble prayers. There is no doubt that these couples are also trying to cultivate and perform perfections.

Writing about the wonders and grace of Sudhamā Hall would find no end. All buildings of the Hall are decorated, most appropriately and artfully with various kinds of precious stones. Flowers from the coral tree[245] near the hall are carried by a breeze, beautifully spread across the floor of the hall. In the centre of the hall is the dhamma throne at which is erected and hoisted a white umbrella. Starting from the sides of the throne, seats are arranged for all the thirty three kings of the deva realm, beginning with King Sakka and other kings such as Pajāpati, Varuna, Isāna and so on

---

243. Land of dragons, a kind of beings from apāya in a reptilian form with supernatural powers of devas.
244. Cetis in common language is for pagodas.
245. It is *pinle kathit* in Myanmar, a tree bearing clusters of very large, bright, red flowers.

(those who were associates of the young Māgha[246]). Seats for other devas, prominent as well as mediocre, are also organized. [There is one each of this Sudhamma Dhamma Hall in Tāvatimsā and the 4 other higher deva realms.]

At the signal from King Sakka, the great "Vijayuttara" conch gives out its sound that spreads throughout the ten thousand yojanās of Sudassana City[247]; it hangs on for a period of 4 human months, it is said. When all devas who come to attend the congregation are inside the hall, it is bright with red radiance from precious stones and pink hues throughout the hall. Sometimes, King Sanakumāra from the Brahma realm came down to deliver dhamma talks. Sometimes, King Sakka talks. Therefore, seeing and kowtowing at the Culamani Ceti and hearing dhamma talks at Sudhamma Congregations give rise to some meagre hope. "Hope" here does not mean the type of hope one holds for magga/phala wisdom. It is only a hope for the maintenance and sustenance of the noble type of mind, and to keep away to a certain extent from the muddy pools of kāmaguna (sensual pleasures).

In the up-coming waning kappa, there is no reason to hold hopes for the bhikkhus and laity to be fully wise. We are now witnessing general foolishness. If the vatta dukkhas (cyclic sufferings) are really abhorred, now is the time to try to work for magga/phala and Nibbāna at any cost. Those, who hope to await from the deva bhumi the coming of Arinmetteyya Buddha and hear his dhamma to attain magga/phala ñāna, must remember to keep and not to lose the hold on whatever dhamma one may have at the entrance gate of the Nandavana Garden. Those, who forget this and aim deeply to enjoy life to their heart's content in the deva bhumi, will miss the Arinmetteyya Buddha, being too busy enjoying pleasures of life to the extreme. So, excepting those who, with their own capabilities in the practice of dhamma, are future saviours, Aggasāvakas and Mahāsāvakas, all other people should begin now to work very hard towards that end.

---

246. Young Māga and his 33 friends who, in human existence previously, had done great voluntary services such as building and maintaining roads, brid0ges and public rest houses.

247. It is only a few hours in the Tāvatimsā-deva standard of time.

"Facing danger, with inner sincerity,
Everyone should work diligently with humility;
But then, for this reason and that,
Vision of the future is that
There is none too clever
And so,
Meditation is thrown away so clear.

The Forgetful King Sakka

Once in the lifetime of our Lord Buddha, Sakka, the Sotāpana[248] king of Tāvatimsā, intending to view a grand garden gala of festivities, came out with a royal entourage, riding the elephant named Eravana. At the gate of the garden, a thought came across his mind to ask Lord Buddha a certain question: how would an arahanta have conducted his life to free himself completely from all sensual desires and enter Nibbāna?

Because the thought could be lost once he got into the garden, he took off invisible from the elephant, with a second thought, "I will go and see the Lord now," and went straight to the Buddha. The elephant was left standing at the gate. So also was the whole entourage.

He got in audience with the Buddha who was then in temporary residence at the Pubbārammana monastery. With the garden festivities in the back of his mind, he asked, "Kindly give me a brief discourse on how arahantas have conducted their living to free themselves completely from all sensual desires and enter Nibbāna? The Lord gave a short sermon in accord with his request:

"King Sakka, the bhikkhu who is to become an arahanta listens to dhamma talks as 'all the tenets of dhamma should not be taken to heart as me, my own, and my knowledge, attaching himself to them'. The bhikkhu exerts diligent efforts to know all the five aspects of khandā (or nāma and rupa formations). And then he knows they are nothing but dukkha. And then he keeps watch of every sensation or interest, and recognizes that as anicca, etc.[249], repeating the watching over and over. Watching so a great many times over and over, clinging is eliminated, leading finally to arahantaship, attaining Nibbāna that has exhausted all attachments and desires, completely free from all defilements." [This is only a brief translation.]

---

248. Sotapana is the first magga/phala ñāna, often referred to as Stream Winner.
249. That is Sayadawgyi's way of writing the three characteristics (lakkhanas) of anicca, dukkha and anatta.

King Sakka was very much satisfied and delighted with the brief answer so given, and saying "sādhu, sādhu" went back to Tāvatimsā.

Ashin Moggalāna who was staying in the room on the left side of the audience hall heard the calling of sādhu. He thought, "Did that Sakka say sādhu because he really knew the teaching, or did he say that without any understanding?" So, to find out the truth, he followed Sakka to Tāvatimsā soon after the latter left.

The sotāpana Sakka, after hearing dhamma from the Buddha, was enjoying the music and dancing in the garden, when he saw Ashin Moggalāna approaching. Like the monastery-donor who was enjoying a dance show when he saw the abbot, feeling much embarrassed, Sakka welcomed the Ashin, saying pleasant words of greetings.

As they met, Ashin Moggalāna said, "How was the *tanhāsankhaya vimutti* dhamma that Lord Buddha talked to you about? Kindly, let us hear the teaching?" The king tried to recall, but was unable to. He could not recall any thing at all, in spite of thinking again and again for some time. So, hoping to escape from shame, he told the Ashin that, although he had carefully committed the teaching to memory, he had now totally forgotten as he had been too busy with the affairs of the state. [Quoted from Mulapannāsa, Cula Tanhāsankhaya Sutta]

Food for Thought

If we think in line with this teaching, we can understand how sensual pleasures of deva bhumi can allure us, making our minds cloudy so as to forget any dhamma. That is true. King Sakka was, in his original nature, alert and sharp, and quick to any situation. He was already a sotāpana then. The dhamma he had heard was what he wanted to know, and was given him in brief. The time gap between hearing of the dhamma and being asked about it by Ashin Moggalāna was only a few minutes. But then, he had forgotten the dhamma totally because of the enchantment of the garden party.

1. Considering this story, we should think deeply of its import. Those of us who can admit ourselves to be "virtuous and upright", if we are what we think we are, are likely to be destined well (sugati) hereafter. But the destinations are only human and deva. We cannot be Brahmas as we have not attained any jhāna. We cannot enter Nibbāna as we are not arahantas. If ever we are in one of the heavenly deva bhumis,

considering how King Sakka had forgotten, shouldn't there be a concern for us about forgetting whatever dhamma we might have learned?

2. If one's time is up for cuti at the moment when one is forgetful of dhamma and happy with the luxurious habits of devas, i.e. happy with the life of a common anybody (puthujana), then one would be clinging to those pleasures, sad, wan and drawn from exhaustion as cuti approaches. The four bhumis of apāya are not very far away for one who dies under such circumstances. Once upon a time, five hundred devis were picking flowers and singing on trees in a garden, when suddenly cuti came and took them to avici niraya.

3. There are also concerns as to the next human life. There are four factors that influence the value of life in terms of moral uprightness: The person will have to be born (1) in the Buddha Sāsanā, (2) in the community most members of which, if not all, are morally upright, (3) to parents and teachers who are morally upright, (4) in a family reasonably well off. Only if these factors are satisfied, human life is worth living.

4. Concerning the Buddha Sāsanā, nowadays it is not an easy matter to seek out virtuous and morally upright people; they are far too few, if any. Lure of sensual pleasures is rampant. Falsehoods, shows of status, rivalries and jealousies, briberies and corruptions are the prevailing winds. Laity also approach and pay respects to influential monks rather than those with sila, samādhi and paññā[250], and try to curry favour with high offices, also spreading glorious news to enhance influence of their devoted monks and teachers. "Holes in the ridge of the roof lets in rainwater" that has wetted those in the service of the Sāsanā.

5. The sons and daughters of those who called themselves devotees of the Sāsanā are gradually losing monastic learning, and now in some monasteries there remain no students. Without monastic students, there can be no resident novices (sāmaneras). Without novices, there can be no scholar monks who have first learned the literature as novices. In a not too distant future, there will remain in the villages *taw'htwet* monks[251] who will

---

250. Moral uprightness, steadiness of character and wisdom, respectively

251. These are the monks with very little learning, joining the Order very late in their lives, having left their households for various reasons.

be taking naps here and there in the monasteries and on the embankments of ponds around them.

6. Concerning donors of the four paccayas[252], the education their children are receiving is likely to be good for living a lifetime. But does that education include any learning to understand kamma and its effects, even leaving out the wisdom of magga-phala-ñāna and Nibbāna? If so, would they believe in such things as deva and Brahma bhumis? If not, would they believe in niraya and peta bhumis? Would such non-believers remember to offer alms food to the Sanghā, even leaving out donating the four essentials (paccayas)?

7. Besides, when those school-going children grow up to adulthood, they would not inherit much from their parents like in earlier times. Most of their parents now can only barely cope with costs of their education. Their utilities, cosmetics and ostentations are already too many. Even when they finish schooling or any higher education, they must work rather very hard (or else, earn more, illegitimately) so as to make ends meet in feeding and bringing up a family. How could material support be found for the Sāsanā under such difficult circumstances?

8. Thinking in one other way, monks who are servants of the Sāsanā are responsible for giving the children some proper religious as well as basic vocational training. With thorough preparation, that could be done. But then, with some exceptions, many monasteries have not begun to think in that direction. Besides, they are not trying, being lax in the conduct of their life, to draw the attention of modern population; most of them are not in public esteem. If that were so, would those modern educated people give the Sāsanā some support? Thoughts on those problems lead one to the vision of the Sāsanā drawing closer to a waning stage.

9. In the life after here, most people can hardly be morally righteous. This calls for an explanation. The age of morally righteous people is signified by general practice of the three virtues, namely mettā, karunā and muditā. Now, it is seen that there is little genuine mettā and little sincere wish of one to see another person prosper. Without mettā, there can be

252. The 4 paccayas are food, robes, dwelling and medicine for the Sanghā.

no compassion (karunā) toward the poor lot, and no gladness (muditā) to see prosperity of the more fortunate. What is happening now is that one is jealous (issā) of another person in good fortune; that one is apprehensive (micchariya) of another person's rise in fortune; that one in high position is proud (māna) of one's status while one other in lower position is also proud with a thinking of "what do I care?" about another more fortunate person.

10. Apart from all that, there are so many attractive household and personal commodities, and so many objects of sensuous pleasure on the increase day by day that greed, like the fire that runs after the fuel, in the consciousness continuum jumps up in leaps and bounds. When the greed is not satisfied, robberies, murders and wars are born out of the uncontrollable greed. In the midst of tempting material surroundings, virtuous men are getting fewer and fewer in number. In that general view, is it not reasonable to assume that the future will be worse than ever?

11. As there will be very few morally righteous people in the future, there will be no virtuous parents and teachers. Without dependable parents and teachers, it is not easy for one amongst bad people to be a morally right person. So, just as it is difficult to avoid enchanting pleasures in the land of the devas, so also it is very difficult for one, in the midst of prevailing corruptions, to be reborn as a human being after this life.

12. Here I would like to point out something that comes across my mind. In January, 1957, I traveled to Rangoon for consecration of a *sima*[253]. I was early at Rangoon Railway Station on the day I was to return. I was talking to the bhikkhu who was seeing me off, with my back to the rail line where the coaches were to be parked for embarkation. When the coaches came in, I heard some commotion among the travelers. I turned and saw people jostling against each other, trying to get into seats as a matter of daily routine.

13. I thought then that these people were on a journey that would take almost 36 hours[254]. They were gravely concerned about discomfort on the way if they could get no proper seats. Some

253. An Ordination Hall

254. In those days trains ran in day light with an overnight stop at Toungoo or Tharzi. Tickets were not allotted with seat numbers...

tried to get reserved seats. Apart from that, they had to look for reliable companions on the train. Otherwise, they were going to be gravely distressed. Security seemed to be zero if one's next-seat neighbour was a dishonest sort.

14. Why did these people, who now were trying to get ahead of every body to get proper seats on the train, not try to meet good company and proper accommodations in the next life and thereafter right up to Nibbāna? If one slips with a wrong step, and goes to one of the 4 apāya bhumis, one would not only suffer for a lifetime once, but also akusala kammas would multiply in all the existences down the line. Even if the next life is human, one would be handicapped in the intellect and very poor, always at the bottom of the social strata. In spite of all those possibilities, they did not try to get proper seats in the next life, i.e. not as hard as they were trying to get good seats on the train now. This was sheer bungling, without a vision for the future, so utterly stupid. This thought was conveyed to the bhikkhu who was seeing me off.

15. Considering the points given above, readers should think deeply and try to gain some wisdom. Those fulfilling higher paramis should take care to be involved in as little akusala kamma as possible and try very hard to be steadfast in the noble practice. Such hard work would result in a virtuous deva in the heavenly realm, and an extraordinarily righteous man if born in the human world. Such extraordinary human being will be able to fulfill paramis to maturity, like the way the by-gone Bhodhisattas had fulfilled their paramis.

THE GOOD LIFE OF A BRAHMA

To be one in the realm of Brahmas, one puts up great efforts in the practice of jhāna, living alone at peaceful and quiet places, away from all sensuous, worldly life and human habitat. Brahmas in their realm are similarly absorbed in jhāna, very quiet and restful. There are no husband and wife and no offspring. All Brahmas are males in form, but with neither male nor female parts. So, they are nothing to do with sensuous pleasures. Because the wrongfulness of all these kāmagunas (sensual pleasures) were seen to their depths when jhāna was pracrised as human beings, the mental attitude here is absolutely pure, and completely devoid of any sensuous desire.

In the mansions much grander than those in the deva realm, Brahmas live in absolute quietness and peace like the most virtuous human yogis, some in mettā kammatthāna, and the others absorbed in jhāna. But then, like in the human realm, Brahmas have their own classes also. Some Brahmas are kings while others take lesser official positions. Still others are the king's servants and companions. All the Brahmas of lower echelons cannot see the king unless shown on purpose.

Asaññasatta Brahmas (Unconscious Beings)

It is citta viññāna (knowing) and saññā cetasika (cognition) that make man to want to see, hear, smell, eat, meet, touch and think. The man or woman who, after attaining jhāna, reflects on that and comes to think, "If citta and saññā were not there, it would be very peaceful," consequently finding faults with the mind and its cognitive process. Thus the man in jhāna becomes so sick and tired of the mind and the saññā that he begins to concentrate his mental powers on the idea that "the mind is hateful, the mind is hateful . . . ." Then there appears a kammatthāna practice known as *"saññāvirāga bhāvanā"*. When such people die in that state of the mind, they appear in the *asaññatta Brahma bhumi* where they would live for 500 kappas, knowing nothing of whatever is happening. Motionless, like golden statues, some are standing, others sitting and still others reclining.

Arupa Brahmas (Beings without Material Bodies)

The people who would become these Brahmas think, after attaining the regular jhāna[255], "Only on account of rupa, everything is in chaos and dukkha. If it were only the citta viññāna alone, life would be in blissful happiness," thus finding faults with rupa., ushering in the kammathāna practice called *"rupavirāga bhāvanā"*, founded on the view of horror for rupa. When that kind of person passes away, he becomes a Brahma in open space called arupa bhumi, where he would live with citta viññāna but without any physical body for a great many kappas. This viññāna continuum is called *arupa Brahma*. [It would be difficult for people in other faiths to believe in these 2 types of Brahma.]

---

255. This would mean the first to the 4th (or the 5th) normal jhāna.

From Brahma Bhumi to a Piggery

Some of those who reach the realm of Brahma are ariyas (if some magga-phala has been attained) - they ascend in ñāna in regular stages to become arahantas and then enter Nibbāna, never reverting back to the lower sensuous worlds. If they are not ariyas (holiness), when their jhāna powers are exhausted, they take patisandhi (conception) and are reborn in the sensuous worlds such as deva and human realms. But, due to the powers of kusala kamma before the attainment of any jhāna, they do not suddenly go lower down; they become dvihetuka and tihetuka persons (man or deva). From then on, they may slide down, as dictated by former kamma, to the apāya bhumis, the worlds of niraya prisoners, petas and tiricchāna (animals).

What it all means is that those who are still puthujana (common anybody), although they may now be Brahmas, can be conceived and reborn in the apāya bhumi such as tiricchāna. So, in spite of having been a "shining Brahma, bright with own radiance," one may one day be reborn a pig "eating noisily from a manger". To be a puthujāna is very abhorrent and horrible. Even a Brahma in *"bhavagga"* (zenith), the highest level of all bhumis, may come down to the lowly worlds (duggati). Just as the rocket shot to the highest attainable point in the sky must come down as its thrust is exhausted, so also Brahmas, when the power of their jhāna is exhausted, must come down to lower bhumis. [bhava-agga (bhavagga) = highest life. *"Nevasaññā nāsaññā yatana"* bhumi is called bhavagga.]

The power of kusala kamma, as opportunity may allow, raises beings to deva or Brahma bhumi, living in grand mansions with own radiance. In spite of the fact that they may live for a great many kappas, enjoying the life of the noblest Brahmas in their highest realm as if lasting forever, but for being puthujāna, once the power of their kusala kamma is exhausted, they do fall to the original lowly bhumis they belong to.[256]

[This ends all there is to know about bhumis]

---

256 This last paragraph is a brief translation of original Pali that runs:*ukhittā puññatejena, kāmarupagatim gatā;bhavaggaantimpi sampattā, puna āuanti dukkatim.*

CHAPTER TWELVE

[ON NIBBĀNA]

Nibbāna in its exhaustive details could only be treated in a huge treatise so that the author may have done justice to his duty. In this book, however, such an opportunity is hardly practicable. I neglected this topic in my earlier books as I had thought that writing not at all is better than writing briefly here and there, rendering it ineffectual. But then in the book printed in 1320[257], I have included the section on *Upasamānussati*[258] excerpted from *Sangaha Tikā Pali*[259] so as to provide some useful knowledge.

Upasamānussati (Absorption in Nibbāna)

Being aware of and watching over and over, the bliss of the serene Nibbāna is called *upasamānussati*. Nibbāna is often described variously in personal fancies as "extraordinary qualities of rupa and nāma "[260]; also "there is inside the body something lasting forever, like the indestructible *amate*[261], imperishable and permanent. When rupa and nāma entities are no more, there remains only that amate. And the existence in such a state of the *amate* is Nibbāna." and also "since there are no rupa and nāma, there is no feeling and so how can there be happiness?" Just as one can know very well about an object in mind only if one has seen that object inside-out, so also only the ariya people know about Nibbāna as they have gained the knowledge of Nibbāna by personal experience. It is impossible for puthujana persons to get at the truth about the profound meaning and significance of Nibbāna. By referring to Pali literature, however, I will attempt to write and explain the subject as far as I can possibly see in its profoundness.

"Nibbāna" is a paramattha entity separate from the other three, namely citta, cetasika and rupa. Since it has no connection with rupa-nāma

---

257. 1958 CE
258. Recollections of the Peace of Nibbāna
259. Expanded Explanation of the Book of Abridged Abhdhamma in the Pali language
260. *"Rupa visesa, nāma visesa"*
261. (M) A derivative of Pali *Amata*: Deathlessness, also a never-perishing hard stone

formations, it cannot be some special aspects of rupa or nāma. Out of the two aspects of dhamma, namely *ijjhatta* and *bahiddha*[262], it is bahiddha dhamma (entity outside of body) as it is included in Mātikā Pāda called "Bahiddhādhammo"[263]. Nibbāna cannot be extant inside the body like the *amate* element. It is also not capable of feeling anything the way human and other beings do. Since it does not take sights, sounds, etc. for sensual perceptions and so, there is no sensuality-related happiness (*vedayita sukha*), but only the bliss of serenity (*santi sukha*[264]) in Nibbāna.

This calls for further explanation. As sensations called vedayita sukha are exhaustible after consumption, they need to be set up anew for further enjoyment. The pleasures so gained are hardly worth the troubles in setting them up afresh. There is no contentment in consuming the sukha so gained by way of so much dukkha, thus making more attempts to gain access to fresh excitements and for further consumption. This is enjoyment of sensuous pleasures more than fairness would allow, thus resulting in indebtedness and so, it will have to be paid back with interest in the villages of apāya. It really is something to be sorry about. Santi sukha, on the other hand, being not mixed up with this kind of sensations, is serenity and peace, free from all rupa-nāma formations. To make it clearer, let us consider the case of the son of a rich man. This young man led a life of all sensual pleasures. One day he was soundly asleep. When his servants. after preparation of all worldly delights for him, woke him up, he would scold them for "spoiling his sleep". While asleep, he had no object of attention. He had enjoyed the peaceful sleep better than any other delight of life. That non-sensual sukha of sleep is appreciated and praised as "wonderful sleep". So, it could better be guessed how holy and wonderful it would be to experience santi sukha, the real peace and happiness, free of all rupa-nāma agitations.

Anāgāmis and arahantas consider rupa-nāma khandhā as heavy burden and so, they enter and stay in holy-men's absorption (*nirodha samāpatti*[265]) to keep as far away as possible from rupa-nāma khandhā. In that samāpatti there is no sensation. The nāma elements such as citta and cetasika, and some rupas do not appear anew in the state of nirodha (nothingness). Such a state of freedom from rupa-nāma formations is a great happiness (sukha) for those ariyas, and so, they very often take to and stay in nirodha

---

262. Inside (ijjhatta)and outside (bahiddha) of body
263. "Entities outside of body"
264. The former sukha (happiness) is subjective whereas the latter is not subject to change.
265. Nirodha samāpatti is temporary suspension of all consciousness and mental activity.

samāpatti. Apart from that, considering the cases of *asaññasatta* and *arupa Brahmas*, the idea of peace and tranquility is quite evident: asaññasatta Brahmas have no nāma processes (consciousness) and so no feeling; for about 500 kappas they have no consciousness whatsoever.

Arupa Brahmas have no rupa (physical body) and so, peace reigns. The nāma element is only slightly discernable in the consciousness continuum of arupa Brahmas of the highest plane of existence. Arahantas have only 12 cittas[266], namely *manodvārāvejjana* 1, *mahākiriyā* 8, *nevasaññāyatana vipakka* 1, *kiriyā* 1 and *arahanta phala citta* 1, together with co-nascent cetasikas. The 12 cittas can occur only one at a time. If one citta element does not appear, all rupa-nāma formations disappear altogether. Then, the Nibbāna dhātu called Santisukha is evident to the arahanta without a doubt.

Santisukha Nibbāna dhātu is not an entity common to some communal domain. It is individualistic, separate and independent. Therefore, the venerable arahantas keep and stay in phala samāpatti while they still have their individual bodies. It is said that while absorbed in phala samāpatti, having and keeping Nibbāna in their mind's sight, they are absolutely happy indeed. Many theras and theris[267] joyfully declared utter disregard for body-kāyas when about to enter Nibbāna, and then left them with absolute zest, putting us, the common puthujana people, to shame for loving and clinging at all times to these rupa-nāma khandhas.

I the ignorant puthujanas, take pleasant sights, sounds, etc. as pleasures of life, the good things to cling to. But in Nibbāna, the Noble Entity ariyas so adore and desire, all rupa-nāma khandhas are no more: For them khandha has gone extinct. The ignorant puthujana people, however, condemn Nibbāna as dukkha, for lack of sensations and feelings.[268]

Venerable ariya bhikkhus, the holy people, have seen with the eye of their experiential wisdom the extinction in totality of rupa and nāma formations distinctly in person (while alive), and the realization of the true happiness in Nibbāna dhātu. The Ariyas see in person this Nibbāna dhātu while the ignorant puthujanas and the whole Avijja[269]-covered satta-loka cannot see it. So the two types are, in fact, like two men running back

266. 12 out of a total of 89 cittas.; see Chapter on Citta; details have been neglected for brevity.
267. Theras = Ariya bikkhus (men); Theris = Ariya bikkhunis (ladies)
268. This paragraph is a translation of Pali verse: *sadevakassa lokasa, ete wo sukhasampatam; yattha ce te nirujjhanti, tam tesam dukkhasampatam.*
269. Avijja is ignorance of The Four Noble Truths, namely Dukkha Saccā, Samudaya Saccā, Noridha Saccā and Magga Saccā. (Definitions are shown elsewhere - see also the Glossary of Pali terms)

to back, always facing in opposite directions.[270] [Salāyatanam Samyugtta, Devadaha Vagga]

Is it difficult to be a Sotapana?

Translation of Pali[271] - One who observes the five precepts, and believes in true experiential wisdom and in the 9 Attributes of the Buddha[272], the 6 Attributes of Dhamma and the 9 Attributes of Sangha, can come to a decision as to have truly become a Sotāpana.

Not difficult to be a Sotapana

As we look into this dhamma mirror, the two factors involved in becoming a Sotāpana are to revere the properties of the Buddha, Dhamma and Sangha, and for lay people, to observe the five precepts to their purity. Lady Visākhā, the Buddha's monastery-donor, was thus a sotapana at the age of seven when she first saw the Buddha. Asandhimittā Devi, queen of Emperor Dhammāsoka, together with her seven hundred companions, became Sotapana when she heard a Crane, said to sound somewhat like the voice of the Buddha, as she felt deep reverence for the Buddha she had never seen. For those lay people who are naturally adept and keep the five precepts, there should be no difficulty to be a Sotāpana.

> Maxim - Just like looking daily into a mirror,
> To prepare oneself to look proper,
> So also into the mirror of dhamma one looks,
> Sees, keeps precepts and character to be good,
> Revere the Buddha, Dhamma and Sangha,
> The properties in true respect of the ariyas;
> Then with joy
> One would be saved from apāya,
> As shown in the mirror of dhamma.

The purpose of kammatthāna

When we come to know that we go round in the samsāra with various kinds of dukkha due to avijjā and tanhā, we try to find a method capable

---

270. This paragraph is a translation of Pali verse: *sukham ditthamariyebi, sakkāyassa nirodhanam; paccanika midam hoti, sabbalokena passatam:*

271. The Pali Verse: *tsamatihā nanda dhammādāsamnāma dhammapariyāyam desessāmi, "yena sammannāto ariya sāvako ākankhamāno attanāva attānam byākareya, khinanirayomhi khina tiricchānayoni khinapetti vusayo khinapāyaduggati vinipāto, sotāpanno hama samiavinipāta dhammo niyato sambodhiparāyanoti.* (Mahāvaggasamyutta Pāli - p. 311)

272. For the Attributes of the Buddha, Dhamma and Sangha, see in Appendix C.

of ending them. That method is only made known on the appearance of a Buddha who discovered and showed it to the world. Just as there are many ports to get to an ocean, so also there are many ports of call called kammatthāna to get across the ocean of the Samsāra to the shores of Nibbāna on the other side of it. Only if practice in that kammatthāna results in gradual reduction of avijjā and tanhā, it is a correct method. If the result would not be so, then it is not a correct method. Or else, the practitioner should have little or no wish to reduce avijjā and tanhā. If the kammatthāna method is correct and one genuinely wishes to make the end of avijjā and tanhā, then that kammatthāna method would make avijjā and tanhā less and less, and finally exhausted. So this point is also to be noted as a dhamma mirror to see if tanhā gets less and less as kammatthāna practice is carried on.

Nibbāna and Parinibbāna

3 types of Parinibbāna

Nibbāna and Parinibbāna are the same in principle. Parinibbāna is of 3 types. One is dissolution (peace with freedom) of all defilements (kilesā) and so it is called *Kilesaparinibbāna*. The second type is *Khandhaparinibbāna* by virtue of the dissolution of rupa khandha (physical body). The third is *Dhātuparinibbāna* by virtue of the dissolution of all dhātu (material) relics.

Kilesa Parinibbāna

Defilements (kilesā) in all beings, such as lobha, dosa and moha are the source of burning heat in their minds. The flames of tanhā, rāga and lobha are the cause for youngsters to disregard counsel of parents and teachers and carry on with what they might. Because of extreme dosa (anger) due to unfulfilled lobha (greed), there are people who try to commit suicide. These examples show how hot the heats of lobha and dosa are. The reason why these lobha and dosa heats consume people is moha (ignorance of moral rights) that hides true causes and effects. For example, a child, not knowing it is hot, wants to touch a fire (some would touch it). When the Buddha attained arahanta magga-phala, all these fires, the defilements (kilesā), were completely extinguished. So, the Buddha had said, "The Kilesaparinibbāna of the Buddha has occurred at the Mahābodhi Pallanka (seat)." [Ñānavibanga atthakathā (page 413)]

Khandha Parinibbāna

This body-kāya, a restless lump of heat, is a combined effect of rupa and nāma. The eleven kinds of fires[273] such as *jāti* (birth), *jarā* (age), *marana* (death), shown earlier, are burning this body, in one way after another. As quoted from Dhammacakka Pali, dukkhas resulting from parting with a loved one, having to associate with a hateful one, and non-fulfillment of one's wishes are all burning fires inside. So, the bodies of all beings are burning with fires of these dukkhas.

Even the body of Lord Buddha did not escape the burns from these fires. The Lord was weak since the time He was struck with the debilitating diarrhea that made Him rest too often in traveling on foot a distance of 3 gāvuttas[274], needing to drink some water often, very gravely tired due to the body heat. The Buddha rose from the fourth jhāna, after repeated absorption time and again, and entered Parinibbāna with the sub-conscious (bhavanga-citta) that is similar in kind to the consciousness-continuum at the time of conception (the first mahāvipāka-citta[275]). This Parinibbāna was of the kind whereby the flaming rupa-nāma khandha was extinguished to a state of peace and tranquility that is called Khandha Parinibbāna.

[*"khandha -prinibbānam kusinārāyam* = Khandha Parinibbāna had occurred at Kusināra," Ñānavibhanga atthakathā - page 413]

Parable of a fire that dies

With an aim to explain this Parinibbāna, Lord Buddha had said in Ratana Sutta thus: "*nibbāntidhirā yathayam padipo* = Buddhas, paccekabudhas and arahantas in their ultimate wisdom passed away in peace with cessation of cuti citta, the last viññāna. It is, for instance, like the flame that dies when the fuel oil is completely consumed." In Mahāparinibbāna Sutta (page 129): "*pajjotassava nibbānam vimokkho ceta so ahu* = the way Parinibbāna cuti citta is liberated is like the way a fire dies," said Ahshin Anuruddhā,

Dhātu Parinibbāna

When all the dhātu (material) relics of the Buddha are gathered and collected into a reunited dhātu-body, it would burn automatically, entering into Dhātu Parinibbāna. It is prophesied that when the Buddha Mission comes near its end, that is when there is almost no one worshipping the Buddha, the dhātu relics that are now spread in places very widely apart

---

273. For a full list of the 11 kinds of fire, please see Appendix F,
274. A gāvutta (a quarter of a yojana) is about 3 miles
275. Subconscious mind, natural and automatic, to begin kamma-resultant life

would gather at the foot of the Mahābodhi Tree to form into a lump like that of gold, radiating the Buddha's Rays of Light.

When devas and Brahmas see the Buddha Rays, they would come down and gather at the foot of the Bodhi Tree to watch the golden lump of the relics burn. Then they would lament, sorrowfully saying, "Now, Lord Buddha enters Parinibbāna. Today, Lord Buddha has entered into Parinibbāna." Saying so again and again, they would weep. Those devas and Brahmas who are sagadāgāmis, anāgāmis and arahantas would bear the weight of heavy bereavement by observing the Law of Impermanence as "whatever that comes into being must perish."

> Verse - Buddha relics were left for worship,
> At sites wide apart in multiple bits;
> But at the time when the Mission dips
> Down to almost no one to worship,
> And the Mission is lost to oblivion,
> The relics return
> And gather at the Bodhi Banyan,
> Forming a lump like gold bullion;
> It emits the six rays of the Buddha
> To make notice the Brahmas-devas
> Who come down, weep and meditate,
> Lamenting with tired mental state,
> And mark the end of the Sāsanā,
> Which is known as Dhātu Parinibbāna.

The one kind of Nibbāna

The Buddha had urged, "Oh monks, wish for the Nibbāna that is free from all harms. For the purpose of Nibbāna, carry out works of charity (*dāna*), observe moral discipline (*sila*), and keep up insight meditation (*bhāvanā*)." The two kinds of Parinibbāna, namely Kilesa Parinibbāna and Khandha Parinibbāna that all arahantas can attain to are not yet the type of Nibbāna that the Buddha had thus urged.

The two kinds of Nibbānas as already shown are not the *asankhatadhātu*[276] Nibbāna that is desired and prayed for by the multitude as "the imperishable Nibbāna, free from all dukkhas, and attainable in the shortest possible time".

---

276. The entity that is unformed, unoriginated and unconditioned, beyond all becoming and conditionality

The two kinds of Nibbāna cited above are not the type of Nibbāna that makes the Buddha say, "My mind is very clear upon contemplation of entering into *amata*[277] Nibbāna before daybreak just as all other Buddhas before me had done."

The two kinds of Nibbāna cited are not the kind of *santisukha amata* - Mahā Nibbāna in the way the Lord had intended to mean, according to Ashin Anuruddhā when he said, *"Anejo santimārubba, yam kāla makarimuni* = having been liberated from clinging to, and never would again be disturbed by, the five objects of sensual pleasures, Lord Buddha, the real *Muni*[278], has now come to the time of passing away with the purpose of entering Nibbāna that is truly peaceful, being free from all dukkhas."

The two kinds of Nibbāna cited are not the type of Nibbāna defined in the book of Abhidhammattha Sangaha as "Nibbāna is the object of *magga-phala ñāna*"[279]; or the type defined in Dhammapada Atthakathā, Sukha Vagga Ekapāsana Vatthu as "Nibbāna is the holiest sukha"[280]; or the type defined in Dhamma Sangani, Rupa kanta, Uddesa as *"asankhata dhātu* (immutable element)[281].

The two kinds of Nibbāna cited are not the type of Nibbāna sighted once and attained as a result of Sotāpatti magga ñāna that is part of the nirodha sacca of the 4 Noble Truths. young Visākhā of Sāvutthi gained this Sotāpatti ñāna at the age of seven, on the foundation of secure observation of the five precepts with freedom from wrong views and doubts about the Buddha, Dhamma and Sangha.

Therefore, now that causal kammas have been cut out, not only the Buddha, but also all arahantas are called *"Asankhatadhātu"*[282], I will write, in devotion and veneration, on Nibbāna that is often the object of absorption these Ariyas observe and dwell in before Parinibbāna, the samāpatti (absorption) that carries on as the absolute Entity, real and immutable, after entering Parinibbāna, the Entity we should all wish and pray for as the Buddha had urged us to do.

277. *amata* = immutable and noble
278. *Muni* = Holy Man, the holiest being the Buddha
279. *"Nibbānam pana lokuttara sankhātam catu magga ñānena sacchikātabbam, maggaphalana marammunubhutam vānasankhātāya tanhāya nikkhantattā nibbānanti pavuccati"*
280. *"Nibbānam paramam sukham"*
281. *"Asankhatā sa dhātu"*
282. Asankhatadhātu is the absolute Entity that is "Unformed, Unoriginated, Uncondi-tioned", the Beyond of all becoming and conditionality. It is real and immutable. It is Nibbāna.

Lakkhana, Rasa and Paccupatthāna[283] of Nibbāna
That people pray for

Explanation by ancient scholars

The elements of paramattha dhamma, namely citta, cetasika, rupa and Nibbāna, with the exception of rupa, are the kinds of dhamma that cannot be seen with the eye. Although they cannot be seen, generations of wise elders, the commentary writers, have explained them[284] so as to make them clear and discernable to the mind's eye[285] by showing, in one way or another, their characteristics (*lakkhana*), functional qualities (*kicca rasa*), or prepared qualities (*sampatti rasa*); or, objects in contemplation as may appear in the consciousness of yogis in meditation or other wise people; or, immediate conditionality (*padathāna*). Nibbāna must also be explained by way of *lakkhana*, *rasa* and *paccupathāna*. But before doing so, I will show the distance between the Nibbāna that is peaceful and tranquil (*santi lakkhana*) (on one side) and the rupa-nāma formations that bear the signs of commotion and disquiet (on the other side of the samsāric ocean).

Sankhata dhātu (Elements subject to change)

Rupa and nāma elements have been shown earlier (in "The Last Ten Months of Lord Buddha"). These elements are *sankhata dhātus* (changeable elements) subject to avijjā, tanhā, kamma, etc. When an element appears, it disappears immediately after appearance. After disappearance, it appears again. After appearance, it perishes again. This continuum of appearing and disappearing takes place hundreds of hundred-thousand times in the flicker of a moment[286]. (While citta-citasika perishes seventeen times, only once rupa perishes.) Since the rupa-nāma elements perishe that many times in such a short duration of time, how can they be restful, cool and happy? Because of this perennial harassment by appearing-disappearing phenomenon of rupa and nāma, there is dukkha at all times. *Udayabbaya patipitthanatthena dukkho* = Because of the harassment by their appearing-disappearing behaviour, all rup-nāma formations are dukkha only.

---

283. Lakkhana = signs or characteristics; Rasa = characteristic quality; paccuppatthāna = real view resulting from insight (experiential view)
284. In treatises called Atthakathās
285. Insightful mind, intellect, not the fanciful imagination
286. An infinitesimally small fraction of the duration of time made by two fingers making a sharp sound once

Santi Lakkhanā (Characteristic of Peacefulness)

By "lakkhanā" is meant note-worthy sign or mark, a characteristic nature. Just as a man has some nature peculiar to him, a characteristic, so also each of the four paramattha truths has its own characteristic feature, distinctive and unlike others. The characteristic of Nibbāna is santi lakkhanā.

How to recognize santi

Rupa, citta, cetasika and nāma are always popping up and popping out, restless at all times, always on fire, never cooling down. The asankhata dhātu Nibbāna, however, is perfect and so not perishable. As there is no becoming and perishing, and no moving about, it is very peaceful. That peace is the characteristic of Nibbāna, and called "*santi*".

Iccuta rasa (the characteristic of non-changeability)

Rupa-nāma khandhas come into being first and foremost. After coming into being, they perish, leaving no trace of their first becoming. The santi nature of Nibbāna, however, is never lost or destroyed, possessing the characteristic rasa of non-changeability with time from its original status.

Animitta paccupatthāna (the characteristic of seeing the truth)

Whether it is a yogi in meditation or a wise man of thought, when he looks into rupa-nāma processes, he would see through the phenomena in true perspective. Such a vision as this is called "*paccupatthāna*". When looking through the nature of Nibbāna, it is seen in the mind's eye (ñāna) to "have no material body", unlike citta, cetasika and rupa that have material bodies.[287]

Padatthāna (immediate causal factor)

An immediate causal factor is called "*padatthāna*". Citta has cetasika as associates (influencing factors) and rupa as residence (conditioning factor). Unlike them, Nibbāna has no immediate condition or cause. For Nibbāna to arise in the consciousness continuum of the ariyas, however, there are causal factors such as dāna, sila, bhāvanā and many others that are far behind in time and space.

The amata Nibbāna has the characteristic of equanimity and peace. It has the sampatti rasa that does not change from its original status. It is

---

287. This paragraph is a translation from Pali verse, "*Nimitta dhammā sankhārā tehi sanimittā saviggahā viya upatthahanti.*" Atthasālini Lokuttarā Commentary - Anutikā (page 121)

seen in the mind's eye (ñāna) to have no material body. And there is no immediate cause for Nibbāna.[288]

Some Attributes (*Gunas*) of Nibbāna

Khaya guna (Dissolution)

At the instant Nibbāna is sighted with sotāpatti magga[289], some defilements (kilesas) such as rāga, etc. as well as rupa-nāma dhātus of every such person for the seven existences to come are all dissolved. When attaining upper maggas also, more defilements are similarly dissolved. Nibbāna that is santi, therefore, has the attribute of *khaya guna* that means the dissolution of all defilements as well as rupas and nāmas.

Virāga guna (Non-desire)

Sensual desire is called "*rāga*". It arises out of rupa-nāma khandhā, and also designated terms and concepts (paññatti) connected with khandhā. Nibbāna is the end of all rupa-nāma entities, and so it has absolutely no connection with rāga. So the guna-attribute is "*virāga* (no rāga)".

Amata guna (Non-death)

"Death" is the last perishing of rupa-nāma formations for one span of life. The perishing takes place after arising. Going forward to be destroyed or preparing to be dissolved is, in principle, called "getting old or decaying". "Jāti, jarā, marana in Pali, or birth (arising), growth (growing old), death (perishing)" are the natural way of rupa and nāma formations. Nibbāna that has ended all rupa-nāma dhammas has no "*mata*" or death. So, deathlessness is the guna attribute of *amata*.

Panita guna (insatiable joy in absorption)

For arahantas, Nibbāna, like food that is as tasty as not to be satiable in eating it, is the kind of joy whereby it is insatiable to be absorbed with one's attention on It. Lord Buddha often used to be absorbed in phala samāpatti, with Nibbāna in His mind. In delivering a sermon, the Buddha would be in phala samāpatti while the audience was saying "Sādhu, sādhu, sādhu", and would continue His sermon after that chorus. Nibbāna is a noble, unique Entity that carries a unique joy for all those who have attained Nibbāna. Hence, this attribute of this unique joy is called *panita guna*.

---

288. This paragraph is a translation of Pali verse: "*santi lakkhanam iccuta Rasam nibbāna amatam;*
animitta upatthānam, padatthānam na labbhati." Visuddhi Magga Vol. 2. page 126; Abi. (tawunbe) 79
289. The first stage of Magga (the first time sighting of Nibbāna)

Yadajjhagā (time and place of the Enlightenment)

The Lord Buddha discovered and saw through the entirety, from the beginning to the end, of that Nibbāna dhamma in this Sāsanā. The place of enlightenment was the Mahābodhi Tree, and the time the night of the Full-Moon of Kason (May) as daylight was about to dawn (in the year 589 BC).

Nirodha Saccā (The Truth of Extinction)

At the time, Lord Buddha came to know in absolute clarity and thoroughness the Four Noble Truths of Dukkha Saccā, Samudaya Saccā, Magga Saccā, and Nirodha Saccā. In that wisdom, *"Nirodha Saccā"* is the Noble Truth of Nibbāna. Then, Lord Buddha saw in His magga ñāna (holy wisdom) the Nirodha Saccā, complete with all the attributes of khaya, virāga, amata and others.

I will give examples to clarify the point.

The world's scientists found nuclear energy at the expense of many attempts in search of it. That energy did not come out only when they found it. It was there as an intrinsic property of nature. In a similar way, scholars sought to understand the correct meaning of a profound treatise for a great many days till they unraveled it; the true meaning of the book was there all the time. Noble yogis also have to work very, very hard to get the experiential meaning of Nibbāna together with the Four Noble Truths. The Nibbāna dhamma that the yogis come to know do not arise at the time of their understanding it; it is there at all times as Santi Sukha, the intrinsic, unique property of nature.

Samamnatthi (Nothing like Nibbāna)

There is no other dhamma entity that is on the same level as Nibbāna, be it all the forty-eight thousand articles of dhammakkhanda contained in the pariyatti literature, or be it jhāna that can, in its own way, discard defilements, or be it the abiññā psychic powers that enable traveling through earth and sky, or be it the magga-phala ñāna attainments that can discard all the kilesa defilements. These dhamma entities may be great sources of various benefits, but none that is comparable with Nibbāna.

Ditthadhammika Nibbāna (The Immediate Nibbāna)

While in phala samāpatti before entering Parinibbāna, Lord Buddha often had Nibbāna in His mind. This is the kind of Nibbāna known (experienced) in the present life time and so, called *"Ditthadhammika Nibbāna"*. Vipāka citta (sense consciousness) and kammajja rupa (kamma-produced rupa) are called "*upādi*". Because Nibbāna is the object in attention while in the presence of upādi, it is also called "*Sa'upādisesa Nibbāna*".

Samparāyika Nibbāna (Nibbāna in Continuum)

The Nibbāna that remains after the Parinibbāna of the Buddha is called "*Samparāyika Nibbāna*". Because there remains none of *vipāka nāmakkhandhā* (nāma-groups capable of cyclic kamma) and kammaja rupa, it is also called "*anupādisesa Nibbāna*". Therefore, it should be noted that although the Buddha had passed away, the immutable asankhata Nibbāna dhātu is still extant today.

[Itivuttakatthakathā, duka, du-vagga, Nibbānadhātu Sutta]

Two kinds of Sukha

There are two kinds of *sukha* (happiness), namely *vedayita sukha* and *santi sukha*. That happiness or joy that people feel in seeing, hearing, smelling, eating and touching, that is happiness of the mind and body, is called "*vedayita sukha*". The nature of joy, without such feeling, but with absolute bliss (or peace) resulting from extinction of all dukkhas is called "*santi sukha*".

Vedayita sukha (worldly happiness)

The feeling of vedayita sukha is consumptive and exhaustive, so that new materials and more consumptive goods and services have to be sought at the expense of dukkha. The sukha so gained is not worth the dukkha suffered in pursuit of that sukha. Besides, there is no contentment in the pursuit of this kind of happiness, thus needing to borrow sukhas here and there in terms of akusala kammas; the loan for such sukhas will have to be paid back in terms of more dukkha in the villages of apāya.

Santi sukha (happiness in Nibbāna)

The significance of santi sukha, unmixed with such feeling of vedayita sukha, is the nature of absolute peacefulness as a result of extinction of all *rupa-nāma sankhāra dhammas*[290]. To explain it further, suppose a certain wealthy man who has all resources to pursue and gain happiness, complete with all sensual objects, is soundly asleep. If his servants wake him up in the middle of it, he would certainly be angry and rail at them vociferously. While asleep, there is evidently no feeling. And yet, he likes the sound sleep better than any feeling of sukha, saying in appreciation, "Oh, It was such

290. All formation groups of mind and matter

a good sleep!" Free from all rupa-nāma manifestations, it should very well be guessed "how good santi sukha would be".

Nirodha samāpatti[291]

Samāpatti (high absorption) that enables extinction of citta, cetasika and rupas of citta origin and stops them from arising anew is called "*nirodha samāpatti*". Only those anāgāmis and arahantas who have attained jhāna can enter into this samāpatti. Anāgāmis and arahantās take the rupa-nāma khandhā as heavy burden. So, to be as free from the rupa khandhā as possible, they enter into nirodha samāpatti. While in that samāpatti, there is absolutely no feeling. In fact nāma and some rupas stop appearing anew. If such a stop is cause for happiness, then how wouldn't Nibbāna, where all rupa-nāma formations are no more, be a happy affair?

The Self-evident Nibbāna

The santisukha Nibbāna dhātu is not nothingness (*abhāva*[292]) as can be meant in paññatti[293] wisdom. It is not anything that is common to all. It is the Nibbāna that is individualistic and absolutely independent. That is the reason why arahantas, while alive, often have Nibbāna as their object of attention in phala samāpatti. It is said that to keep Nibbāna as object of attention in samāpatti is a very real sukha. So, all the theras and theris[294], at the approach of Parinibbāna, finally throw away their rupa-nāma khandhās with a joyful utterance in praise of such rejection.

Ratana[295] *Sutta Pali*
(Discourse on Preciousness)

> *khayam virāgam amatam panitam?*
> *Yadajjhagā sakyamuni samāhito,*
> *na tena dhammena samatthi kinci,*
> *idhampi dhamme ratanam panitam.*
> *Etena saccena suvatthi hotu.*

Its translation:
Born of Cakya-Sākiya clan, Lord Buddha, our Master, had gained the knowledge of the Four Noble Truths on the throne of the Victory Land

---

291. Attainment of extinction
292. That does not exist in nature
293. Normal everyday language
294. The male and female monks (bhikkhus and bhikkunis)
295. Ratana = Jewel, something held as precious

217

of Mahābodhi, unmixed with anything subject to change, always in cool comfort with peace; with all rupa-nāma formations and their process continuum being extinct and so having exterminated desire; immutable, never aging and dying; gratifying and always insatiable to know, like being insatiable in the eating of the most palatable food; infallible in concentration with unfailing diligence at bhāvanā.

There is no other precious ratana by way of dhamma anywhere in the human world, or in the worlds of devas, however thorough the search may be, which is on equal terms with Nibbāna dhātu that is beyond becoming and conditionality. It is the noblest of all dhamma gunas, such as khaya and virāga that converge to this point of Nibbāna, the immutable dhātu, the best of all the best ratanās, beyond any match in the making. For these truthful words that I say now, I pray for peace with all beings and for their freedom from all harms, without fail.

Conclusion
One's duty
The moral principles, concepts and practice shown in the preceding should suffice for understanding and practical application. The giving of knowledge and wisdom is the duty of the book. The duty of readers is to have and keep mindfulness and the upkeep of diligence in their day-to-day conducts of life according to the knowledge they have gained. This would mean, "Now that the duty of the book has been served, the duty of the readers only remains to accomplish."

Knowledge and practice
Knowledge is only learning, not practice. With no application of knowledge, there can be no wisdom and so no benefits. Books can only give guidance; it cannot enforce practice. Nowadays, those who read much and learn much from instructions are very knowledgeable. But very few of them care about, and observe moral principles. In a world where greater portion of the human race is so careless and unobservant of moral principles, even the good people find it hard to keep up their principles.

That is correct. Even in the works of dāna, there are too many ostentatious displays all around so much so that one has to follow the crowd, even if one wants to do a genuine dāna. The result is that one cannot fulfil the dāna parami in the straight manner of the truly saintly people. Those pretentious people do know they do not really get any lasting benefit, or very little if any, from their false dāna. But it is tanhā that rules and the love of ostentations that make them do it.

The Sly Tiger

The story of a sly old tiger in "Hitopadesa"[296] shows clearly how knowledge and practice can be quite different. The tiger was quite old. It was so slow in its movement that it cannot catch games well. So, it shouted, loud enough for travellers through the wood to hear, "Oh travellers, come, take this gold bangle!"

When a traveller heard it, he approached the tiger and asked, "Where is the gold bangle?" When the tiger opened out its paw and showed the bangle, the traveller said, "You are a killer of games for food. How would I dare come near you and take it?" To this the tiger replied, "When young, I was ignorant of dhamma and so I had killed. Now, all my children and wife are dead as a matter of "vengeance by vipāka vatta[297] hitting back at me", and I am remorseful. Then I met with a holy man who taught, "From today on, you must do charitable works, and meditate." I am now living by his advice. My hand and toe nails are all loose now, and so, how can I be so horrible as to cause harm?" And he added, "I now have very little lobha. Just see how I want to give this bangle away. So, how would I kill you? The dhamma I had heard says, 'Consider another man's wife as for your mother. Think of other man's property as worthless gravel. Be kind to other beings as to yourself. That is the way of holy men.' As I am a saintly creature knowing all these teachings, how can I be so cruel as to kill? So, step into the pond, wash yourself clean and accept this bangle as my charitable gift."

The traveller believed the tiger and walked into the pond for a wash, where he found himself caught in a quagmire. Then the saintly tiger said, "Ha, ha, now you are caught in mud. I will pull you out." So saying, the tiger approached, killed and ate him.

This tale shows how knowledge by itself is nothing more than that and, if knowledge is not translated into practical terms, then it would turn to wickedness that can be quite systematic and more horrible than the ignorant rowdiness. So, I pray for, and again remind, the readers not to be content with learning alone, but to put the knowledge into practice so that they, one and all, nurture themselves as morally good and highly principled characters.

---

296. An ancient book of folk tales
297. The vicious circle of kamma-results, the return attack of deeds done

Concluding Verse

Buddham,
Dhammam,
Sangham, pujemi.

* * *

As a matter of tradition,
I must write a verse in conclusion
To make determinations, and keep in *mana*[298]
For monks and laity to attain to Nibbāna;
But if the root of the mind
Isn't fresh and pure in kind
Far away the goal would be;
Beginning with you and me,
My associates and our posterity,
All those who want to gain dhamma in purity
Should study this book of practical Abbhidhammā
With thorough care to enter the holy land of *khemā*[299]
Like many forefathers who had gone there before us
Hoisting victory banners, just like a victorious army
Hitting the gong of victory to end in the final victory.

[Here ends the book on The Buddhist Morality]

---

298. Mano or mind
299. Land beyond all harms (dukkhas)

APPENDIX A - CATEGORIES OF DUCCARITTA AND SUCARITTA

(1) The 10 Moral Misconducts (Duccaritta) are:
1. Pānātipāta (killing of life)
2. Adinnādānā (taking what is not given)
3. Kāmesumichācāra (amoral sexual conduct)
4. Musāvādā (lies, falsehood)
5. Pisunavācā (slandering)
6. Phrussavācā (saying abusive and rough language)
7. Samphappalāpavācā (frivolous and idle talk)
8. Abhijjhā (wanting to take away others' wellbeing)
9. Vyāpāda (ill will, malice)
10. Micchāditthi (holding wrong views)

These articles are also known as *akusala kammappatha* or *akusala kamma*.

(2) The 10 Morally Righteous Conducts (Sucaritta)
Abstention from the 10 categories of duccaritta is in keeping with observation of 10 sucaritta or *kusala kammapattha* or *kusala kamma*.

APPENDIX B - THE PRECEPTS

(1) The Pancca Sila or 5 Precepts are (to abstain from):
1. Killing of life;
2. Taking what has not been given;
3. Sexual misconduct;
4. Telling lies;
5. Drinking alcohol and taking any intoxicating drug.

(2) The Uposatha Sila or 8 Precepts (to abstain from):
1. Killing of life;
2. Taking what has not been given;
3. Sexual activity;
4. Telling lies;
5. Drinking alcohol and taking any intoxicating drug;
6. Eating after mid-day (until dawn the next day):
7. Dancing, singing, playing and listening to music, seeing shows, wearing flowers and perfuming;
8. Using high and luxurious seats and beds.

(3) The Ājivatthamaka Sila, 8 precepts (to abstain from):
The first 4 of the 5-precepts, added with slandering, rough language, idle talk and wrong livelihood (business in live stocks, weapons, drinks and drugs).

[This sila is said to have been given to men and women of rough characters in the days of the Buddha sāsanā, judging from exclusion of abstention from drinks and drugs and inclusion of all 4 improper speeches and livelihood devoid of kindness to living beings.]

APPENDIX C - ATTRIBUTES OF THE BUDDHA, DHAMMA AND SANGHA

(1) The Nine Attributes of the Buddha:

1. *Arahan*: The Buddha is one worthy of worship, especial veneration, exaltation to the loftiest esteem and devotion by
man, gods and Brahmas;

2. *Sammāsambuddho*: The Buddha, the self-perfected Man, knows
by virtue of His own effort and diligence in perfection,
by Himself and without assistance from any teacher, all
the phenomenal worlds of *sankhata* (ceaselessly changing) rupa-nāma formations and *asankhata* (never changing) Nibbāna dhātu;

3. *Vijjācarana sampanno*: The Buddha is perfectly endowed with 3
articles of *vijja*, 8 articles of *vijjā* (knowledge) and 15 articles of *carana* (conduct)[300];

4. *Sugato*: The Buddha says only what is righteous and virtuous;

5. *Lokavidu*: The Buddha knows all the three worlds (*lokas*) of the living
beings (*sattaloka*), rupa-nāma formations (*sankhāraloka*)
and the inanimate (*okāsaloka*);

6. *Anuttaro purisa dhamma sārathi*: The Buddha can tame wild males
of mankind, gods and animals:

---

300. *Vijjā* or Knowledge: *Vijjā* refers to either 3-fold Knowledge (Remembering Past Existences, Divine Eye and Extinction of all defilements) or the 8-fold Knowledge, namely
(1) the 6 Higher Spiritual Powers (*abhiññā*, consisting of Magical Powers, Divine Ear,
Knowing others minds, Divine Eye, Remembering Former Existences, Extinction of
all defilements), (2) Insight (*vipassanā*) and (3) Magical Power (*iddhividha*);
Carana or Conduct: there are 15 items of *carana*, namely moral restraint, watching over
sense doors, moderation in eating, wakefulness, faith, moral shame, moral dread,
great learning, energy, mindfulness, wisdom and the 4 absorptions.

7. *Sattādeva manussānam*: The Buddha is Teacher to man and gods for their wellbeing and development in the present existence as well as the lives hereafter;

8. *Buddho*: A Buddha knows the Four Noble Truths thoroughly and analytically with absolute certainty and clarity;

9. *Bhagavā*: The Buddha is fully endowed with the Six Psychic Powers[301].

(2) The Six Attributes of the Dhamma:

1. *Savakkhāto bhagavatā dhammo*: The Natural Law or Dhamma that Lord Buddha had delivered and left us with is blessed with goodness and grace, right from the beginning to the end;

2. *Sanditthiko*: The tenets of Dhamma are clearly evident now, at this very moment;

3. *Akāliko*: Practice of the Dhamma can bring about resultant benefits immediately after the deed is done;

4. *Ehipassiko*: The Dhamma invites those who are interested to come and see the Truth of the Law for themselves by practising its tenets;

5. *Opāneyiko*; The Dhamma, if extant in the consciousness continuum of a being, would carry that being to Nibbāna without fail;

6. *Paccatam veditabbo viñuhi*: The Dhamma is the noble Natural Law that the noble ariya practitioners experience and get benefits from in accordance with the level of parami and wisdom they have reached.

---

301. The Six Psychic Powers of Bhagavā: (1) *issariya* (power that enables assumption of the Buddha's body as small as an atom or so large as to fill the cosmos); (2) *dhamma* (power of wisdom); (3) *yasa* (power of companionship and popularity); (4) *Siri* (power of grace and glory), (5) *kāma* (power of satisfying all wishes); (6) *payatta* (power of strength and energy)..

(3) The Nine Attributes of the Sangha

1. *Suppatippanno bhagavato sāvaka sangho*: The Sangha, disciples of the Buddha, whose aim is Nibbāna, attend well to the conduct of life according to the nine-fold magginga-Nibbāna course of dhamma[302];

2. *Ujuppatippanno bhagavato sāvaka sangho*: The Sangha, disciples of the Buddha, genuinely engage themselves with the practice of the Eightfold Middle Path, the *athingika magginga*.

3. *Ñāyappatippanno bhagavato sāvaka sangho*: The Sangha, disciples of the Buddha, work for progressive development of knowledge and wisdom in the practice of insight meditation.

4. *Sāmicippatippanno bhagavato sāvaka sangho*: The Sangha, disciples of the Buddha, are well worthy of worship with veneration by all man, devas, brahmas and other beings.

5. *Yadidam cattāri purisayugāni attha purisapuggalā esā bhagavato sāvaka sangho āhuneyo*: The eight-some Sangha[303], disciples of the Buddha, may, with kindness, accept alms and donations brought in from afar.

6. *Pāhuneyo*: The Sangha, disciples of the Buddha, may gladly accept alms and donations meant for visiting Sangha.

7. *Dakkhineyo*: The Sangha, disciples of the Buddha, may, with compassion, accept alms and donations offered to them.

8. *Ancali kariniyo*: The Sangha, disciples of the Buddha, may accept bowing down in veneration from people.

9. *Anuttaram puññakhettam lokassa*: The Sangha, disciples of the Buddha, are like the unmatched fertile field where man, devas, brahmas and other beings sow their seeds of wholesome, meritorious deeds.

---

302. The course consists of the 4 magga ñāna, the 4 phala ñāna, and the one goal Nibbāna.
303. This refers to the Sangha at the 8 stages of ñāna development in insight meditation

225

APPENDIX D QUESTIONS BY MANLE SAYADW AND ANSWERS BY MINKUN ALE TAWYA SAYADAW, REGARDING THE SUBJECT OF MALE AND FEMALE DEVAS:

Q1 - Are deva ladies like our lassies? Does the monthly flower bloom there too?

A1 - Deva ladies are unlike human lassies, wearing no monthly flowers that bloom not.

Q2 - Would you mind this mischievous question? But you do know what I mean. In all the 6 homes, how do they go about you-know-what-I-mean when two of them are in pleasant agreement?

Like human beings?
A2 - No, I wouldn't mind. Yes, I know what. When the two are in pleasant agreement, they do the same way human beings do.

Q3 - Tell me if you know. Do those deva ladies, like human ladies, feed their children from their breasts?

A3 - No! Not like human beings. They don't feed children from their breasts.

Note: These questions and answers were asked and answered in a delightful poetic form, humorous in content, to the artistry of which this rendering may not have matched

APPENDIX E PĀRAMI - THE TEN PERFECTIONS PRACTISED BY BODHISATTAS LEADING TO BUDDHAHOOD

(1) *dāna pārami* - Perfection in Giving

(2) *sila pārami* - Perfection in Moral Conduct

(3) *nekkhamma pārami* - Perfection in Renunciation

(4) *paññā pārami* - Perfection in Wisdom

(5) *viriya* - Perfection in energy

(6) *khanti pārami* - Perfection in Forbearance

(7) *saccā pārami* - Perfection in Truthfulness

(8) *additthāna* - Perfection in Resolution

(9) *mettā pārami* - Perfection in Good Will and Loving Kindness

(10) *upekkhā pārami* - Perfection in Equanimity

[Some people claim themselves to be *"Phayaalaung"* , meaning to be Bodhisatta. They would be so only if they qualify on the criteria of perfection in any one or combination of these ten points. When all these Perfections have been fulfilled, the Bodhisatta would be a Buddha.]

APPENDIX F - THE ELEVEN FIRES

The eleven fires that burn beings:

(1) *Rāga*, the fire of lust

(2) *Dosa*, the fire of anger and hatred

(3) *Moha*, the fire of delusion and ignorance

(4) *Jāti*, the fire of birth

(5) *Jarā*, the fire of decay (or old age)

(6) *Marana*, the fire of death

(7) *Soka*, the fire of anxiety

(8) *Parideva*, the fire of weeping

(9) *Dukkha*, the fire of physical pains and miseries

(10) *Domanasa*, the fire of mental pains and miseries

(11) *Upāyāsa*, the fire of extreme grief (to the point of faints and fits)

APPENDIX G: GLOSSARY OF SOME
PALI TERMS AND CONCEPTS

A Suggested Phonetic Scheme:

A or a without a diacritical mark has the sound of '**a**' as in par, without the end sound being stretched out for '-ar'; say only a crisp 'pa', e.g. *loba, dosa, sutta.* If **A** or **a** is the first character (not followed by a double consonant) of a word, its sound is shorter still, as in *avijjā, anatta, adosa, aloba.*

(Note: in *adosa* and *alobha*, the sound on '*a*' should be pronounced with a little more emphasis than the first '*a*' in *avijjā* and *anatta* as a matter of form).

Ā or ā has the sound of '-**ar**' in par with the ending sound, stretched out for ' ar' as in *avijjā, saddhā, Nibbāna, ārammana.*

'a' followed by 'j' sounds like '-ij' as in *majjhima.*

'-am' sounds '-um' as in tam and sammāsambuddha.

'-an' sounds like '-un' in 'sun' or rhymed on '-in', respectively, as in *chanda, saññā, asancheyya.*
'-att-' has the sound of '-ut' in put or in rut as in **vatta, sattavā.**

B has the sound of normal 'b' as in *Buddha, sabbaloca.*

Bh has the sound of 'b' followed by slight 'h' as in *bhava, lobha.*

C has the sound of 'c' in 'ice' as in *catu saccā, cetiya.*

Ch has the sound for 'S' in Sun. read as in *chanda, chattha.*

D has the sound of normal 'd' as in *dāna. Ditthi.*

Dh has the sound of 'd' followed slightly by 'h' as in *Buddha, dhamma.*

E has the sound rhymed on 'way' said light as in *tejo, Sena.*

If followed by 't'. it will sound like '-it' as in *mettā.*
G has the sound of normal; 'g' as in *magg, /magginga.*

Gh has the sound of 'g' followed by a slight 'h' as in *Sanghā*.

I sounds as 'i' or '-ai-' in 'it', pain or gait as in *Milinda, mitta*.

j   has the sound of "z" as in *tejo, jarā*.

Jh sounds as of 'z' followed by a slight 'h' as in *jhāna, majjhima*.

Ń or **ñ** has the sound of '-ny-' in canyon as in *ñāna, saññā*.

O sounds like 'aw' or 'au' as in *tejo, bhagavato*.

•   Sounds somewhere between 't' and 's' in **th**under, as in *sila*.
Th has the sound of 't' followed by 'h' as in *Theravāda, ditthi*.

•   has sounds of 'u' in you and 'ut' in put as in *suta, putta*.
V has the sound of 'W' as in *velu, bhava, vipāka*.

Double consonants read both the characters as in '-bb-'. '-cc-', '-gg-', '-tt-', etc.

[There are several diacritical marks, applicable to Latinized Pali, other than those shown here, but here the object is simplicity. The sounds are most akin to Myanmar tongue. Better-learned readers, h.owever, may pursue their own preference.]

GLOSSARY

[Notes: The author, being a native of Myanmar, is in the habit of using Myanmar-styled Pali words that are close derivatives of formal Pali, but peculiar only to Myanmar tongue. E.g. we have a character for 'r', said in the same way as for 'y', both being consonants. Also, we are silent on the last syllable of some Pali words; for instance, we say 'ñān' for Pali 'ñāna'. Similarly, we say '*jhān*' for '*jhāna*', '*Nibbān*' for '*Nibbāna*', '*duccarite*' for '*duccarita*', and so on. Apologies for any unintentional mix-ups, if any.]

Abhidhammā: Analytical explanations of the Ultimate Realities, one of the three

Baskets of Buddhist Texts, *Tipitaka* (Abhidhamma, Sutta and Vinaya)

Abhijjhā: Covetousness, greed

Abhiññā: Higher psychic power, supernormal knowledge.

Adhimokkha; Decision; Determination

Adinnadānā: Taking things not given, stealing and robbery

Aditthāna: Determination; resolution

Adosa: Antithesis of *dosa*, hatelessness, (by extension) loving kindness (*mettā*)

Agga Sāvaka: The two Chief Disciples

Āhāra: *Ojā*, nutrients, food

Ăkāsadhatu: space in-between rupas, space

Akusala: Unwholesome (kamma, duccarita)

Alobha: Antithesis of *lobha*, greedlessness

Amoha: Antonym of *moha*, non-delusion, (by extension) wisdom

Ahirika: Lack of moral shame

Ājivatthamaka sila: The eight (non-Sabbath) precepts – vows from (1) killing; (2) stealing and robbing; (3) wrongful sex; (4) lying; (5) slandering; (6) abusive language; (7) idle talk; (8) wrongful livelihood such as raising and selling livestock, dealing in drugs and intoxicants, weapons and ammunition, slave trade, and so on.

Akālika: Now in this present life term, the idea that the truth would be evident now in this lifetime (the akālika guna of the Buddha's Teaching)

Akāla marana: Untimely death, death before end of life span and exhaustion of kammic support, sudden and often violent death due to *uppacchedaka kamma*

Akusala (kamma): Unwholesome kamma; any or all unwholesome mental, verbal and physical acts

Amate*, *Amata: Something imperishable, immortality, deathlessness, Nirvana, Nibbāna

Amangala: antithesis of mangala, things that bring misfortune, horror

Anāgāmi: the non-returner, having attained the 3rd stage of holiness (Enlightenment)

Ānāpānasati: Mindfulness on in- and out-breathing; keeping a continuous, constant watch on the point of contact between in/out air currents and the tip of the nose.

Anatta: Non-self; non-ego; non-personality; the characteristic of the world of nāma-rupa

being nothing but phenomenal, not subject to any creation, or the will of any personality

Anicca: impermanence, the phenomenon of perennial change inherent in matter and mind

Anitthārammana: undesirable sense objects

Anottappa: Lack of moral dread (***Ahirika*** is a companion character)

Anumaru – Extremely fine elemental matter; ***Paramāanumaru*** – sub-atomic particles. (These terms are, presumably, Pali-derived words of Myanmar origin)

Anusaya: Potential or inherent defilements – 7 articles: sensuous greed (*kāma-raga*); grudge (*patigha or vyāpāda*); speculative opinion (*ditthi*); skeptical doubt (*vicikicchā*); Conceit (*māna*); Craving for rebirth in kāma-bhumis (*bhava-rāga*); Ignorance (*avijjā*)

Apacayana: Giving respects to elders, homage to the Buddha and the bhikkhus

Apara cetana: Reflection on one's willfulness (volition) on act of charity already done

Apāya: The four lower worlds – the animal world, ghost-world, demon-world, and hell

Āpo dhātu: element of cohesion, fluidity

Arahanta also *arahat*: the pure one, who has destroyed all defilements, having attained the 4th and final stage of holiness.

Ariya or *Ariya puggala*: Noble person, usually one who has attained at least the first-stage magga/phala ñāna (*sotapana magga*)

Ārammana, also *aruna* (Myan.): Sense objects such as sight, sound, smell, and taste, physical or mental objects

Asankhata dhatu: Immutable element, non-changing nature

Asancheya: A unit of cosmic time, uncountable in number of earth years

Ashin: (M) The venerable one, the one worthy of homage (form of address to bhikkhus)

Asubha kammatthāna: meditation with attention on corpses, unpleasant sights

Asurā, asurakāya: Beings in the demonic world, one of the four apāya worlds

Atta: the self, ego, personality or soul (*anatta* is the antithesis of atta)

Attānuvāda: Self-accusation, disrespect for self, censuring one-self for one's own wrongful deeds, although no other people accuse him

Atthanga sila: The eight (Sabbath) precepts: vows from (1) taking of life; (2) taking things not given; (3) breach of celibacy; (4) lies; (5) taking of intoxicants and drugs; (6) eating after noon; (7) indulgence in beautification, perfumes and other cosmetics, music, dancing and watching of shows; (8) using high and luxurious seats and beds.

Atthukkamsana: self-praise

Atthagika magga: The Eight-Fold Path, the Middle Way or *majjhima-patipadā*

Avijjā: Ignorance of the Four Noble Truths, the darkness of delusion

Āyatana: The six sense bases (*salāyatana*) and the six sense objects (*ārammana*)

Āyu: Long life, life span

Bahiddha: External to bodies

Bala: Power, strength, powerful strength, great resources (5 categories, namely physical, intellectual, economic, moral and social)

Bhāvanā: Meditation; continuously repeated contemplation or watching of an object for a certain length of time – there are two kinds, namely: *samatha* and *vipassanā* (insight). ***Samāpatti***: Absorption higher than *vipassanā*, by which the *ariya* person contemplates the path he has taken or the neroda sacca he has attained.

Bhava rāga: attachment to continued existence, craving for life, love of life

Bhāva rupa: Physical forms of male (*purisa bhāva*) and female (*itthi bhāva*)

Bhikkhu: One practicing austerity, dressed in bark-dyed rough robes, going on alms rounds, committed to end recurring rebirth, member of the Buddha's Order, follower of the 227 Rules of Conduct (*Vinaya*), carrier and propagator of the Buddha's Teaching

Bhikkhuni: Properly ordained female member of the Buddha's Order

Bhivamsa: Title of a highly learned bikkhu; a public recognition by having this title put after the bikkhu's designated name, e.g. *Sayādaw Ashin Janakā Bhimvamsa*

Bhumi: Place of birth, abode of beings – there are 31 bhumis, namely: one of mankind, four of *apāya*, six of *devas*, and twenty of *Brahmas*.

Bimāna: Lar4ge luxurious mansions and palaces

Brahma: a celestial being on higher planes of existence, and of longer lifespan, than the six deva bhumis (There are 20 planes of Brahma realm). A person of the noblest character.

Brahmacariya: The way of living of a Pure One, the way monks live

Brahmavihara: The four 'Divine Abodes', also called the four 'Boundless States'

Bhumi: Home land, realm of existence

Cakkāvalā: The universe; the expanse of space throughout which is distributed all the uncountable worlds and uncountable living beings. There are uncountable universes.

Cakkhu: The eye, the sensual base of sight

Carita: Habitual thoughts, talks and behaviours, nature, inborn traits, character

Catudhātuva vutthāna: Contemplation (in absorption) of the four elements of *mahābhuta*, a samatha meditation.

Catumahārāja deva: A god of the celestial realm where the four Great Deva Kings reigned, the lowest of the six deva realms, closest to or contiguous with the human realm

Cetanā; Volition, it is an associate of the mind, inseparably bound up with consciousness.

Cetasika: The mental factors, the mind associates that act on and influence the mind

Chanda: A mere wish, will, intention

Citta: Mind, consciousness

Cula sotapana: the lesser kind of *sotapana* (the first stage of magga/phala wisdom)

Cuti: Death; *cuti citta*, the 7th *javana*, is awareness at the time of passing away

Dāna: Charity; donation; alms giving to the monks and in obeisance to the Buddha

Danta: return of suffering (punishment) for one's wrongful deeds in the past

Devaduta: Yamamin's messengers, namely the child, the old person, the sick person, the dead person and the prisoner, the manner of Yamamin questioning some new arrivals to his kingdom i.e. Niraya (the infernal world)

Dhamma: The natural law of all rupa-nāma phenomena, The Buddha's Teaching

Dhammadesanā: Delivering talks on dhamma

Dhammassavana: Listening to dhamma talks (or study in any form, including reading)

Dhātu: Elements, constituents of a whole; intrinsic, fundamental nature

Dhana: wealth, possessions,

Ditthi: Its meaning is 'view', but without the qualifying *sammā-*, it is interpreted as wrong contemplation and wrong view, and misled faith

Dipankarā: A Buddha millions of kappas ago, from whom our Lord Gotama Buddha took blessing for His Buddhahood.

Domanasa: grief, mentally painful feeling due to unpleasant sights, sounds, smells, tastes and thoughts

Dosa: anger, hatred, aversion, sorrow, despair (antithesis of *mettā*)

Dubbhikkhantara Kappa: The hard times of prevailing hunger

Duccarita: Evil conducts – three kinds: in deeds, words and thoughts

Dukkaracariya: The hardest of all hard practices in austerity, mainly by way of self mortification. Prince Siddhattha was in this practice for six years, before becoming a Buddha. That was his *atthakilamathā nuyoga* that he discarded eventually (because it was no way to Bodhi ñāna, he found out), to follow the Middle Way.

Duggati: destination to the 4 lowly worlds of woe (*apāya*)

Dukkha: Pain, suffering; unsatisfactoriness or liability to suffering as meant by the "*dukkha*," the first of the 4 Noble Truths and the second of the 3 Characteristics

Dussila: Corrupt monk, one who has breached monks' rules of conduct

Dvihetuka-patisandhi – Conception carrying a continuum of only two out of the 3 noble root-conditions (***Tihetu***), the two being *alobha* (greed-lessness) and *adosa* (hatelessness)

Ekaggata: One-pointedness of the mind; the highest of the five parts of rupāvacara jhāna, which is only possible with the presence of upekkhā cetasika.

Gandha: Smell

Gati: Destination, life hereafter

Gati bhava: The form of life to be born in after the present life

Gehassita pema: Home-dependent love

Gottarabhu: Maturity ñāna immediately preceding the entry into magga ñāna

Ijjhatta: Dhamma formations inside of body, mental qualities of a person

Issā: Envy, an unwholesome mental factor

Itthamajjhattarammana: The sense object that is neither attractive nor repulsive

Itthārammana: Desirable sense objects

Jarā: Aging; decay; old age – what is born is bound to grow old, and will surely die.

Jataka: life stories of the Buddha

Javana: 'Impulsion' is the phase of full cognition in the perceiving process (*vithi-citta*); it is only at this phase that kamma is produced. 'Impulsive moments' = There are seven stages of javana or the seven impulsive moments – the first javana may take effect immediately or in the present life; if that is missed, the seventh javana will occur at the time of cuti, which will take effect in the next life; the second to the 6th will take effect in any of subsequent lives.

Jhāna: Absorption; there are two types of jhāna, namely: rupāvacara (concentration on material objects); arupavacara jhāna (concentration on non-material objects)

Jāti: birth comprising the entire embryonic process beginning with conception and ending with parturition

Jāti paññā: Inborn intelligence

Jinvhā pasāda: Taste sensors on the tongue

Jivitindriya: Faculty of vitality, controlling factor of life, mind-matter continuum

Hiri-ottappa: *Hiri is* moral shame; *ottappa* is moral dread. The combination word would mean a virtue somewhat greater than the principle of 'integrity'. The two words are also known as the 2 Protectors of Human Society.

Issā: Jealousy, envy

Kalāpa: The smallest units in pathavi dhātu, e.g. attha-calāpa, the eight particles of matter split from the paramā-anumaru (sub-atomic particles).

Kalyana: Noble; *kalyāna mitta* means noble friends, e.g., the Buddha, the bikkhus and the kammatthāna teachers, as well as other associates in dharma

Kāma: Pleasure of the senses; sensuality; the 5 sense objects

Kāma bhava: Sensuous existence; life full of sensual pleasures

Kāma rāga: sensuous lust

Kamma: Actions (bodily, verbal, mental); wholesome and unwholesome actions that carry corresponding effects immediately or sometime after commitment of such acts

Kamma bhava: The present commitment of actions on account of upadānā (obsessive preoccupation with sensual desires), resulting in effects in this life and hereafter

Kammaguna: active properties of kamma conducive to unwholesome willful actions (akusala kamma)

Kammasakā: Kamma is the source or the root of one's destiny, one's own property

Kamma sakata sammāditthi: The Right View that the past kāya kamma, vaci kamma and mano kamma are the causes of the present fortune or misfortune; the present kammas wholesome or unwholesome) are the causes of future effects (good or miserable). .

Kammatthāna: Meditation – two types: samattha and vipassanā

Kāmesumicchācāra: Wrongful sex: adultery and other sexual misconducts

Karuna: compassion for all, kindness to the less fortunate

Kāya pasāda: Sensors on body to receive signals of various touches and contacts

Kappa, also *Gabar* in Myanmar: world period, world cycle, (inconceivably long period of time) - a world cycle has a beginning, upward expansion in life forms and spans, stay, downward slide, and destruction by fire or water, involving an immeasurably long time in terms of earth years.

Khanti vāda: The view and practice of patience and forbearance

Khanti parami: One of the ten perfections to be practised and fulfilled by a Buddha-to-be

Kasina: A material object of attention to hold concentration on. There are ten types.

Khandha: Aggregates or groups often referred to as formations, of rupa and nāma (citta and cetasika) that are sense receptors that in their turns cause attachments and so miseries. (Paticcasamuppāda Sutta)

Khaya guna: A property of Nibbāna, dissolution of all defilements, rupa and nāma

Kusala (kamma): Wholesome actions, meritorious deeds

Kusala citta: whole some thought, wholesome mind, wholesome action of the mind

Lakkhanā: Characteristic signs; characterisatics – the three characteristics of anicca, dukkha and anatta.

Lobha: Greed, sensuous desire

Loka: 'World', denoting the 3 spheres of existence, the whole universe: (1) Sensuous World (*kāma-loka*), or the world of the 5 senses (2) the Fine Material World (*rupa-loka*), or the 4 *rupāvacara jhānas* (absorptions) (3) the Immeterial World (*arupa-loka*), or the 4 immaterial *jhānas* (absorptions);

240

also the 3 worlds of (1) all beings (*satta-loka*) (2) rupa-nāma formations (*sankhā-loka*), and (3) the inanimate (*okāsa-loka*)

Lokadhamma: The ups and downs of life; the eight vicissitudes – gain and loss, honor and dishonor, happiness and misery, praise and blame.

Lokaniti: Books of Buddhistic instructions on ethics and civic

Lokapāla dhamma: The two guardian laws of mankind: hiri (moral shame) and ottappa (moral dread).

Lokiya: The worldly, that belonging to human (the mundane) world

Lokuttarā: Beyond the world, super-mundane- the four magga and the four phala ñāna.

Macchariya: Stinginess, avarice (usually combined with Issā as issā-macchariya)

Magga: Path; the four super mundane paths (the four maggas); the Eightfold Path (atthangika magga)

Magginga: See magga.

Magga ñāna: The four attainments of magga: sotapana magga, sagadāgāmi magga, anāgāmi magga, arahatta magga)

Mahābhuta: The four primary elements of matter: properties (in principles) of earth, water, heat, and air; the bases of rupa, the objective matter.

Mahā Sāvaka: Great saintly disciple (classed as great ariya puggala)

Majjhima-patipadā: The Mddle Way, devoid of extremities of pleasurable life and self-mortification

Māna: Conceit, pride

Manasikāra: Attention, reflection, conceptual approach to decision

Mangala: (joy from) blessed deeds that are truly auspicious, conducive to great benefits, now and hereafter, all along the samsāra, ending with Nibbāna finally

Māra: Evil god, evil, the god from Paranimmitavasavatti, who tried to tempt the Buddha

Marana: Death,

Maru: (M) Fine mist

Māyā: Deceit, pretence, false presentation

Methuna: the act and the joy of sexual union

Mettā: universal goodwill, loving kindness applicable equally to all living beings

Middha: sloth, laziness, indolence used in combination with *thina*, torpor, as *thina-middh*

Makkha: a kind of dosa that does not know the gratitude one owes to others

Mittadhubbhi: dosa that does not know friendship and may do damage to benefactors

Moha: delusion, ignorance, darkness (antithesis of *paññā, amoha*)

Muditā: sympathetic joy in seeing the more fortunate people

Munca cetanā: Volition or willfulness during act of charity

Musāvāda: Telling lies, falsehood

Muttacāgi: Donor completely detached from dāna materials or the recipients.

Nāma: Mind. Mentality, a collective name for the groups of cetasika and citta as khandha is classified.

Ñāna: Wisdom, *paññā*, insight, experiential knowledge

Napantuka: persons with indistinct male or female sex organs

Natthibo paññatti: Designated emptiness as object of absorption

Nekkhama: Perfection in renunciation, one of ten perfections of a Buddha

Nibbāna: Enlightenment, the attainment of wisdom that signifies entry into a state of the mind that knows it is past the dangers and miseries of rebirth, decay and aging, sorrows of all kinds and death, not returning to the next life. The real Nibbāna is attained upon Parinibbāna (passing away) of the arahanta, the highest and ultimate achiever.

Nimitta: Signs apparent in the mind as a result of practice on mind concentration; sense object (material or mental); mental image

Niraya: The nether or infernal world, hell, is one of the four low destinations (gati), apāya. This existence like any other bhumi existence lasts only as far or as long as past kammic (unwholesome) effects have their impacts to exhaustion.

Niyata micchāditthi Wrong views with fixed destiny, which include the views of un-causedness of existence (*ahetuka ditthi*), inefficiency of action (*akiriya ditthi*), and nihilism (*natthika ditthi*)

Ojā: *Āhāra,* nutrients, food

Okkatha kusala: Noble wholesome deed

Omaka kusala: Inferior wholesome deed

Paccaya: Condition, conditionality, mode of conditionality

Paccaya pariggaha ñāna: The knowledge of dependent origination of nāma and rupa.

Paccekabuddha; a self-enlightened *arahanta* not in connection with any Buddha sāsanā

Padathāna: The closest conditionality of citta by co-nascent cetasika and rupa

Palāsa: the kind of dosa that tries to keep up with the Joneses

Panita guna: A property of Nibbāna, the unique joy in phala samāpatti

Paññā: Knowledge and wisdom, understanding, insight (vipassanā ñāna)

Paññatti paññā: Wisdom attained on the basis of *samuti saccā* or day-to-day worldly language built of designated terms and concepts

Pānātipātā: Killing of a living being

Paramattha saccā: The Objective Truths: rupa, citta, cetasika and Nibbāna. They are true in the highest or ultimate sense, natural and universal, never changing their inherent, intrinsic properties and characteristics as contrasted with the conventional truth (sammuti saccā) which bear names and designations (paññatti).

Pārami, Pārimita: 'Perfection' (the 10 qualities of), leading to Buddhahood

Parami dhātu: strength of character as per Perfections accomplished in past lives

Parānuvāda: other people's accusation of one for wrongful deeds

Paravambhana: condemnation of others

Parideva: deep sorrow resulting in weeping with sound, crying (a kind of dosa)

Parikamma nimitta: The image objects perceived in early stages of concentration

Parikamma: Preparatory moment, preparatory duties

Parinibbāna: Entry into Nibbāna; passing away of the Buddhas and arahantas

Pariyatti sāsanā: Teaching of the contents of all Buddha dhamma, the textual learning

Pariyutthāna: That appears together with the mind, active *cetasikas* such as *moha,* thoughts of sensual desire, ill-will and cruelty

Pasāda rupa: Sensual elements (sensors) in eye, ear, nose, tongue, and body that receive signals of sight, sound, smell, taste, and touch

Pathāna: The pathāna desanā – listing and explanation of the twenty four modes of paccaya, the conditionality of khandha (the world of nāma and rupa)

Pathavi dhātu: The element of earth, the principle of hardness and softness applied to the level of atthacalāpa, a subdivision of sub-atomic particles which carry energy, but no discernable mass or shape. It is at this level of rupa where the arising and passing away of rupa (its all other attributes) and, together with it, viññāna, i.e. nāma, comes into view in the vipassanā meditator's ñāna cakkhu (eye of wisdom developed by way of experience)

Pātimokkha: Disciplinary code for monks, recited on all new-moon and full-moon days, before an assembly of fully ordained monks.

Patibhāna: Great power in knowledge and wisdom

Patibhāga nimitta: Clear and immobile mental image or images 'seen' at a high level of mind concentration known as near-jhāna or upacāra Samadhi.

Paticcasmuppāda sutta: The Discourse on Dependent Origination, the Teaching that explains conditionality of all material and mental phenomena, also seeking how and where in the vicious circle of that conditionality liberation may be led out.

Patigha: repugnance, aversion, ill will, hatred (a synonym of *vyāpāda*)

Patipatti sāasanā: Teaching in the practice of samattha/vipassanā meditation

Patirupa desa: Place of advantage for one's living (or livelihood)

Patisandhi: Kamma-resultant type of consciousness at the moment of conception in a mother's womb; rebirth. It is linked to the previous bhava by kamma only.

Pativedha: Realization of the Truth of the Dhamma, as distinguished from the mere acquisition of textual and literary knowledge (***pariyatti***), or the practice (***patipatti***) of it

Pativedha sāsanā: The message of pativedha

Patti dāna: Wishing and calling others to share one's merits of dāna and other kusalas

Pattānumodana: Blessing and taking a share in the merits of others' kusala kamma

Pavatti paññā: Acquired knowledge

Pema: liking with attachment (a form of lobha)

Peta: ghosts, perpetually hungry beings

Phala ñāna: Knowledge of fruiting or benefit; fruition immediately following magga ñāna. There are four stages of phala ñāna corresponding to the four of magga ñāna.

Phassa: Sense of impact, the sense of touch (contact) – six classes, namely: sight, sound, smell, taste, body-contact and thought.

Photthabba: Sensation of touch

Phra: (Myan.) A salutation in reverence, an address in homage (to a venerable monk), usually combined with and following ***Ashin***

Pisunavācā: slander, calumny

Pitaka, Ti-Pitaka: the 3 Baskets of Buddhist learning: *Vinaya* (Rules of Conduct), *Sutta* (Discourses) and *Abhidhamma* (Analytical Studies of the Teaching).

Pubba cetanā: Volition or willfulness before an act of charity

Puggala, puggalika: Personality (person), individuality (individual)

Puthujjana: The ordinary men and women. Many a member of the ordinary sanghā, are still puthujana persons as they have not yet attained any stage in the domain of the ariyas, but still worthy of worship by virtue of their moral conduct and Noble Service.

Rāga: lust, greed (a form of lobha)

Rakkhasa (deva-rakkhasa): A race of Catumahārāja devas, often called ogres

Rasā, rasārupa: The six tastes: sweet, sour, hot, acrid, bitter and salty

Rupa: Matter (fine matter), corporeality, material objects that have the property of becoming and unbecoming, arising and passing away – that what appears will disappear.

Rupakkhandhā: Rupa or corporeal group

Rupāvācara jhāna: Absorption in the fine-material sphere (one of kammā-, rupā- and arupā-vācara jhānas)

Sabbaññuta ñāna: The Omniscience of the Buddha

Saddhā: Confidence, faith, and worship in the Buddha, Dhammā and Sanghā.

Sadda: (usually in adj. form) to do with hearing, e.g. *saddārammana, or sotārammana*

Saddārammana (Sotāruna): The sound object.

Sādhu: 'Very well'; 'Well done'

Sakadagami Magga: The second stage of magga attainment, by virtue of which the ariya will return to kāma-bhumi for only once before entering Nibbāna

Sakkāya ditthi: Holding the idea of 'I', 'he', 'she', 'male', 'female', sattavā, and so on

Salāyatana: The six sense bases of the material body.

Samanera: A novice, a young monk before proper ordination at the age of 20

Samādhi: Concentration, the state of the mind firmly fixed on an object of attention

Samāpatti: Attainment, a name for the 8 absorptions (rupa- and arupa-jhānas); also the 9th attainment after the 8 magga-phala ñānas, absorption in extinction of rupa-nāma formations (nirodha-samāpatti)

Samatha: Methods by which samādhi is achieved, for purposes of absorption or insight meditation.

Sammuti sacca: The truth of designated terms of speech, the conventional truth.

Sammā-ditthi: The Right View, paññā magginga.

Sammādāna virati: Keeping precepts and refraining from committing duccarita

Sammā-sankappa: the Right Thought, paññā magginga

Sammā-kammanta: The Right Action, sila magginga.

Sammā- vācā: The Right Speech, sila magginga

Sammā-ājhiva: The Right Livelihood, sila magginga.

Sammā-vāyama: The Right Effort, samādhi magginga

Sammā-sati: The Right Mindfulness, samādhi magginga

Sammā-samādhi: The Right Concentration, samādhi magginga

Sampatta virati: Avoidance of doing duccarita, without deliberately keeping precepts

Sampatti: Fortunate situation, circumstances complete with blessedness

Samsāra: round of rebirths, cycle of rebirths, relentless arising (and vanishing) of rupa-nāma formations

Samuti saccā: The day-to-day language dealing with worldly expressions as designated

Samudaya: attachment to the 5 aggregates of khandhā (rupa-nāma formations)

Samvega: Emotional or moral lesson drawn from (superficial) observation of sources of anicca, dukkha and anatta

Samyojana: literally the rope that binds people together, fetters, the love and fondness

Sanghika dāna: Dāna proffered for Sanghā in general, not for any person in particular

Sankhārakkhandha: Aggregate of volitional activities

Sankhata dhātu: Perishable element, changeable nature

Saññā: perception

Saññakkhandhā: Aggregate of perceptions

Santi sukha: The kind of joy without sensual feeling, but with absolute bliss that results from extinction of all dukkhas

Saranaguna* (M)** or ***Sarana gamana : Properties or domains of the Three Refuges called The Three Jewels, namely the Buddha, the Dhamma and the Sangha; also called *Ti-Sarana Gamana*.

Sāsanā: Mission, propagation and maintenance of the teaching; in Buddhism there are three classes of sāsanā, namely: the learning (***pariyatti***), the practice (***paripatti***) and fruition of the practice (***pativedha***).

Sassata ditthi: The belief in soul or personality existing independently of the five groups (khandha) of existence, the belief in eternity as distinct from 'annihilation belief' (*uccheda ditthi*) in which death is the end of everything.

Sātheyya: A type of deceit that signifies pretence of possessing qualities or virtues that one does not have.

Satipatthāna: Foundation of mindfulness, the sutta that expounds all the facets and methods of practicing mindfulness

Sattantara kappa: The era of destruction by means of weapons

Sattavā: A living being whether that be a human being, a deva, a Brahma or an animal

Sāvaka: A noble disciple (ariya puggala)

Sila: Moral conduct, keeping of precepts

Silabhatupadan: Belief that it is purity of morality to live like animals

Sita tejo: coolness, coldness, the nature of coldness

Soka: a kind of dosa (depressive), sorrow, unhappiness,

Sota: to do with hearing or ear, e.g. *sotāruna or sotarammana*

Somanasa vedanā: Feeling of happiness due to sensations of pleasant sight, sound, smell, taste and thoughts.

Sotāpana: or ***sotāpan*** is the Stream-Winner, the lowest stage of the 8 noble persons (the 8 ariya persons or magga/phala puggala)

Sotapatti maggatha puggala: One who attains ***sotapatti magga ñāna***, in sight of Nibbāna in a fleeting moment for the first time

Sucarita: Good, moral conduct in deeds, words and mind, consisting of the ten wholesome courses of action (avoidance of the ten moral misconducts – Appendix C)

Subha: Pleasant feeling of attractive objects of senses.

Sukha: Happiness, satisfaction due to pleasant senses and thoughts (*sukha vedanā*)

Suññata: Literally, void, nothingness. An arahanta's mind is void of all defilements and cankers (all kilesās); it is often referred to as arrival of the ariya at the state of suññata.

Surapāna (Surameraya): Taking intoxicants, drugs

Sutta: Discourse, one of the three classes of the Teaching: sutta, vinaya and abhidhamma.

Tanhā: Thirst, craving, sensual desire (the origin of lobha)

Tāvatimsā: A level (abode) of the celestial beings called devas (2nd of the 6 levels)

Tejo dhātu: element of heat, fire

Thera: the elders, the elderly bhikkhus

Thina: Torpor, sleepiness, used in combination with *middha*, sloth, as *thina-middha*

Tihetuka-patisandhi: Conception carrying a continuum of the 3 kammically whole-some root-conditions, namely *adosa, alobha,* and *amoha*

Tiracchanna: The realm of aimals

Titthiya: Those holding wrong views, followers of those faiths

Ubatobyi: Persons with both male and female sex organs

Uccheda ditthi: Annihilation view, the belief that death is the end of everything **Udayabhaya ñāna**: The fourth stage of thirteen-level vipassanā ñāna and three-level ariyā ñāna series. At this stage, the on/off incidents of fine khandha are evident experientially.

Uddhacca: Restlessness, the sign of a highly disturbed mind.

U-nha tejo: heat or hotness, the nature of fire

Upacāra nimitta: Acquired image sign, the still unsteady and unclear mental image 'seen' at low levels of concentration

Upacchedaka kamma: Certain very serious akusala kamma that brings about sudden, violent death

Upādāna: Clinging to desires and views, chasing after lust and passion

Upekkhā: Equanimity, a state of the mind neutral to all sensations; it is the state of the mind achieved after applying samādhi to a very high level (as distinct from indifference)

U-tu: The tejo element, heat or cold, climate

Vanna: Good looks, handsome appearance

Vāsanā: The trait or inclination of a character towards certain tendencies, a property of the consciousness continuum that carries it from existence to existence

Vatta: Round trips, cycle of rebirths

Vatta nissita kusala: Round-trip supportive kusala kamma

Vivatta: Absence of round trips, not supportive of the samsāra

Vivatta nissita kusala: kusala kamma free of the samsāric rounding

Vāyo dhātu: Air element, the nature of air (pressure, tension, contraction and expansion)

Vedanā: Sensation, excitement of the mental faculties by impacts of the six types of sense objects on the sense bases, the six *dvaras*. (eye, ear, nose, tongue, body and mind).

Vedanakkhandhā: The second group of khandha, signifying feeling and sensations corresponding to the impact of sense objects (the six types) on the sense bases (the six dvaras). Reactions to the sensations will cause pleasure or aversion. By virtue of samādhi and vipassanā practice, these reactions can be kept at bay, thereby breaking the chain of causes and effects in the paticcasamuppāda circle.

Vedayika sukha: Happiness or joy that people feel, in the mind and body, in perceiving desirable and pleasant sights, sounds, smells, tastes, touch and thoughts

Veramani: Abstain from killing, thieving, etc. as in the 5 Precepts

Veyyāvacca: Sundry services, assistance in general chores at shrines, monasteries, etc.

Vicāra: Sustained application of a thought after *vitakka* has initiated it.

Vicikicchā: Skeptical doubt about khandha-paticcasamuppada, the four Noble Truths and the Eightfold Path to magga/phala ñāna.

Vihimsa: Thinking of tormenting others. (Avihimsa is antonym)

Viññāna: Consciousness, the knowing, the mind

Viññānakkhandhā: The khandha comprising viññāna or the citta.

Virati: The three deliberate, as distinct from automatic, abstentions: abstention from wrong speech, from wrong bodily actions and wrong livelihood.

Vipassanā: Insight, the intuition that sees experientially the mind-matter reality, their interactions and mutual dependency, impermanency of all mind-matter formations, and progressive ascendancy of wisdom to the door of Nibbāna

Vipatti: Deficiency, misfortune, unfortunate circumstances

Virāga: A property of Nibbāna, the non-connection with all sensual pursuits

Visuddhi: Purity of the mind. Visuddhi Magga enumerates on the seven stages of purity of the mind as can be achieved by means of the vipassanā practice.

Vitakka: Initial application of the mind, initiation of thought that can only be maintained and sustained by *vicāra*

Vithi = *citta vithi*: Process of consciousness, stages in the process of consciousness

Vitikkama kilesā: Defilement causing extreme greed and anger, evil conduct in deeds, words and thoughts

Vyāpāda: Malice, ill-will (a kind of dosa).

Vyassana: Loss, ruination, misfortune

Yathābhuta: The reality, objective reality

Yojanā: A linear measure of 12 miles approximately.

Unspecified: Many more Pali words used throughout in the main text are left unregistered in this Glossary. But each and every new word (both Pali and Myanmar), hopefully, has been defined on the spot therein. The idea of this appendix is for the reader to find ready reference for the more or less oft-repeated words.

Abbreviations (where indicated)**:** P for Pali; M for Myanmar (Burmese); S for Sanskrit

Printed in Great Britain
by Amazon.co.uk, Ltd.,
Marston Gate.